THE WRITER'S IDEA THESAURUS

An Interactive Guide for Developing Ideas for Novels and Short Stories

FRED
WHITE

WD

WRITER'S DIGEST
BOOKS

writersdigest.com

Cincinnati, Ohio

For more resources for writers, visit www.writersdigest.com/books.

To receive a free weekly e-mail newsletter delivering tips and updates about writing and about Writer's Digest products, register directly at http://newsletters.fwpublications.com.

18 17 16 15 14 5 4 3 2 1

Distributed in Canada by Fraser Direct
100 Armstrong Avenue
Georgetown, Ontario, Canada L7G 5S4
Tel: (905)877-4411

Distributed in the U.K. and Europe by F&W Media International
Brunel House, Newton Abbot, Devon, TQ12 4PU, England
Tel: (+44)1626-323200, Fax: (+44)1626-323319
E-mail: postmaster@davidandcharles.co.uk

Distributed in Australia by Capricorn Link
P.O. Box 704, Windsor, NSW 2756 Australia
Tel: (02)4577-3555

ISBN-13: 978-1-59963-822-5

Edited by **James Duncan**
Designed by **Bethany Rainbolt**
Production coordinated by **Debbie Thomas**

DEDICATION

For Philip and Marion Weyna, with love and admiration.

ACKNOWLEDGMENTS

I wish to thank the editors at Writer's Digest Books—especially James Duncan, Kimberly Catanzarite, and Mike Hanna for their many fine suggestions. I also wish to thank my agent, Rita Rosenkranz, for her excellent advice at the book's formative stage. And to my wife, Terry Weyna: I couldn't have finished this book without you.

BIO

Fred White (Ph.D., University of Iowa) is professor of English, emeritus at Santa Clara University where he taught courses in writing and literature for more than thirty years. In 1997 he received the Louis and Dorina Brutocao Award for teaching excellence. His essays, short stories and plays have appeared in many periodicals and anthologies, including *The Brooklyner*, *The Cambridge Companion to Emily Dickinson*, *The Chronicle of Higher Education*, *College Literature*, *Confrontation*, *Fantastic Odysseys*, *Oregon Literary Review*, *Pleiades*, *Southwest Review*, and *Writer's Digest*. His most recent books include *The Daily Writer*, *The Daily Reader*, *Where Do You Get Your Ideas?*, and *The Well-Crafted Argument*, now in its Fifth Edition. He lives with his wife, Terry, an attorney, near Sacramento, CA.

TABLE OF CONTENTS

INTRODUCTION

Words are all around us, but when we're searching for a precise word, we consult a thesaurus (like Roget's) to find it. Ideas are all around us too, ideas with the potential to become stories and novels, gazillions of ideas—more than enough for every aspiring and veteran writer on the planet. However, that doesn't mean they're easy to identify or to anatomize for their story potential. Sometimes we have just the grain of an idea but need a push to expand it to full form. This is why writers also need an *idea* thesaurus, a central clearinghouse for ideas, you might say—not unlike that imaginary clearinghouse in Schenectady that Harlan Ellison once humorously referred to in response to the question, "Where do you get your ideas?"

Until now, however, such a reference work has not existed. Yes, there are books of prompts on the market, but not story situations, which is what *The Writer's Idea Thesaurus* provides. These situations are organized by subject matter (twenty subjects in all), divided into ten more specific categories, with ten even more specific situations in each category. Let's take a look at how it works.

SO HOW DID I COME UP WITH ALL THESE IDEAS?

Let me first assure you that I did not extract any of these scenarios from existing works, not even from my own. Instead I mined my notebooks—many dozens of them, which I've kept over the years and have stored in a large box in my study. If I had transformed all of these ideas into finished works, I'd probably be the most prolific author in the world. You see, I'm a teacher of writing (now retired) and I enjoy talking about ways to conjure up and work with ideas as much as I do turning ideas into stories. Indeed, in my previous book, *Where Do You Get Your Ideas? A Writer's Guide to Transforming Notions Into Narratives*, I discuss the art of idea conjuring and offer a step-by-step approach to shaping those conjured-up ideas into marketable stories.

Ideas come to me continually, morning and night, even when I don't particularly want them to come, such as when I'm driving, cooking, trying to sleep (I often get up in the middle of the night to jot down ideas), or even getting together with friends, when jotting down ideas is awkward, if not downright rude. Even so, I am never without at least a pocket notebook so I can make surreptitious jottings. *The Writer's Idea Thesaurus* represents a carefully screened and finessed selection of the countless ideas I've conjured up over the years, along with new ideas that continue to stream through my head. By the way, I encourage you to develop this notebook habit too! Ideas have a way of begetting more ideas.

HOW TO USE THIS BOOK

In addition to flicking randomly through *The Writer's Idea Thesaurus* and chancing upon one story situation or another (which can be fun), you might try the following systematic approach.

First, review the Table of Contents to see how the twenty chapters and the ten idea categories under each chapter are organized. Notice that chapters are presented in alphabetical order for easy reference. Flip to an interesting chapter and category and peruse the ten story situations under each category—ten story scenarios for each of the ten idea categories in each of the twenty subjects (chapters)—two thousand story situations in all, enough to keep you swimming in story or novel ideas for a very long time. The breakdown looks a little like this:

CHAPTER 6:

THE CURSE OR PROPHECY OF X

CATEGORY 1: A CURSE FROM THE DEPTHS

The horror factor in Gothic fiction typically stems from its settings: dungeons, cellars, laboratories, caves, grottos, secret passageways—wherever darkness and mystery reign. Similarly there are non-supernatural tales to be told about curses and prophecies. The story premises that follow should help you conjure up your own Gothic chillers or real-life psychodramas stemming from curses or prophecies passed from generation to generation.

> **SITUATION 1:** A rowboat containing a skull washes onto the coast of Spain. Accompanying the skull is a parchment containing a prophecy: Whoever finds the skull must return it to the family of the deceased, or the finders will suffer calamity. Alas, the curse is not taken seriously.

After looking at this example above, some writers might wonder whether I'm offering up too much information or infringing on one's creativity. No, and no. A sourcebook of general story ideas such as this can actually spark creativity, especially when prompted to take those general ideas and spin them in unique ways to create something new, as we'll see below.

Let's take a look at four specific methods you can use to personalize these situations.

THE STARTING POINT

This method uses the situation you settle on as point A and relies upon your imagination to propel the idea into a full-fledged story. Let's imagine that you're itching to write a thriller about the search for a hidden bomb. Chapter 17: "The Search for X" will be the chapter for you. Go there and survey the ten categories in that chapter and find the category that comes closest to the kind of "search" story you'd like to write. Let's say you choose Category 10: "The Search for a Weapon." As with all the other idea categories, this one lists ten story situations specific to searching for weapons for you to choose from. You may finally decide on Situation 2:

> A scientist with top secret information about a new military weapon vanishes. It is up to the protagonist—a CIA agent—to find her. The problem is that the scientist and the CIA agent once worked together, and each knows incriminating things about the other.

This is just the starting point, and there are many ways to approach a story idea such as this based on your own creative intuition, plucked randomly from your own creative juices. Here are three such higher-level changes you may choose to make:

- The scientist and the CIA agent have become double agents, but neither knows of the other's allegiance.
- It is later revealed that they were once lovers.
- The scientist has been kidnapped by a terrorist group—but the alleged secret weapon she is supposed to know about does not exist. The terrorists do not believe her and threaten to kill her. It is up to the CIA agent to find her in time.

You may likely come up with a dozen different ways to change the story. No matter what you choose, the goal here is to take this starting point and run with it into new directions that no other author might ever think of. Think big. Think unique.

DIG INTO THE DETAILS

Of course there are many other ways to manipulate a story, namely, dig into the details and change them around. Instead of making major plot changes, you can simply set the situation we noted in a specific decade. Spies in the 1950s worried about very different things than spies do now, and each kind of spy has access to different clothing styles, slang, weapons, cars, etc. Genders and roles may be swapped. Maybe the scientist and CIA agent aren't lovers but mother and son. Or brother and sister. Or you might change the location. Perhaps the story takes place in Eastern Europe, or California, or Antarctica.

Another detail you can play with is genre. The situation we've used as an example leans toward a thriller and espionage, but what it if were written as romance? We'd referenced the love interest between the scientist and agent, so run with that angle. Or try science fiction. Who says this story couldn't take place in a Ray Bradbury-esque future, or a dystopian war zone and the scientist's new weapon could bring about the much sought after victory? Try a western. Try a hardboiled angle. Try a cozy mystery solved from the confines of the agent's secluded office in the basement of the secret CIA offices beneath the New York Public Library. Who's to say? You are. Play with the details and possibilities of a situation as if it was a Rubik's Cube and you'll soon find a story line that is all yours.

THE SITUATION COMBINATION

It is also possible to combine two or more situations in the same chapter. Take, for example, Chapter 1 ("The Adventures of X"), Category 2 ("Aviation Adventures"), Situation 6:

> A woman aviator in the 1920s embarks on a series of adventures across the country. A male aviator, feeling upstaged by her achievements, tries to discredit her. He even tinkers with her plane.

Now let's combine this with another situation in the same chapter—we'll choose Situation 1 from the same "Aviation Adventures" category:

> A barnstormer in the early days of aviation is determined to win a woman's affection by staging incredible aerial feats—until he suffers a debilitating accident.

4

Combine the two situations and tweak the details a bit in both situations, and you might come up with a new story situation such as the following:

> A woman aviator in the 1920s upstages her male counterparts by performing incredible aerial feats. One male aviator—a barnstormer—is both intimidated by and attracted to the female aviator, and challenges her to a contest. She accepts, not knowing how dangerous the contest is going to be.

This method of combining two situations into one is also helpful if you want to create a longer, more complex story suitable for a novel, although many will be suitable for a short story or novel as they are, depending on what you add from your own imagination.

THE SUBJECT COMBINATION

If you find one situation you like, you can also take another situation from a different chapter altogether to create a deeper story, or one with a powerful subplot. For example, say you select Chapter 20 ("The Transformation of X into Y"), Category 1 ("The Transformation of Addicts and Criminals"), Situation 2:

> A prisoner experiences a vision of himself as a healer. He requests a job in the infirmary and studies nursing in his spare time. But because he has a difficult time controlling his temper, he keeps missing opportunities.

Now you want to put this prisoner-turned-healer in a unique situation. How about Chapter 19 ("The Threat of X"), Category 9 ("The Threat of Natural Disaster"), Situation 8:

> A hurricane is heading straight for a hospital, threatening to flood the area and cause widespread devastation. City officials must decide how to evacuate ill and frail people, many of whom are dependent on facilities only a hospital can provide.

Now you have a special character in a very dangerous situation, with plenty of room for drama, action, and redemption.

By regarding the ideas in this thesaurus as flexible and capable of being combined with other ideas as I've shown here, you will be able to generate many more story situations than by just flipping through and choosing ideas at random. But regardless of the method you choose, the stories you ultimately create will be entirely your own.

With this treasure trove of two thousand story situations at your elbow, you will never again have to grope for ideas to write about. The ideas are here, in embryonic form, waiting for your creative vision to transform them into exciting short stories or novels.

Enough pep talk. It's time for you to get busy and start writing!

CHAPTER 1

THE ADVENTURES OF X

CATEGORY 1: ADVENTURES IN AN ALTERNATE UNIVERSE OR REALITY

Every work of fiction depicts, in a sense, an alternate universe, another reality that could come to pass. Readers love entering different realities, not just because it's fun to escape the reality we're stuck in but because different realities offer new possibilities and fresh insights about the world we know. Use the following situations to help you develop an alternate-reality tale.

SITUATION 1: A Wall Street investment expert in October 1929 struggles to avert the stock market crash—and succeeds. His actions lead to a series of wild investments that never would have occurred otherwise. But another investment bubble looms later in the 1930s, leaving America woefully ill-prepared for the world events to follow.

SITUATION 2: On an alternate Earth, toxic air pollution leads scientists to genetically engineer people who are capable of living underwater. But because the sun is growing hotter and the oceans are drying up, more drastic survival measures as well as genetic alterations must be undertaken.

SITUATION 3: An expedition is sent to Mars—but this Mars exists in an alternate universe, one in which they find a breathable atmosphere on the surface. The narrator and crew find catacombs hinting at an ancient civilization, as well as another that may yet exist.

SITUATION 4: An alternate-Earth Leonardo da Vinci has successfully built a motorized flying machine. When a war breaks out, Leonardo struggles in vain to keep his invention out of the hands of the military.

SITUATION 5: The Walt Disney of this alternate Earth is a creative genius but is also unstable. In his Disneyland, he creates a machine that temporarily transforms visitors into his famous and lesser-known characters, some more ghoulish than anyone expects. One of the visitors avoids the transformation and seeks out the twisted Mr. Disney to get him to return the visitors to normal.

SITUATION 6: In this alternate Earth, a religion known as Disneyism is sweeping the country. Cartoon characters are the disciples who spread the gospel of childhood whimsy everywhere. But when the religion seems to be getting out of hand, a determined parent sets out to demolish the movement.

SITUATION 7: Columbus and his men in this alternate 1492 encounter Native Americans who possess supernatural powers and worship gods that discourage the European explorers from interfering with their culture.

SITUATION 8: An explorer finds an alternate Earth (the gateway to which he discovered by accident) that is dramatically unlike his own Earth and filled with possibilities for adventure. But then he encounters inhabitants that make him want to return to his own world as fast as possible.

SITUATION 9: In this alternate United States, Texas has seceded from the Union. Its citizens are not only permitted but are required to own and be trained to use high-capacity assault rifles. Despite internal conflict, the leadership decides that the only way to preserve their new nation is through expansion.

SITUATION 10: In this alternate Earth, humans are under the control of super-intelligent, upright-walking dogs that are euthanizing humans because they are breeding out of control. After several failed attacks on the dogs, the humans attempt to negotiate a peace treaty.

CATEGORY 2: AVIATION ADVENTURES

Flying is in our genes. For ages we have longed to soar like the birds, and since the eighteenth century we've been able to in hot-air balloons—a feat romanticized by Jules Verne and others—but once the Wright brothers invented motorized flight, our hunger for flying adventures increased tenfold. Here are some flying scenarios to get your readers airborne.

SITUATION 1: A barnstormer in the early days of aviation is determined to win a woman's affection by staging incredible aerial feats—until he suffers a debilitating accident.

SITUATION 2: A hang glider fantasizes about gliding across the Grand Canyon from North Rim to South Rim. The stunt would be suicidal, if not impossible, but he is obsessed with the idea.

SITUATION 3: The year is 2027, and an aviator attempts to replicate Charles Lindbergh's transatlantic flight—from plane to flight path (New York to Paris)—in an effort to call attention to Lindbergh's less-than-popular political views; but the protagonist is determined to publicize the event for a less controversial reason—the need to rekindle the spirit of adventure that people seem to have lost by the centennial year of Lindbergh's flight.

SITUATION 4: Hot-air balloonists embark on a journey across the Atlantic Ocean and encounter several life-threatening challenges along the way. Some are due to natural phenomena, but one is due to rivals who have planted an explosive device on the balloon.

SITUATION 5: Several jet-pack enthusiasts learn to enhance maneuverability to make possible a sport that can be played in midair. Problems arise when some players underestimate the power of their jet packs.

SITUATION 6: A woman aviator in the 1920s embarks on a series of adventures across the country. A male aviator, feeling upstaged by her achievements, tries to discredit her. He even tinkers with her plane.

SITUATION 7: A passenger jet gets hijacked by the copilot, who orders the pilot to divert the plane to an enemy country. The copilot is aware that an air marshal is aboard and tricks him into surrendering his weapon. However, an assistant air marshal (in training) is also aboard.

SITUATION 8: Black Hawk pilots plan an attack against a terrorist cell in the midst of a civilian neighborhood. One of the pilots (the narrator) refuses to carry out the mission unless certain security measures to protect the civilians are carried out—even if it means putting the pilots' own lives at greater risk.

SITUATION 9: During an air show, one of the fighter pilots sees the event as an opportunity to avenge a rival for what he considers to be a terrible injustice. Unfortunately the avenger's plan backfires, causing him to be injured, which in turn leads the rival to rethink his own actions.

SITUATION 10: Massive power blackouts due to off-the-chart solar flares cause air-traffic controls at major airports to go haywire. It takes a combination of savvy pilots and air-traffic controllers to figure out ways to avert disasters.

CATEGORY 3: ADVENTURES OF DEFECTORS, DESERTERS, AND MUTINEERS

People on the run, people protesting injustice, people at the end of their collective ropes: Such people set the stage for exciting reading, and authors like William Bligh (*Mutiny on the Bounty*) and Herman Wouk (*The Caine Mutiny*) have capitalized upon them. World history is filled with examples of heroic resistance against oppressors. The following scenarios should pique your storytelling imagination.

SITUATION 1: A long-suffering laborer leads other workers in a massive strike in sweatshops in her city. But the sweatshop managers retaliate. Not to be deterred, the protagonist (the most experienced of the employees) finds a unique way to convey her fellow workers' needs to the owners and public.

SITUATION 2: In the Deep South, the narrator (a runaway slave) escapes. Just as he is about to walk into a trap, he is assisted in his escape by a plantation owner's son, whose life was once saved by the runaway.

SITUATION 3: Individual teens who have run away from home struggle to create an organization devoted to teaching parenting skills to those about to have children—but their parents, having uncovered clues to their whereabouts, take steps to ensure that they return to their homes instead.

SITUATION 4: A defector from a totalitarian country is given asylum in the United States, but he is actually a spy who plans to sabotage a secret NASA mission. During the mission, however, he has second thoughts.

SITUATION 5: An army deserter about to be executed is given another chance to prove his bravery after convincing his superiors that he knows where an ambush has been set up. The odds of neutralizing the ambush are nil because of high-tech booby traps.

SITUATION 6: Despite being decorated for valor, a soldier deserts his platoon during a raid when his fellow soldiers open fire on civilians whom the enemy

10

combatants have infiltrated. He has a change of heart when he learns that one of his closest buddies in the platoon has been killed.

SITUATION 7: Several of the crew aboard a naval vessel fear that their captain is collaborating with an enemy nation. A female officer thinks she can foil the captain's plans.

SITUATION 8: After receiving intensive training in the use of top-secret military equipment, a soldier defects to an enemy country. A special agent is assigned to intercept him before he has a chance to share his training with the enemy.

SITUATION 9: The most courageous of King Arthur's knights deserts the Round Table and disappears. Arthur recruits one of the other knights to find him and bring him to justice—but it turns out that the deserting knight has disguised himself as a servant to uncover a plot to overthrow the monarchy.

SITUATION 10: Pirates attack a cargo ship carrying ancient artifacts, which they seize. But when two of the pirates are killed as they try to escape, the lead pirate wants to avenge their deaths by destroying the cargo ship.

CATEGORY 4: ADVENTURES WITH GHOSTS

Take your readers on a thrill ride chasing ghosts of one kind or another—or maybe it's the ghost that is doing the chasing. Readers young and old never tire of an exciting and creepy ghost story, such as Peter Straub's *Ghost Story* or Shirley Jackson's *The Haunting of Hill House*. The following situations should pique your creative imagination.

SITUATION 1: The protagonist has a talent for locating rogue ghosts (a talent she discovered as a child during a haunting) but is deathly afraid of ghosts. Her boyfriend helps her to overcome this fear in order to trap an especially dangerous ghost.

SITUATION 2: After years of hunting down mischievous ghosts, the ghost hunter decides to take on one final, dangerous assignment—but the ghost threatens to outsmart him. However, the old ghost hunter has one last trick up his sleeve.

SITUATION 3: A ghost hunted by a nobleman turns out to be the nobleman's lover who died in a house fire set by a jealous rival. The nobleman feels obligated to persuade the ghost not to avenge the rival even though they both want the rival to suffer.

SITUATION 4: A ghost hunter fully understands, and is sympathetic to, the misery of being a ghost. She uses her insight to assuage a rogue ghost, but the ghost makes some startling demands that she cannot imagine being able to fulfill.

SITUATION 5: Several ghosts compete to see who can frighten people most effectively. They have a great time until they encounter individuals who have learned a thing or two about how to frighten ghosts.

SITUATION 6: Several ghosts wreak havoc in a college residence hall or sorority/fraternity house. However, when the students are about to be evicted for gross misconduct, the ghosts offer a truce ... of sorts.

SITUATION 7: An altruistic ghost tries to help a thief see the error of his ways, but the thief doesn't take the ghost seriously—until the ghost demonstrates its remarkable generosity.

SITUATION 8: A ghost offers to trade its supernatural powers with a living person for the opportunity to inhabit that person's body for a year. The person agrees; but after the year is over, the ghost does not want to depart.

SITUATION 9: Infant ghosts haunt a nursery, causing mayhem when they make the infants do things infants are normally not capable of doing. A medium with experience in dealing with infant ghosts intervenes, but she only makes things worse.

SITUATION 10: The ghosts of a Nevada ghost town plan a few surprises for a film crew that's shooting a Western there. Result: an adventure between the actors playing the town's 1880s-era inhabitants and the actual ghosts who lived there and know things the actors do not.

CATEGORY 5: ADVENTURES IN A MAGICAL LAND

Magic exists on many levels in storytelling: There is the magic of magicians, the magic that permeates fantasy worlds, and the magic that emerges from the dark corners of the real world. Think of Lev Grossman's *The Magicians* and, of course, J.K. Rowling's Harry Potter novels. The following ten story situations will give you a chance to make magic real.

SITUATION 1: In this new *Alice in Wonderland* adventure, the Cheshire Cat leads Alice into an unexplored part of Wonderland where she must hold her own against malicious dwarves and carnivorous caterpillars.

SITUATION 2: Using her ESP powers, a child is able to detect portals to magical realms. She is afraid to enter them until her brother, who secretly follows her one day, persuades her to enter with him. Alas, they cannot find their way back.

SITUATION 3: A hypnotist takes the narrator on a wild adventure through dream space, where dream and reality begin to blur for her. To make matters worse, the hypnotist is unable to awake the narrator; as a result she must find a way to navigate back to reality on her own.

SITUATION 4: In an impoverished village, a child is possessed of subtle magical powers that enable the villagers to withstand disease and starvation. One of the adults, witnessing the child's magic, tries to get the child to use her magic for more avaricious ends.

SITUATION 5: Orpheus descends to the realm of Hades to rescue his beloved Eurydice from death, but while he's down there, he is distracted from his task by dead souls and monsters, whom he manages to enchant with his singing ... with one exception: Hades himself.

SITUATION 6: Apollo pursues Cassandra; she will let him make love to her only if he grants her the gift of prophecy, which he does. When she doesn't keep her end of the bargain, he sees to it that her prophecies are never believed. But Cassandra manages to get Apollo to reverse his decision after she stops an invading army from destroying his shrines.

SITUATION 7: Angels appear to mortals and imbue a chosen few (regardless of faith) with magical powers in order to bring peace to a land constantly at war. Things become complicated when one of the angels falls in love with a mortal and is captured by one of the warring parties.

SITUATION 8: The narrator, an exiled king, recruits a magician of unknown reputation to help him restore fertility to the fields of his kingdom, which a sorcerer had rendered sterile. His plan is to retake his throne after the magician replenishes the land—but the magician has a different agenda.

SITUATION 9: This adventure story is set in the Garden of Eden before all that business with the apple. Satan schemes to lure Adam and Eve out of the garden using the seven deadly sins to entice them, with the apple being the final temptation.

SITUATION 10: A sweet old lady rescues a brother and sister from an abusive home by transporting them to a magic land where she is a sorceress ... who also happens to be running from the king's army. It becomes the siblings' turn to help the woman.

CATEGORY 6: ADVENTURES OF MARINERS, MOUNTAIN CLIMBERS, AND SPELUNKERS

The more rigorous and risky the adventure, the more exciting your story will be. Use one or more of the following scenarios to spin a white-knuckle adventure on the open sea (like Yann Martel's *Life of Pi*), on mountains (Jon Krakauer's *Into Thin Air*), or in the bowels of the earth (Jules Verne's *Journey to the Center of the Earth*).

SITUATION 1: A paraplegic climber trains to scale a mountain never before scaled by disabled climbers. Her biggest obstacle is her own self-doubt, which her boyfriend and sister struggle to help her overcome.

SITUATION 2: After two women become trapped while climbing a treacherous mountain, two male rescuers themselves become trapped, and the women not only extricate themselves but also save the male rescuers.

SITUATION 3: In a prequel to *Moby-Dick*, Ahab embarks on the whaling adventure that results in the loss of his leg. [For backstory clues, see *Moby-Dick*, Chapters 28 and 36.]

SITUATION 4: While on a deep-sea fishing trip, fishermen are sucked into a vortex. They emerge in an alternate world filled with strange sea creatures, one of which seems intelligent enough to help them return to their world.

SITUATION 5: A group of classical-literature lovers embark on a voyage that retraces Odysseus's journey from Troy to Ithaca. To their astonishment they encounter some of the mythological beings that appeared in *The Odyssey*. The narrator, a Homer scholar, must figure out how to evade their traps.

SITUATION 6: Interplanetary explorers discover an underground city while exploring a cave on one of Saturn's moons. It appears that the city was founded by interstellar travelers eons ago.

SITUATION 7: When explorers enter a sealed cavern chamber, they discover several caskets containing people in suspended animation—or are they vampires? Should they try to revive them?

SITUATION 8: Divers discover an ancient ship containing artifacts that do not seem to belong to any known ancient culture. It is up to the narrator—an offbeat archaeologist—to determine the nature and origin of these artifacts.

SITUATION 9: Anthropologists exploring a cave on a remote island discover the remains of an unknown species of hominid. While researching the site, they come to realize that this humanoid species is extinct.

SITUATION 10: Pilgrims climbing a sacred mountain in a fantasy land come face-to-face with the gods they've sought—but the gods are more mischievous than benevolent: They like to make the climbers do things against their will.

CATEGORY 7: THE ADVENTURES OF REBELS, ROGUES, AND CRAZIES

All of us carry some rebelliousness in our blood and have brought it to the surface on occasion since early childhood. Characters like Heathcliff in Emily Bronte's *Wuthering Heights* or Holden Caulfield in Salinger's *Catcher in the Rye* are examples. It stands to reason, then, that readers will identify with the heroes or antiheroes in the following situations.

SITUATION 1: An ex-convict breaks his restrictive parole to achieve spiritual wholeness on a pilgrimage. He discovers that his faith isn't as strong as he hoped, but when faced with imminent arrest, he must choose between giving up peacefully or committing further parole violations to help a young idealistic pilgrim on a similar quest.

SITUATION 2: Mental patients escape from a state hospital and embark on a religious quest in a nearby seaside community. But just as they establish a following with local inhabitants, hospital officials try to round them up.

SITUATION 3: In the late nineteenth century, a riverboat captain tries to outsmart a group of thieves who board the vessel and intend to rob the passengers. However, the thieves (veteran lockpickers, pickpockets and card sharks), prove to be more clever than the crew expected.

SITUATION 4: Rebel circus clowns, mistreated by the manager, take over the circus and stage shows never enacted in a circus before. Things get complicated when one of the clowns goes on a rampage and tries to murder the manager.

SITUATION 5: Two college dropouts embark on a train-hopping journey across America to realize their spiritual connection with the land. Their idealism is constantly challenged, however, by the riffraff they encounter.

SITUATION 6: A teenager with three personalities literally splits into three separate persons as a result of a potion or incantation. They go their own ways, and the most rational of the trio attempts to reintegrate the other two (realizing he cannot exist without them), but they prove to be more elusive than anticipated.

SITUATION 7: The court jester of a king secretly hypnotizes the king to be the court jester while he himself assumes the king's identity. Everyone is fooled because the jester, being the king's illegitimate son, resembles his father. When the Queen discovers what has happened, she takes drastic measures to restore normalcy.

SITUATION 8: A homeless eccentric wins a Powerball jackpot of half a billion dollars and uses the money to embark on a worldwide crusade to turn some of his dark fantasies, like gladiatorial combat, into reality.

SITUATION 9: During WWII, an American POW manages to convince one of his captors to launch an attack against their own army. The captor has a change of heart and to demonstrate his loyalty, threatens to execute the POW, unless the POW conducts a covert operation against the Americans.

SITUATION 10: Guardians of an evil king secretly plot with spies dispatched by a good king to cast a spell on the evil king's army. The spell shifts loyalties to the good king at first, but the trance wears off prematurely.

CATEGORY 8: ADVENTURES OF SHAPE CHANGERS

A favorite motif in science fiction, shape changing is actually part of the real world: We change shapes when we embark on weight-loss regimens or don costumes for Halloween or wear prosthetics when we act in plays. Consider developing any of the following shape-changing situations into a serious or amusing tale.

SITUATION 1: The narrator has been abused by one man too many in her life. Now that she has mastered the art of shape-shifting, she avenges these abuses in unorthodox ways.

SITUATION 2: A werewolf's transformation back into human form goes awry: He only partially changes, leaving him half man and half wolf and exhibiting both behavioral and physical manifestations of both.

SITUATION 3: A secret agent kidnaps a key operative in a drug-smuggling ring and then assumes the operative's appearance. But the others suspect the operative of being an informant and plan to kill her.

SITUATION 4: Zeus embarks on a romantic romp to seduce as many women as he can by changing himself into innocuous creatures—but one of the women learns of Zeus's schemes from another god, and she sets a trap.

SITUATION 5: Extraterrestrials change themselves into political and military leaders in order to infiltrate strategic sites. When the plan is set, they launch a coordinated invasion of the earth. The protagonist, one of the few humans whom the ETs think they have brainwashed into assisting them, tries to stop the invasion in its tracks.

SITUATION 6: Fallen angels sneak back into Heaven by disguising themselves as benevolent angels—and once back inside the Pearly Gates, they incite all kinds of mischief until one of the genuine angels works out a plan to drive them out.

SITUATION 7: A woman loses a drastic amount of weight (real-world shape changing) and finds that it does not bring her happiness, so she attempts to lose even more weight. Before her health is irretrievably damaged, a close friend finally makes her see the folly of her behavior.

SITUATION 8: Several shape-shifters embark on an adventure of mischief and mayhem during Mardi Gras in New Orleans. But the shape-changing revelry goes awry when one of the masquerading "normal" people seeks revenge.

SITUATION 9: A cuckolded husband (who is also a shape changer), assumes the shape of his wife's secret lover and gets back at his wife in frightening ways. When she figures out what he's up to, she engages in some shape-changing surprises of her own.

SITUATION 10: A group of shape changers attempt to influence federal legislation. Despite careful planning, however, their plot falls apart when they kidnap key senators, assume their shapes, and try taking over the Senate.

CATEGORY 9: ADVENTURES OF TIME TRAVELERS

Time travel is the quintessential science-fiction/fantasy adventure (typified by H.G. Wells's *The Time Machine*, given a fresh approach by Audrey Niffenegger in *The Time Traveler's Wife*). It satisfies our desire to escape the prison house of now, to change the past awful events, and to peek at things to come. The following situations should help you develop time-travel adventures of your own.

SITUATION 1: A physician travels to 1889 Austria and attempts to prevent Hitler's mother from meeting his father, thereby preventing Hitler from being born. However, this only reshuffles the deck of potential Nazi leaders. Undaunted, the physician tries again, this time targeting the mothers of Goebbels, Goring, and Himmler, but each attempt leads to the same tragic events Finally he tries a simpler tactic: ensuring that one of the assassination attempts on Hitler succeeds.

SITUATION 2: Time travelers journey to the future to obtain secrets about how to keep the human race from destroying itself. When they return to their own times with their insights, nobody believes their solutions can work. On the contrary, they're convinced the time travelers' solutions could change humankind in disturbing ways.

SITUATION 3: Two bibliophiles travel back to ancient Alexandria (fifth century C.E.) determined to prevent the Great Library from being destroyed. In the process they become entangled in the uprising between Christians and Pagans.

SITUATION 4: A time traveler jumps fifteen years into the future and encounters himself in a wretched state. He asks his future self to explain what had happened to him and then returns to the present to prevent those events from occurring. However, things do not work out as planned.

SITUATION 5: A governor, desperate to find a way to reverse the bad political decisions that led to her downfall, travels back in time to change key decisions. Although these changes will lead to improvements, they will also be the cause of new problems.

SITUATION 6: A time-traveling teenager winds up in the twenty-third century, when virtual reality has overtaken physical reality. In trying to escape one nightmare scenario after another, she keeps confusing one reality with the other.

SITUATION 7: A time traveler decides to live her life over, starting at age seventeen, when she became infatuated with a man who steered her in the wrong direction. Seeking revenge, she re-encounters the man, but she is swept up by his charm all over again—until he does something that snaps her out of it.

SITUATION 8: An orphan travels back in time to rescue his parents from the accident that took their lives. But as a result of his interference with the timeline, his life becomes more troubled than before. He must now choose between being an orphan or keeping his parents and having a more difficult life. Or perhaps there is a third alternative ...

SITUATION 9: Traveling to late-sixteenth-century England, a playwright befriends Shakespeare. The friendship results in the two of them collaborating on a play whose reception has far-reaching consequences.

SITUATION 10: A small cruising vessel in the Mediterranean is swept off course by a bizarre weather system and winds up in ancient Greece. After overcoming suspicions that they are invaders, the passengers gradually become part of Athenian culture during its Golden Age.

CATEGORY 10: ADVENTURES OF TREASURE SEEKERS

Treasure: The very word stirs our spirit of adventure. We all dream of finding a gold nugget, a precious artifact from a vanished civilization. Literature is filled with treasure-seeking adventures, from *Treasure Island* to *The Da Vinci Code*. Such finds can have a life-changing influence on individuals and can even change history. Here are ten treasure-hunting adventures for you to spin stories from.

SITUATION 1: A homeless man learns prospecting secrets from an old friend, and he decides to test them out in an abandoned gold-prospecting site in the Sierra foothills. He meets up with unsavory prospectors who try to force his secrets from him.

SITUATION 2: Two prospectors, once close friends, become bitter rivals. When one of them discovers a silver lode in an abandoned Nevada mine, the other tries to sabotage the mine.

SITUATION 3: An archaeologist uncovers the remnants of a Paleo-Indian culture—but local Native Americans on whose land the archaeologist was digging refuse to allow the skeletons discovered there to be examined scientifically.

SITUATION 4: A group of wildlife preservationists, motivated by a large reward, set out to prevent ivory poachers from attacking elephants. To have any chance of succeeding, they must lure the poachers away from the elephants and toward an even greater treasure source: rhino horns—but these rhino horns are fake.

SITUATION 5: After a long-lost painting is discovered in a warehouse used for hiding valuables during World War II, art thieves steal it. After tracking down the thieves, the discoverers make an even more valuable discovery.

SITUATION 6: Divers try to salvage treasure from a cargo ship that sank more than a hundred years ago. However, one of them gets trapped inside, and the narrator struggles to save his life before the sunken ship slips into a deep trench beside it.

SITUATION 7: Astronauts fifty years in the future attempt to drill through the ice crust on Jupiter's moon Europa and reach the underlying ocean. Preliminary evidence suggests that a treasure trove of exotic organisms awaits their discovery—although some of them might be deadly. The challenge is to break through before Jupiter's potentially lethal radiation prevents the astronauts from completing the mission.

SITUATION 8: A group of adventurers dares to rescue precious artifacts from an ancient village facing imminent destruction from a volcano about to erupt, while also avoiding others seeking their own fortunes in the abandoned village.

SITUATION 9: A billionaire offers a $100 million reward to anyone able to infiltrate and destroy a gang of militants who wiped out the billionaire's family decades earlier.

SITUATION 10: Archaeologists have a vague idea where treasure from an ancient Mediterranean culture is buried, but they must outwit pirates who know for certain where the treasure is but do not know how to retrieve it.

CHAPTER 2

THE CLASH OR COMPETITION BETWEEN X AND Y

CATEGORY 1: ATHLETIC OR GAMING COMPETITION

Competition is elemental to life: We compete in school, at work, and on the playing field. From family games to major-league sports, competition generates fun and excitement. A game is like a story: It has a central purpose, is energized by strong conflict and suspense, and is tightly structured. Draw from the following situations to build a gripping story that will force readers to choose sides.

SITUATION 1: A gifted prizefighter, retired from the ring because of repeated blows to his head that left him partially brain damaged (unable to keep his balance without help), prepares to make a dramatic comeback in order to defeat the rival responsible for that injury.

SITUATION 2: Climbers compete for a hefty prize to scale a treacherous mountain; one of them (the protagonist) is an amateur—but he is the one who has studied the mountain most carefully.

SITUATION 3: An overpaid pitcher helps put his team in last place by becoming a laughingstock of blunders. He embarks on a retraining program without much progress until his old nemesis ridicules him publicly.

SITUATION 4: Taunted for her love of boxing, a college undergraduate organizes a tournament for female boxers designed to raise the status of boxing in her region. But finding qualified female boxers and serious financial backers becomes troublesome, especially when a she falls victim to an unexpected disease that might prohibit her from ever boxing again.

SITUATION 5: A former softball star, exiled from the game for a serious infraction, wishes to redeem herself by playing for a worthy cause. But she must first regain the trust of the softball community as well as her family.

SITUATION 6: Socially awkward among her high-school peers, the protagonist tries to gain respect by honing her already considerable chess-playing skills and challenging the school's grandmaster: one of the teachers. She defeats the teacher in a match but her plan for social acceptance backfires.

SITUATION 7: The narrator sponsors basketball competitions for gang members to reduce gang violence and drug trafficking. At first the scheme fails, but then the narrator (with the help of a gang member) turns the project into what promises to be a success—but not before a gang member commits a crime.

SITUATION 8: A teenager gifted at Scrabble is bullied into losing a tournament. The organizer, discovering the scheme, tries to set things right by siding with the teenager, but he discovers that the conflict is more complicated than it appears on the surface.

SITUATION 9: A Halloween costume competition at a public venue goes awry when the competitors realize that, due to some spell, they have actually become the persons or creatures they have dressed up to resemble. Only one person, dressed up as a Sherlock-Holmes-type detective, will find a way to undo the spell.

SITUATION 10: A woman plans to compete in a dangerous snowmobile race though friends try to dissuade her because she is a woman. The narrator is determined to win, thereby demonstrating that gender has nothing to do with skill.

CATEGORY 2: BATTLEFIELD CLASHES

Wartime conflict is archetypal—so much so that it has become a metaphor for other kinds of conflict. Arguments are often described as battles—the word *debate* even comes from *battre*, the French word for *battle*. Literature is filled with war stories; here are ten situations for you to add to your repertoire.

SITUATION 1: In the midst of combat, a sergeant has a premonition of defeat so powerful that he orders a retreat. Even after being reprimanded by his commanding officer, he continues to have premonitions but is determined to follow orders. Finally, he is driven to act on one of his newest premonitions.

SITUATION 2: During World War II, a German soldier encounters a platoon that includes his estranged American brother, who left Germany in 1933, just before Hitler became Chancellor. Despite their fierce loyalty for their respective countries, they cannot bring themselves to fight. They spend a long night together sharing a foxhole and must make their final choices on fighting or fleeing by dawn.

SITUATION 3: Despite being well-trained to follow orders, a soldier refuses to open fire on an enemy camp because he's sure civilians are inside. Facing a court martial, the soldier must convince his superiors that his decision was correct.

SITUATION 4: A former slave fighting in a regiment of the Union Army liberates a slave family and tries to persuade them to torch their master's plantation and murder him and his family. When they resist, the Union soldier attempts the deed instead, but he runs into complications when he encounters the owner's wife.

SITUATION 5: As he lies wounded, a soldier on the Mexican side in the Mexican-American war envisions a future in which, following a United States victory, California and Nevada are ceded to the U.S. just as the Gold Rush and Silver Rush get underway. The vision not only resuscitates him but ignites his resolve to ensure that Mexico wins the war instead of the United States.

SITUATION 6: Just as he is about to be struck down in battle, a general in an ancient war is transported into the future where modern people show him instruments of warfare far beyond his time. The reason: They want him to change the course of history. The soldier is returned to the battlefield with a super-advanced weapon, but it falls into the enemy's hands.

SITUATION 7: The fighting on this alternate-earth battlefield is between two species of humans, the only physical difference being that of size. The war was triggered by the smaller species' claim that the larger was unlawfully settling on the other's land.

SITUATION 8: A Native-American militia in possession of a powerful secret weapon invades a Great Plains town and holds it hostage. Their demands include return of Indian territory—a vast amount of territory—wrongfully confiscated 150 years ago.

SITUATION 9: The battlefield in this future war exists in cyberspace, but the consequences of winning or losing a cyber battle influence physical reality—not through consensus but through mind control. Everyone in this future world is born with a neural chip that keeps them connected to events occurring in cyberspace.

SITUATION 10: In this fantasy world, battles are fought on chessboards the size of a small town and must follow the rules of chess. However, some of the soldiers/chess pieces have illegal tricks up their costumed sleeves.

CATEGORY 3: BUSINESS-WORLD CONFLICTS

In the modern world, the workplace is the preeminent battleground. Here there may be no bloodshed (well, almost none), but heads will nonetheless roll, if only metaphorically. And if the threat of heads rolling is not imminent, there are plenty of other causes for job-related trepidation, as you'll find in these situations.

SITUATION 1: Feeling that her marketing schemes are not taken seriously because of her gender, the narrator looks for ways to discredit her principal male competitor. Alas, he uncovers her schemes and attempts to discredit her.

SITUATION 2: No longer able to tolerate his boss's insensitive managerial tactics, an employee is determined to make the boss see the error of his ways. However, the boss discovers the scheme and becomes even more draconian—and the employee is in danger of losing his lucrative job.

SITUATION 3: An ambitious but reckless, low-ranking company executive takes over the presidency of the organization after his father falls ill—but his plans violate the original mission of the company and trigger a bitter clash between father and son.

SITUATION 4: A recently fired, disgruntled employee seeks revenge by luring clients away from his old employer to the new company that hired him. But after doing so, the new employer begins treating him unfairly.

SITUATION 5: Despite her years of loyal service, a technician is laid off due to lack of seniority. Tempted to blackmail the CEO (she had an affair with him, a married man), she opts for an even more potent form of retaliation: whistleblowing. But matters get complicated when the CEO discovers her plan and threatens a counter-blackmail.

SITUATION 6: Something sinister is brewing in management. Employees are suspicious of massive overhauls but have nothing tangible to go on, until one of them overhears a chilling conversation between the CEO and the vice president and discovers something far worse.

SITUATION 7: Healthy competition between rival companies turns unhealthy after each company releases a new product of similar (but not identical) attributes. Things become more complicated when the designers of the respective products discover they are distantly related.

SITUATION 8: A copywriter persuades a company to adopt a clever but controversial advertising campaign that leads to a lawsuit. The copywriter looks for a way to persuade the filers of the lawsuit to withdraw, but the filers refuse to back down.

SITUATION 9: An accountant embezzles funds from her company to finance a medical experiment designed to combat a deadly disease her husband is suffering from. Just when the experiment gets underway, her embezzlement is uncovered.

SITUATION 10: The narrator has a crush on a female employee who accuses him of sexual harassment after he compliments her on her appearance. He demands that she retract the accusation, but she files a second complaint instead. Fearing that he may lose his job, he resorts to an unorthodox way of vindicating himself.

CATEGORY 4: DEMOCRACY VS. DICTATORSHIP, MONARCHY, OR THEOCRACY

> Can there be such a thing as a benevolent dictator or a philosopher king? Is democracy truly the best safeguard against tyranny? Consider developing one or more of the following story situations designed to immerse you in the fascinating, thorny issues of governance.

SITUATION 1: In an imaginary country, a civil war is about to break out between those who insist on government by the people as the best hope for social harmony and those who insist that government by a "philosopher king" offers the best hope. The protagonist rallies support for the former, while a former friend rallies support for the latter.

SITUATION 2: What sort of leader will the people prefer—a conservative who vows to preserve traditional marriage at all costs or a liberal who vows to support alternative marital relationships at all costs? In this future society, a government insider is able to get an up-close look at both candidates and subsequently makes a passionate case for one over the other.

SITUATION 3: When a theocratic leader issues a mandate that all citizens must attend worship services, the citizens revolt—but their aesthetic agenda is as radical as the theocratic leader's.

SITUATION 4: Sensing that his theocratic government is crumbling, a monarch implores the deity on which his government is based to manifest himself to the populace as a means of winning their trust. When the deity does not heed the request, the monarch stages a series of "miracles," hoping the people will regard them as divine manifestations.

SITUATION 5: Despite having a bounty on his hide for "disturbing the peace," a minister in the Reconstruction-era South argues for a reform democracy that sees women, minorities, and homosexuals as equal to whites. When several white supremacists beat him severely, a covert ally pledges to carry out the reformer's dream.

SITUATION 6: A secret branch of a country's defense department is scheming to stage a military coup of the government, but one of the schemers has second thoughts and, together with a partner in the secret branch, plans to divulge the scheme to the Premier.

SITUATION 7: Matriarchy, anyone? A newly independent country decides to form a government ruled only by women, on the grounds that women have a far better track record of maintaining peace and harmonious international relations than men do. But an all-male oversight committee sets out to prove that no matriarchy can last.

SITUATION 8: A coven of witches attempts to form its own government—a wiccocracy? But to make it happen, the members need to recruit "normal" politicians to gain a socially acceptable foothold, especially those politicians who have shown (secretly or publicly) an interest in sorcery.

SITUATION 9: Vampires assemble to form their own government, their own army, and their own internal security in order to withstand ongoing onslaughts by the living.

SITUATION 10: The president of a small nation tries to change her government into a theocracy after she experiences a divine epiphany. She appoints herself as supreme leader, claiming that an angel so instructed her. When the citizens threaten to revolt, she implores the angel to address the people. The angel consents, but the people accuse her of being a fake.

CATEGORY 5: THE CLASH BETWEEN INDUSTRIALISTS, ENVIRONMENTALISTS, AND NATURE LOVERS

> Traditional thinking assumes that industry and nature are incompatible, and while that may sometimes be the case, there are such things as "green" industries. Even so, the clash between the use of natural resources for urban and technological development and preservation of the wild continues. Many timely stories are possible here.

SITUATION 1: Wishing to capitalize on the market potential of solar power, an entrepreneur who promotes herself as "green" aims to cut environmental corners. Despite warnings that her plans would endanger natural resources, she forges ahead and triggers an environmental disaster.

SITUATION 2: A manufacturer has been secretly disposing of hazardous materials illegally to avoid the cost of recycling them properly. When children playing near the illegal dump site become ill, the narrator (a parent of one of the children), with the help of an environmental activist, traces the source. The manufacturer, however, fights back.

SITUATION 3: A petroleum refinery sits on ecologically sensitive land. Despite the refinery's efforts to cooperate with environmentalists (by establishing a nature preserve nearby), some of the more radical environmentalists do all they can to get rid of the refinery altogether.

SITUATION 4: Environmentalists try to stop a dam from being built on an ecologically sensitive river. The dam would deliver desperately needed water and electricity to a nearby community, but it would also result in extinction for several animal species.

SITUATION 5: A shape-shifting polar bear changes into a human and tells a large group the sad story of his rapidly shrinking habitat. When several of the audience members threaten him, he changes back into a bear—but that angers the people even more.

SITUATION 6: A group of nature lovers wishes to live free from industry and technology. Before too long, they discover just how difficult it is to live that way. They give up electronic communication, including radio, television, and the Internet; they give up motorized vehicles and even high-tech hospitals, choosing to rely on folk medicine. The protagonist is torn between embracing the ideal and keeping a foothold in the twenty-first century.

SITUATION 7: The owners of a nature sanctuary battle the state over plans to build a highway nearby. The proposed highway would generate millions in tourist revenue; but the nature sanctuary has succeeded in protecting endangered but little known species.

SITUATION 8: Militant environmentalists take over an endangered ecosystem and prohibit visitors in motorized vehicles from entering. But a group of hunters with SUVs scheme to attack the environmentalists—who have anticipated such an attack.

SITUATION 9: A developer wishes to build a golf course in an ecologically sensitive region, resulting in a battle between golf enthusiasts (who would otherwise have to travel many miles to the nearest golf course) and environmentalists. But one of the golfers, sympathetic to the environmentalists' cause, suggests a way to serve both needs.

SITUATION 10: Ecologists try to prevent a lumber company from cutting down a forested area that harbors an endangered species. When the company proceeds with deforesting (despite government warnings), the ecologists sabotage their equipment, leading to a violent confrontation that the narrator struggles to resolve.

CATEGORY 6: THE CLASH BETWEEN LOVERS (CURRENT OR FORMER)

Can there be a more commonplace source of conflict than between the romantically involved? It is likely that more stories are based on the conflict between lovers and spouses than on any other source. The ten scenarios that follow should whet your appetite for a rousing clash between those who profess—or once professed—to love each other.

SITUATION 1: Two trapeze artists/lovers turn on each other after a new performer enters the picture. The new performer schemes to seduce the male trapeze artist, an old rival—not because she has fallen in love with him but because she wants to undermine his ability to perform. The female trapeze artist, however, has a scheme of her own.

SITUATION 2: After remarrying, the narrator regrets his decision to divorce his first wife and tries to win her back. Meanwhile his second wife learns of her new husband's sentiments and tries in vain to resolve the matter. The husband is lured back, but is it out of rekindled love or the desire for retribution?

SITUATION 3: Former tennis rivals are in love with the same woman, a tennis champ. But the rivalry threatens to undermine all three of their performances on the tennis court. The woman comes up with a clever situation to get everyone up to speed for upcoming tournaments.

SITUATION 4: Scientists working on a research project fall in love; when they disagree on the details of their research, their relationship threatens to cloud their judgment, and they wonder whether to suspend their relationship or suspend their collaboration on the project. The urgency of the research may help them make this decision.

SITUATION 5: After having pledged undying love to his Iraqi sweetheart, an American soldier does not maintain communication with the woman after he returns to the United States. But the Iraqi woman, pregnant with his child, flees her country and seeks out the soldier.

SITUATION 6: Despite the professional distance a psychiatrist keeps from his patients, one of them, a severely bipolar woman, falls in love with him. He knows he must proceed with great caution because the woman has exhibited suicidal tendencies.

SITUATION 7: A marriage counselor falls in love with the man whose marriage she is trying to save. The harder she tries to quell her growing attraction, the stronger it grows, especially after the man's wife ridicules him in her presence.

SITUATION 8: When a young college professor falls in love with one of her graduate students (who is only five years younger), the graduate student's current live-in partner becomes insanely jealous and threatens violence against the professor. But the professor harbors a violent streak herself.

SITUATION 9: A gay couple is harassed when they move into a conservative neighborhood. But the gay couple's relationship is more harmonious than most

29

of the heterosexual relationships in the neighborhood. Discovering this, the gay couple makes an effort to educate the other couples.

SITUATION 10: Two couples whose marriages are shaky go on a cruise in an effort to rekindle romance. Everything goes wrong until an incident onboard offers them an unexpected opportunity to resolve their problems.

CATEGORY 7: THE CLASH BETWEEN GANGS AND GANGSTERS

Gangs and crime families are subcultures unto themselves, with their own sets of rules and rituals, any violation of which can lead to enmity and violent reprisals. Stories highlighting the actions of organized crime groups—past, present, and future—make for absorbing reading.

SITUATION 1: In a postapocalyptic world, humanity has been reduced to roving gangs in search of food. When one gang encounters another, they fight for each other's resources. One of the gang leaders wants to integrate outside gangs into her own as a better way to pool resources, but the gang members are reluctant to cooperate.

SITUATION 2: Two gangs fight for supremacy in an embattled region of an American city. One of the gangs wants to establish brothels, casinos, free-narcotics dispensaries, and illegal activities; the other gang wants to purge all such illegal activities and set up a dictatorship based on a strict moral code, one that includes violence to enforce the code. Somehow the city must rid itself of both gangs.

SITUATION 3: A gang of vampires clash with a nearby gang of witches. Things get complicated when a group of vampires abducts some of the witches and turns them into vampires. The vampires underestimated how much more powerful the witches would become as hybrids.

SITUATION 4: Several young women train themselves in kickboxing and form a street gang to even the score with a gang of thugs who assaulted one of the women. The thugs laugh off the threat ... until the women send two of them to the hospital with broken jaws. Tensions escalate.

SITUATION 5: In postapocalyptic America, the only way to ensure survival is to join a gang, but some gang leaders require their members do things that are morally questionable. The narrator joins a gang dedicated to getting rid of the more violent gangs—a task requiring rigorous training.

SITUATION 6: By the twenty-second century, global crop failure has led to widespread famine and the rise of black marketeering of foodstuffs, which is controlled by rival gangs. A major gang war over corn is underway in the Midwest—and the victor could decide the fate of millions.

SITUATION 7: Religious gangs clash in a future world where the ruling gang controls religious beliefs. Each gang must gain recruits in order to succeed at overthrowing the existing gang. To gain new members, the gangs offer promises (of rewards in the afterlife, of divine favor in this life, etc.)

SITUATION 8: Rival gangs of robots duke it out in the twenty-second century. One gang is dedicated to protecting humans; the other is dedicated to ridding the world of humans. Complicating matters are spy robots that infiltrate each gang. Humans disguised as robots also infiltrate the enemy gang.

SITUATION 9: Female gangs are widespread in this future world, where men are sickly because of a genetic disorder. The female gangs clash over what roles the men, given their disabled condition, should play. One gang wants men to serve as slaves; another wants them to become mere breeders; a third gang wants to do all they can to restore men to good genetic health.

SITUATION 10: The narrator is a counselor who is working with street gangs, trying to re-channel their intragang ethics into community-action ethics (using job opportunities as an incentive). However, two of the gangs she is working with do not easily dispel their hostilities toward one another.

CATEGORY 8: RELIGIOUS OR SPIRITUAL CONFLICTS

It has been argued that conflicting religious views have caused more strife throughout history than any other source of conflict. True or not, such conflicts have resulted in great works of literature: George Bernard Shaw's *Saint Joan*; T.S. Eliot's *Murder in the Cathedral*, Hermann Hesse's *Siddhartha*, Salman Rushdie's *Satanic Verses*, Yann Martel's *Life of Pi*, and others. The possibilities for stories based on religious or spiritual conflict remain vast.

SITUATION 1: A religious cult that has attracted thousands of followers has fortified itself in the mountains. In the valley, young people are leaving their homes for the mountain compound, and no one can figure out how to stop them. Finally, agents attempt to infiltrate the compound.

SITUATION 2: A biology teacher at a church-affiliated school is laid off on the pretext that her classroom performance is not satisfactory (even though her student evaluations are stellar). She suspects that she is being let go because she refuses to teach creationism or intelligent design as "alternative" theories to evolution. A colleague thinks he can help her out of the dilemma.

SITUATION 3: After researching the scientific experiments conducted on the Shroud of Turin since 1978, a chemist who had never before had any spiritual convictions experiences a "Saul becoming Paul on the Road to Damascus" conversion. Now his colleagues ridicule him and even hint at discrediting him in the scientific community.

SITUATION 4: In this fictional society, it is a felony to criticize the state religion on grounds that such criticism causes social instability. The protagonist is a free thinker who defies the State by encouraging debates about the state religion, on the grounds that open discussion of religion contributes to much greater stability. The State disagrees and threatens to arrest the protagonist.

SITUATION 5: A minister who has struggled with the issue of gay marriage counsels a young man with homosexual tendencies. The minister is inclined to tell him that, in accordance with Scripture, he must regard those feelings as unnatural and pray to be relieved of them. Yet the more the minister interacts with the man, the more inclined he is to disavow those Scriptural teachings.

SITUATION 6: God pays a visit to a reclusive atheist, but the atheist convinces himself it was a hallucination. After God visits him again, the man asks a female colleague to stay with him for a few days, but she assumes he just wants to seduce her. Finally, he devises a plan that will help him decide once and for all whether these visits are real.

SITUATION 7: Five religious people who have become friends at work get together to discuss their respective religious convictions and share their conflicting feelings—especially with regard to how best to place those convictions in the context of the other religions.

SITUATION 8: The lives of three narrators who have suffered hardships are transformed in three different ways after visiting a shrine to the Virgin Mary. The transformations are not blatant but occur subtly and gradually. Each narrator must figure out what he or she is being called to do.

SITUATION 9: An atheist couple attends a religious event that doesn't affect the wife but deeply affects the husband—to the point where he experiences a divine revelation and renounces his atheism. The wife is deeply troubled by this change in her husband.

SITUATION 10: In a small town, church attendance suddenly declines precipitously. The town's clergy visits families of those who've dropped away—in an effort to learn the cause—and what they discover enables them to launch a campaign to win back the flock.

CATEGORY 9: SCIENCE VS. SUPERSTITION

> We assume that one of the reasons the Dark Ages were dark was that superstition dominated so much of everyday life. Yet even today we see how superstition still governs some people's lives. Be that as it may, the clash between science (or rationality) and superstition can generate fascinating stories that probe the human psyche.

SITUATION 1: A family refuses medical treatment for their seriously ill children. Insisting that any effort to force the children to take medication would offend their guardian spirits, the parents threaten violence to anyone who interferes. However, one of the children, who is desperate to survive, conspires with one of the physicians.

SITUATION 2: What we consider superstitious beliefs are observable phenomenon in this alternate world. People who break mirrors really do suffer seven years of bad luck, and so on. Thus, people are paranoid about violating any of the many taboos associated with these odd occurrences. One day, a "mad" scientist insists he can put an end to superstition-grounded phenomena.

SITUATION 3: A scientific-minded owl tries to introduce superstitious birds to the laws of nature, but they will have no part of such seditious nonsense. When the owl persists, the others plot to silence him for good ... but then a pragmatic crow, seeing value in both science and superstition, intervenes.

SITUATION 4: A brother and sister with opposing worldviews: One sees the world governed by scientifically demonstrable laws, the other, by magical and divine forces. They argue endlessly, each trying to convince the other that their way of apprehending the world is the best way. Then something happens to convince them that their respective worldviews are both correct in different ways.

SITUATION 5: In a postapocalyptic world, people have resorted to superstitious beliefs, having condemned science and technology as evil forces. The narrator strives to convince people of the opposite—that it was the irrational misuse of science and technology that led to Armageddon.

SITUATION 6: Superstition governs the relationship between two lovers. When one of them decides it is time to stop relying on superstition, things start to go wrong. One sees this as evidence that superstitions are real; the other sees it as a psychological aberration. Finally something happens to resolve the matter for them.

SITUATION 7: Although a prehistoric village nears starvation after a fire destroys their food sources, the people fear crossing the sea, believing it to be the gods abode. An outcast member of the group (she refuses to believe in the gods) is willing to cross the sea in search of food—but she needs a courageous crew.

SITUATION 8: The narrator, deciding never to let superstitious thinking influence her decisions, makes a heroic effort to ignore the superstitions she once believed in, if only subconsciously. But she soon discovers that vanquishing thirty years of belief is easier said than done.

SITUATION 9: Two communities have evolved on a small island: one governed by superstition (but enjoying fun and games); the other governed by logic (with no time for fun). The two societies never interact. A visitor realizes how one society could help the other, if only they could get along. He thinks of a way to pull it off.

SITUATION 10: A black cat is superstitious of people crossing its path; a rabbit keeps a human finger attached to its leg for good luck. In this world, animals suffer the superstitions of humans, and their lives are topsy-turvy because of it.

CATEGORY 10: SUPERHERO VS. SUPERVILLAIN

The more powerful the hero, the more powerful his or her nemesis must be for the story to work. Superman must have his Lex Luthor, Batman his Joker, and so on. Here are ten story scenarios that require you to pit a superhero against a supervillain in ways that should keep your readers glued to the page.

SITUATION 1: Samson, just prior to his unfortunate encounter with Delilah, is forced to confront a Philistine warrior with superhuman powers bestowed upon him by the Philistine god Dagon—powers that are equal in magnitude to Samson's.

SITUATION 2: A visiting angel tells a teenager that she is destined to save humanity with her supernatural powers. The girl asks, "What powers do I have?" But the angel refuses to tell her. "What am I supposed to save humanity from?" The angel merely points up at the night sky.

SITUATION 3: A creature claiming to be a paranormal superhero inhabits the body of a teenager to hide from a supervillain who is chasing him through many parallel universes. The teen wonders if these creatures are actually video-game-generated beings that found a way into the real world, if he's going crazy, or if the superhero's story is true.

SITUATION 4: Hercules has his work cut out for him in this unrecorded eighth labor in which he must battle an ogre living in a cavern far below the Acropolis. But the ogre has powers exceeding those of Hercules. Desperate, Hercules begs the gods for additional strength or cunning. He receives neither and instead finds a new gift within himself.

SITUATION 5: Here's a scenario that Homer never included in his *Odyssey*: After blinding Polyphemus (the cannibalistic Cylops), Odysseus must battle Polyphemus's brother Steropes, who is even more ferocious.

SITUATION 6: Oedipus's sons Polynices and Eteocles inherit their father's throne at Thebes, agreeing to rule in alternate years. But after Eteocles's term expires, he refuses to step down. Polynices responds with an army (the fabled Seven against Thebes). Legend has it that the brothers killed each other in battle—but in this scenario things turn out differently.

SITUATION 7: Two monarchs from enemy kingdoms face each other in a unique battle staged to avoid massive loss of life through regular warfare. The losing side agrees to vacate the island. When it looks as if his monarch is losing, however, the commander deploys his army in violation of the monarch's orders.

SITUATION 8: Two would-be superheroes battle it out in a contest to become the chosen Super Guardian. They must demonstrate not only extraordinary physical strength but cleverness as well. Things become complicated when both resort to dirty tricks—albeit clever ones.

SITUATION 9: A T-Rex challenges his opponent for supremacy, but they are equally matched. Bleeding heavily, they are on the verge of doing each other in when the female T-Rexes convince the contenders to work toward being cooperative—for their food supplies are running low and other, smaller competitors are moving into their hunting territories.

SITUATION 10: A homeless man, unaware that he is considered a superhero in a parallel universe, plunges through a portal that materializes during a fierce electrical storm. He is greeted by residents of a strange world who expect him to battle one of the most formidable villains ever.

CHAPTER 3

CONFESSIONS OF X

CATEGORY 1: CONFESSIONS OF ARTISTS, AUTHORS, AND MUSICIANS

Artistic expression can be a kind of confession or spiritual catharsis. Sometimes artists are driven to confess transgressions that their art only partially satisfies, if at all. Sometimes they become so haunted by their artistically rendered confessions that they are driven to commit even more transgressions.

SITUATION 1: A portrait painter tends to fall in love with his female models, no matter how hard he tries not to let that happen. He now faces his worst predicament—the governor's wife has asked him to paint her portrait, and she seems just as interested in him as he is in her.

SITUATION 2: A writer confesses that her stories are coming true. Because of this, she tries to write only happy stories—but halfway through their telling, a demonic force takes over. When her husband discovers the draft of a story in progress about a homicidal wife, he fears for his life.

SITUATION 3: Whenever a pianist performs, moments from his traumatic childhood surface and interfere with his concentration. He confesses these private experiences to his wife, but it doesn't help. He then sets out to confront those responsible for these traumatic events.

SITUATION 4: A mystery novelist confesses to using actual cold cases as premises for his stories. This strategy puts his own life in jeopardy when his fictional resolution for one book turns out to be true and the killer confesses other crimes to the novelist while evading detection from the police.

SITUATION 5: The rock-star narrator of this tale wants to confess his sins but is unable to come right out and do so. Instead he uses a coded language embedded in his lyrics. One of his ex-girlfriends is savvy enough to decode some of the lyrics, which she uses to blackmail the singer.

SITUATION 6: A painter confesses a terrible crime via symbolic images in her paintings. It is the task of the narrator, a detective with a knack for interpreting complex clues, to decipher them. Meanwhile, the painter has escaped abroad with her lover.

SITUATION 7: The narrator is a songwriter who has mastered his skills to the point where he can confess his sins through song lyrics without anyone realizing. Although he moves millions with his songs, one person is able to interpret what he is really expressing and confronts him.

SITUATION 8: Years after being found innocent for a crime he actually did commit, a poet confesses his guilt to a woman with whom he has fallen in love. Torn between wanting to protect him and wanting to turn him in, the woman considers a way to achieve both goals.

SITUATION 9: After describing to a friend the monster that has been haunting her for years, a sculptor, acting on the friend's advice, depicts the monster in a clay sculpture. This opens a mental doorway to a traumatic moment in her past that the friend helps her to confront.

SITUATION 10: Facing what seems like certain death aboard a sinking ship, passengers, all of whom are aspiring writers, confess their sins to one another; but at the last minute, when they are rescued, they realize they must figure out how to live with their confessions.

CATEGORY 2: CONFESSIONS OF CRIMINALS

Bad guys experience guilt too—sometimes to the point of confessing (often obliquely) their transgressions. Some people confess to committing crimes they never committed—or tried to commit but couldn't—as if they aspired to a life of crime. Try your hand at developing any of the following scenarios that focus on the psychopathology of criminals.

SITUATION 1: The head of a mob family is visited by an angel who tells him to stop his criminal activities and confess. The angel also says that if he does so, there will be a reward in store for him and his family once he gets out of prison. The mob boss is torn between heeding the angel and continuing his successful business operations.

SITUATION 2: After burglars break into a gun shop, steal the automatic weapons, and go on a shooting rampage, a group of gun-rights advocates have a change of heart and launch a gun-control campaign. Ironically their lives are threatened by radical members of the anti-gun-control lobby.

SITUATION 3: A jewel thief is mesmerized by one of the gems she has stolen: It reflects the image of a saint to whom she always prayed as a child. She confesses her thievery to the saint, who tells her to return the gem to the owner—which she does. But when the owner presses charges, something strange happens.

SITUATION 4: Mutual crook confessions: Two roommates, a cop and a burglar, confess their secret lives of crime to each other. They also castigate each other for their choices in life and reach a deep level of understanding about human motivation.

SITUATION 5: The viewpoint character confesses to a crime he did not commit. Perhaps it's his way of getting media attention after a lifetime of being invisible; perhaps he is harboring a death wish or is insane. Or perhaps he is being crafty—crying wolf so that nobody will believe him when he really does commit a crime.

SITUATION 6: During Prohibition, the owner of a speakeasy confesses his crime to the police in exchange for leniency. The cops still demolish his place, and he avenges the betrayal by setting up a dozen speakeasies when he gets out of jail.

SITUATION 7: The narrator dreams of robbing a bank with a beautiful woman as his partner in crime, Bonnie-and-Clyde–style. When the opportunity comes, though, his supposed girlfriend (who is secretly in love with an ex-con who did rob a bank) beats him to the punch and is caught. The narrator confesses to the crime to protect her and then later learns whom she really loves.

SITUATION 8: Several criminals get together every week to confess their petty (or not so petty) crimes. Afterward, they vote on who committed the most outrageous crime and the others pick up his beer tab. However, each feels tempted to outdo the others by committing a more serious crime.

SITUATION 9: Now advanced in age, a former KKK member confesses his crimes committed during the pre-Civil Rights era, but instead of just asking forgiveness, he asks the African-American community to help him decide how to best donate his vast fortune to their community before he dies. Will they accept the offer?

SITUATION 10: A presidential candidate confesses in private to obtaining documents about her opponent's personal life and falsifying them before leaking them to the press. When the confession is also leaked, her opponent goes on the offensive.

CATEGORY 3: CONFESSIONS OF THE DISSATISFIED

Everyone wishes that some aspect of his or her life were different, whether it involves physical appearance, intelligence, particular skills, or temperament. We often keep these "grudges" private, but every now and then, we confess them to someone, sometimes simply to ourselves.

SITUATION 1: All his life, the protagonist wished he could play a musical instrument but never had the drive or dedication. He confesses his wish to a genie that offers to grant him his wish to become a gifted pianist—but he must give up two of his other skills to accomplish this.

SITUATION 2: In this scenario for a children's story, a cat confesses to her mother that she wants to be a dog. From her window perch, she notices how the dog next door always gets attention, plays with neighborhood children, etc. Despite her mother's warnings about the disadvantages of being a dog, the cat arranges the transformation with a magician.

SITUATION 3: A recently married woman reveals to her husband that she is bisexual and wishes to take a female lover while continuing with her marriage. The husband agrees, but their relationship soon begins to fall apart.

SITUATION 4: After a year of bliss in Heaven, the narrator confesses to St. Peter that she is bored with harps and basking in divine golden light. She wants out. St. Peter agrees to return her to earth but only as an animal (her choice of species).

SITUATION 5: A woman tells a specialist in sex-change operations that her life would be happier as a man. But the surgery leaves her without any functioning gender characteristics. She demands to be changed back into a woman, but the surgeon confesses that he wasn't actually qualified to operate and is being sued by others in her situation.

SITUATION 6: A genie with a sense of ethics grants one wish to whoever confesses, and subsequently atones for, one transgression. However, anyone who is granted the wish but does not atone for the transgression he or she confessed to will be severely punished.

SITUATION 7: Like most goddesses, the narrator is immortal, but she tells a magician that she is willing to give up her immortality in exchange for someone to love. He arranges it, but after her relationship crumbles, the goddess expects the magician to give her back her immortality.

SITUATION 8: Zeus is bored with being ruler of the universe and lord of the Olympian gods, and he confesses as much to his wife Hera. Hera, on the other hand, has been looking for a way to get even with Zeus for all his philandering. She wouldn't mind taking Zeus's place at the top of the pantheon.

SITUATION 9: No matter what his wife does to please him, the husband is never pleased. He finally confesses his dissatisfaction to his closest friend, who offers him unconventional advice on what he needs to do to spice up his marriage.

SITUATION 10: Now that she is a multimillionaire, the protagonist misses the days when she struggled to make ends meet. She decides to give away her millions to charities. Ironically, her benefactors help her to become even richer than before.

CATEGORY 4: CONFESSIONS/DISCLOSURES OF HEALTHCARE WORKERS

Medical and health-care professionals, from candy stripers to brain surgeons, have many stories to tell about lapses in judgment, fears, cover-ups, accidents, loss of confidence, and so on. What stories can you develop out of the following situations?

SITUATION 1: An orderly has been keeping close track of an intern who seems to be harboring ill will toward a certain kind of hospital patient. Finally, he divulges his suspicions to his supervisor, but the gesture backfires.

SITUATION 2: After being condescended to one time too many, a surgical nurse plots a way of getting even with an arrogant, bullying surgeon during a surgical procedure. When she realizes she has inadvertently endangered the life of the patient, she confesses her plot to the surgeon.

SITUATION 3: A therapist confesses to disclosing confidential information about one of her patients after learning that patient might be endangering someone's life. When the patient gets wind of the breach of confidentiality, he seeks revenge.

SITUATION 4: After years of mistreating nurses, a surgeon confesses his wrongdoing to the press and then goes a step further by organizing a fight for nurse's rights and for the profession of nursing itself. Meanwhile, he must overcome resistance from fellow surgeons.

SITUATION 5: When a surgical nurse confesses her frustrations to the hospital administrator regarding the erratic behavior of a distinguished surgeon during an operation, she is chastised for speaking out of her area of expertise. But after the patient lapses into a coma, her concerns are taken more seriously.

SITUATION 6: The director of a nursing home confesses substandard conditions to a reporter working undercover. But the exposé the reporter publishes is greatly exaggerated. When nursing-home staff members come to the director's rescue, he vows to make the facility a model example.

SITUATION 7: A country doctor confesses to a journalist about his role in the deaths of local children due to the intolerance of those in his community who spurn modern medicine in favor of divine intervention. He tells stories of children who died because their parents refused treatment, situations made worse because he did not push harder or seek outside advice even though he knew better. His lack of resolve has eaten away at him and he is now determined to make up for these past mistakes.

SITUATION 8: The nurse assigned to a famous patient confesses to using unorthodox healing techniques after the standard ones failed to work. She is threatened with losing her job if she uses those healing techniques again—but when the patient seems about to die, she decides to use them anyway.

SITUATION 9: A physical trainer confesses to less-than-ethical choices he made working one-on-one with men and women who were driven to achieve top physical condition for any number of reasons—and how some of his efforts backfired.

SITUATION 10: Afflicted by psychotic episodes of increasing frequency, a respected surgeon confesses to his therapist of episodes that have occurred in the operating room. Despite the therapist's advice that he take a leave of absence, the surgeon continues to operate on patients.

CATEGORY 5: CONFESSIONS/DISCLOSURES OF EMPLOYEES AND EMPLOYERS

Most workplaces these days are guided by clearly defined ethical standards, but that does not mean that all injustices have been wiped out. There are still plenty of stories to tell about the unjust relationships between employers and employees.

SITUATION 1: An airline attendant confesses her true feelings about the passengers she must deal with every day. In a series of flashbacks we vicariously experience her ordeal with rude, paranoid, belligerent individuals. Ironically, the person to whom she confesses these incidents is an airlines informer, who concludes that the attendant hates her job.

SITUATION 2: A sweatshop manager in a third-world country confesses to a local newspaper reporter that the owner forced him to neglect fire-safety measures, which led to the deaths of three workers. When the manager's confession leaks, the owner tries to exact revenge.

SITUATION 3: After years of emptying wastebaskets and shredders in the office building where he works, a night janitor discloses incriminating evidence about certain employees, culled from shredded documents he had painstakingly reassembled.

SITUATION 4: Disguised as a computer technician, an industry spy gains access to a competitor's confidential documents. When caught red-handed by a member of the rival company, he discloses the materials but also offers the rival a proposition he cannot refuse.

SITUATION 5: A boss who has imposed draconian working conditions on her employees has a change of heart when one of her best workers becomes seriously ill. After disclosing her dysfunctional work conditions to the owner of the business, she decides to improve conditions—but her past improprieties have resulted in lawsuits.

SITUATION 6: Despite her disdain for standardized tests, a popular teacher begins "teaching to the test" when the superintendent warns the teachers that they will be fired unless their students achieve a certain ranking. When the teacher discloses this tactic, the superintendent threatens to fire her ... unless she agrees to help manipulate the test results.

SITUATION 7: Following a catastrophic oil rig explosion, a supervisor pins the blame on a subordinate (who was guilty of other, more minor problems), when he himself was responsible. But when the subordinate, a family man, is threatened with imprisonment, the supervisor confesses his guilt. In gratitude, the subordinate does all he can to absolve him.

SITUATION 8: Convinced that he could never be prosecuted for sexual harassment, a manager finds clever excuses for harassing his female subordinates. The harassed women find a way to get even: during a party they trick him into confessing his "boys-will-be-boys" tactics ... which they capture on tape.

SITUATION 9: A dock worker confesses to helping drug smugglers get their shipments through customs, but word of his confession leaks to the drug cartel, endangering his life. An FBI agent promises to give him immunity (and protection) in exchange for helping the FBI flush out the cartel members.

SITUATION 10: After his employer fires dozens of employees and then outsources those same jobs for much lower wages, an employee divulges his tactics to state officials. Ironically, the state officials are in collusion with the employer, and now the employee's job (and even his safety) is being threatened.

CATEGORY 6: CONFESSIONS OF LOVERS AND SPOUSES

Lovers and spouses usually have a lot they'd like to confess about their love lives. Romantic and marital relationships are complicated, virtually by definition. Good stories about such conflicts, however, can help shed light on how to resolve them.

SITUATION 1: The narrator falls in love with a woman who is secretly a transsexual. When the transsexual discloses that she was born male, he is initially shocked. But the more he learns about her early life, the more accustomed he becomes to her transgendered nature.

SITUATION 2: A woman obsessed with jewels confesses to her therapist how she got men to steal (not purchase) precious jewelry for the romantic thrill of wearing stolen property—and how her childhood experiences led her to develop such a need.

SITUATION 3: Two cooks in a restaurant express their love for each other through their cooking prowess. The more amazing the dishes they create, the more romantically attached they become. But then one of them takes a liking to exotic dishes that the other finds unappetizing.

SITUATION 4: Once they were formidable rivals in the fashion world; now they are lovers, confessing their respective past indiscretions to each other. But at least one of these indiscretions triggers another round of rivalry and distrust.

SITUATION 5: An idyllic love relationship goes terribly wrong when one confesses to the other that he is capable of reading minds. But the mind-reading lover is also capable of bestowing that gift on his beloved.

SITUATION 6: The graduate student of a famous scientist confesses her love for the scientist while working on a secret experiment with him. When he shuns her, she threatens to blackmail him. Because of the secret nature of the experiment, he wants to stay in her good graces.

SITUATION 7: Several years into their marriage, just as it is on the brink of collapse, a husband confesses to his wife that he is bisexual. His wife acts shocked, even though she herself has secretly held back bisexual urges. The event gives her the courage to explore her bisexuality.

SITUATION 8: After a parishioner confesses to the local priest that she is in love with him, the priest, after much hesitation, leaves the priesthood to pursue a relationship with her. By then, the woman has fallen out of love with him. Mortified, the now former priest takes extreme steps to reignite her affection for him.

SITUATION 9: Two dragons confess their love for each other but are repelled by each other's bad habits: One cannot stop exhaling fire when he's angry, and the other cannot stop herself from eating people when she's angry. Together they sign up for relationship therapy with a dragon therapist—who has issues of his own to deal with.

SITUATION 10: The chauffeur of a wealthy widow admits that he has been in love with her all the time he worked for her—thirty years, before she had even met her late husband. Assuming he is just after her money, she ignores the admission—but then he does something astonishing for her that changes her mind.

CATEGORY 7: CONFESSIONS/DISCLOSURES FROM THE MILITARY

Clear communication is vital in the military, but misunderstandings, even deceptions, do occur—usually inadvertently, but sometimes deliberately for complex reasons. The dynamics of trust, obedience, and strict protocols in tense and dangerous situations can become the basis for suspenseful tales.

SITUATION 1: When a decorated combat veteran suddenly relives horrific moments on the battlefield after having suppressed them for years, he decides to return his medals and confess that not only did he not deserve them but that he had committed war crimes.

SITUATION 2: A sergeant suffers from guilt after assigning a private to a dangerous mission that leaves him severely wounded. In confessing his decision, the sergeant reveals that he held a grudge against the private, one that now seems silly. However, the sergeant also vows that he will do all he can to make up for his lapse in judgment.

SITUATION 3: After threatening to report sexual harassment, a female cadet suddenly becomes seriously ill. Her roommate suspects that she was poisoned. When an investigation is launched, the sexual-abuse problem turns out to be widespread and more female cadets' lives are put in jeopardy.

SITUATION 4: To get even with his sergeant for not recognizing his valor, a soldier divulges that sergeant's inappropriate activities. The sergeant finds out about it and threatens the soldier with a court martial, unless the soldier agrees to aid him with inappropriate activities.

SITUATION 5: Top-secret military files describing highly controversial chemical experiments have gone missing. Officials must disclose the contents of the documents to investigators if they hope to get them back, but one of the documents is so sensitive that the officials continue to keep it secret—yet it is the one document that could lead investigators to the culprits.

SITUATION 6: When a female sergeant replaces her male counterpart, the soldiers under her command have difficulty taking her seriously, and she confesses to a soldier that she abhors the draconian philosophies of the male sergeant. Working with her in private, the soldier helps her to become a stern leader who motivates soldiers humanely.

SITUATION 7: After American soldiers open fire on their own troops, thinking that they are the enemy, an investigation is held to determine the cause of the accident—and (secretly) to determine whether one of the soldiers is an enemy infiltrator who'd disseminated false information.

SITUATION 8: A specialist in the psychopathology of soldiers investigates allegations that some soldiers are after the thrill of killing—a syndrome that could result in premature judgment about when or when not to open fire.

SITUATION 9: Rumors of a sex scandal in a military academy are being investigated by the narrator, who discovers that the alleged scandal is merely the tip of the iceberg: An officer requesting immunity confesses drug trafficking, gambling, and extortion.

SITUATION 10: During an underwater test run, a submarine technician uncovers a conspiracy to mutiny against the captain, who is alleged to have a drinking problem. But the technician discovers that the rumor is false and that a more sinister motive for mutiny is afoot.

CATEGORY 8: CONFESSIONS/DISCLOSURES FROM THE POLITICAL WORLD

Politicians, like salespeople, must spend much of their careers wheeling and dealing, learning to be specific but not too specific, compromising on issues while still appearing to support them without compromise. Sometimes the line between sincerity and insincerity can be blurry indeed.

SITUATION 1: A senator running for re-election confesses to a friend that she has always hidden her real views on a particular issue, on grounds that disclosing them would cost her the election. But having confessed in private, she now feels that she should confess in public because she feels like a hypocrite.

SITUATION 2: A popular, young conservative candidate thrills his base by championing traditional values (marriage not being extended to same-sex couples, prayer being returned to the schools, etc.) and wins a landslide gubernatorial race, but later confesses that he is truly moderate, and even liberal, on most issues and misled the overwhelmingly conservative voter base in the state to win the election. While calls come forth for a new election, the young governor races to push through his once-hidden agenda with a sympathetic state congress.

SITUATION 3: During the second-term presidential campaign, one of the President's advisors confesses to leaking sensitive information to the rival candidate about the President's re-election strategies. When the rival candidate uses that information to his own advantage, it backfires. Was this the plan all along? A journalist explores this theory.

SITUATION 4: Having been neglecting his duties, a senator confesses to having an affair with someone on his staff. Despite calls for his resignation, he makes a valiant effort to redeem himself, arguing that a sinner who confesses his sins his more trustworthy than those who appear not to sin and are not as devoted to their jobs as he.

SITUATION 5: After having won the respect of her party, a congresswoman confesses to the media that the motives behind her policies were self-serving, that she has one issue she wishes to fix, and then she plans to step down. When her party turns on her she is determined to raise their consciousness on the issue.

SITUATION 6: The mayor of a Midwestern city confesses to shady dealings with a crime syndicate. Now, as members of the syndicate are being brought to justice, other members are attempting to kill the mayor for ratting on them.

SITUATION 7: In this totalitarian state, confessions are obtained through drugs and hypnosis. A journalist gets herself arrested on purpose, hoping to capture the state's brutal methods of interrogation, but her captors discover her scheme.

SITUATION 8: An administrative assistant to a state legislator discloses evidence of corruption in her department, but the agent to whom she discloses the evidence is himself part of the corruption operation and her life is now in danger.

SITUATION 9: A popular congressman suffers a nervous breakdown. When he recovers, he confesses to being a warlock. Although his colleagues are outraged and try to run him out of office, the people in the district he represents support him more than before.

SITUATION 10: After championing a bill that the President wants to push through Congress, a senator changes his mind and attacks the bill. He confesses that he was exacting vengeance on the President for not appointing him to a post once promised to him. But then, when the bill looks as if it will fail, the senator has a second change of heart.

CATEGORY 9: CONFESSIONS OF RELIGIOUS PERSONS

Because they are regarded as exemplars, religious leaders may harbor the darkest secrets of all—and the guilt that accompanies these pent-up secrets can be overwhelming. Here are ten scenarios for you to devise your own clergy-generated confessions.

SITUATION 1: A priest devoted to his calling experiences a crisis of faith, which he confesses to a fellow priest—who in turn (for various reasons) shares this confession with the Archbishop. It turns out that the Archbishop, too, has had a crisis of faith, which he confesses to the troubled priest.

SITUATION 2: After attracting a large following, a faith healer confesses to her congregation that she is a fraud—but they refuse to believe her, insisting that she truly had healed at least three of her followers.

SITUATION 3: A shaman living in the U.S. confesses to using voodoo to cast spells on people whose policies he disagrees with. The spells seem to work—but is it possible, the narrator (a detective) wonders, to prosecute someone for practicing voodoo?

SITUATION 4: Haunted by intense visions of Heaven and Hell, a monk turns to therapeutic techniques, such as capturing the visions through paintings, poems, and journal entries. When some of the works go viral, they cause mayhem.

SITUATION 5: After years in the pulpit, and having gathered a large following a charismatic preacher is exposed as a fraud: he had never been ordained. But after he is driven out of town, some of his followers stage a protest in support of his good deeds over the years.

SITUATION 6: A priest consumed by guilt confesses his sins—a few each week—from the pulpit, despite his certain knowledge that his congregation (already diminishing) will disappear altogether. But to his astonishment, his congregations increases dramatically. "Keep confessing!" they seem to be telling him.

SITUATION 7: Despite her valiant effort to be an exemplary spiritual leader, a minister cannot entirely escape her past—especially when she becomes widely known for her ability to renew the faith of members who have fallen away from the church.

SITUATION 8: A self-appointed religious leader "confesses" a completely imaginary life of crime as a way of gaining fame, or rather, infamy. Once he gains that attention, he stops confessing—but his followers insist that he continue confessing or they will expose him as a fraud. However, some former members of the faith are on to his lies.

SITUATION 9: A nun confesses to being the author of murder mysteries featuring serial killers, deranged sadists, terrorists, and the like. A recluse, she refuses interviews, but that just intensifies the public desperation to learn more about her—and whether she is hiding some terrible secret.

SITUATION 10: Certain events have led a devout religious leader to doubt the existence of God. This revelation first comes to him in a nightmare, and is reinforced by events taking place over the next several days. He confesses these experiences to a confidant who suggests that the events may be God's way of testing his faith.

CATEGORY 10: CONFESSIONS OF TRAITORS AND DECEIVERS

> Dante reserved the lowest circle of hell for those guilty of treachery. But perhaps they can at least partially redeem themselves by confessing their deceptions and betrayals. Here are ten situations for you to transform into stories that explore the depth of this particularly vile brand of villainy.

SITUATION 1: During the American Revolution, a soldier everyone thought to be devoted to the Colonists' cause switches loyalties and serves as an informant for the British, but soon, consumed by guilt, he switches back and confesses all to General Washington. Before being executed as a traitor, he engages in a heroic deed.

SITUATION 2: A con artist maintains dual identities with two women, pledging allegiance to each of them. One of the women uncovers the deception and decides to get even by informing the other woman—but the other woman intends to keep the relationship going and decides to do away with the first woman.

SITUATION 3: When an attorney discovers evidence (loot from a burglary) that the client she is defending is actually guilty (even though he swore to her that he was innocent), she threatens to drop the case unless he gives her most of the cash (to pay for her daughter's exorbitant hospital bills)—but the attorney's blackmail scheme backfires.

SITUATION 4: Lacking a sense of ethics, a sales manager orders her employees to use deceptive techniques in selling their products. Her scheme is to uncover dirt on each of them and blackmail them into complying with her sales tactics. But one salesperson confesses all that is going on to an ethics board.

SITUATION 5: A 1950s movie star confesses her secrets in old age to her biographer. Her special talent was mind control, which she used to sway studio executives into giving her contracts. But one executive was immune to her powers, and he still wants to get even with her.

SITUATION 6: A contest of confessions to see which deceiver can out-confess the others. Deceiver A bets he can out-deceive Deceiver B; Deceiver C bets she can out-deceive them both ... and so on, until the most deceptive one of all wins a trip anywhere in the world, all expenses paid. The twist: The deceivers are all local leaders of differing faiths.

SITUATION 7: In exchange for leniency, a traitor confesses to his espionage activities, but he withholds confessing the most serious acts—just in case the request for leniency is rejected—which is what happens. Will he receive leniency in exchange for confessing that serious act, even though such a confession could compromise national security?

SITUATION 8: An expatriate writer renounces his past jeremiads against the publishing industry in open-letter confessions; not surprisingly, when he asks his former publisher to re-publish his books, they refuse. But then a newfound friend agrees to serve as an intermediary.

SITUATION 9: Pretending to renounce her American citizenship, a double-agent "confesses" military secrets to the nation to which she appears to be defecting in order to gain secrets from them. Unlike the Paul Newman character in Hitchcock's *Torn Curtain*, this agent intends to sell her information to a third country for a huge sum. However, a colleague discovers her motive.

SITUATION 10: After renouncing his citizenship over international policies, an American expatriate confesses to being bribed. In exchange for amnesty, he agrees to disclose the names of those who have been plotting to share sensitive information to an enemy nation.

CHAPTER 4

THE CONQUEST OF X

CATEGORY 1: CONQUERING A BAD OR DANGEROUS HABIT

Stories about addictions and habits aren't limited to "interior" drama. For example, an alcoholic's struggle to stop drinking (see Situation 2) contains a psychological torment but also the external struggle with family, friends, work, etc. A good story about breaking a bad habit will likely contain both interior and exterior drama.

SITUATION 1: A guidance counselor cannot control her kleptomania. Friends and family cannot stop her from pilfering small items from shopping establishments. But one day, she gets caught and her career is threatened.

SITUATION 2: Although a police detective manages to control his alcoholism by following Alcoholics Anonymous directives and taking medication, he lapses during a traumatic investigation. His only hope is for a friend to rescue him but that friend has developed a drinking problem herself.

SITUATION 3: Unable to break the habit of stealing jewelry at arts and crafts shows, the narrator seeks help from a therapist who suffers from the same affliction. Together they vow to rid themselves of the habit—but their growing romantic feelings for each other complicate matters.

SITUATION 4: To help break her boyfriend's habit of losing his temper at the least provocation, a psychology student tries to get to the root of his problems by asking him to describe certain moments in his childhood. She soon realizes, however, that she has put herself at risk by doing so.

SITUATION 5: The narrator is at her wit's end about to how to break her clever dog's habit of digging up neighbors' yards in search of bones. Then one day the bone he brings home a human bone.

SITUATION 6: A private elementary-school teacher who espouses the idea that smoking and drinking are signs of immorality is secretly addicted to both and vows to give them up. But the addiction and cycle of guilt worsens. One day she gets careless and several children not only catch her drinking in the school, but they tell the principal.

SITUATION 7: Bad habit or good? A billionaire hands out hundred-dollar bills to homeless people. On the surface, it appears to be a charitable act, but ironically her generosity triggers greater woes for many recipients who use the money to buy drugs—or purchase guns.

SITUATION 8: A teenager cannot stop abusing her telekinetic powers (e.g., levitating bullies or transporting her parents to the rooftop when they quarrel). No one dares to help her ... except an old boyfriend.

SITUATION 9: To stabilize her violent mood swings, a woman asks her therapist to hypnotize her. When he does, he discovers a dangerous personality within. Unsure of how to treat her, he knows he must try something before the dangerous side of her personality takes over for good.

SITUATION 10: A respected CEO, who is also a compulsive gambler, embezzles funds to feed his habit. Just when he is about to gamble an entire pension fund, a friend intervenes with a scheme to help him quit gambling for good.

CATEGORY 2: CONQUERING INTIMIDATION

Many of our toughest "interior" battles stem from our desire to stand up for what we believe in spite of the threat of ridicule or harm. It's difficult to fight these battles alone. The situations that follow should help you create dramas in which characters young and old strive to become the courageous individuals they dream of being.

SITUATION 1: After being bullied repeatedly, a student is rescued from despair by a friend who encourages him to get even without bullying back. After the ploy backfires and he becomes depressed, the friend has one more plan up her sleeve.

53

SITUATION 2: To overcome extreme stage fight, an aspiring actor tries various mind games to help him become more comfortable before an audience. It is only when he faces a crisis situation that he manages to vanquish his fears.

SITUATION 3: A politician retains confidence in her causes despite great dissension, but after her marriage breaks up, her resilience crumbles. Ironically, her estranged husband does all he can to restore her confidence and maybe even their marriage.

SITUATION 4: Ridiculed for her musical tastes, an accordionist abandons her instrument. But one of those ridiculing friends repents and finds a way to get her to perform again.

SITUATION 5: An avant-garde artist sometimes ridiculed for his paintings is ready to give up when a former teacher has second thoughts about his work. Now the teacher must convince the artist—who's in the process of destroying his paintings—why his work has merit.

SITUATION 6: A near-drowning accident prevents a talented swimmer from entering an Olympic Games elimination competition. It takes a therapist who experienced a similar trauma herself to help him overcome his fear of reentering the water.

SITUATION 7: Driven by a rival's intimidation and daring, a former circus performer plans to walk a tightrope from one skyscraper to another, blindfolded and without a net. The rival's intimidations become sinister when it appears that the former circus performer just might pull it off.

SITUATION 8: Two sisters, fierce rivals when growing up, become rival businesswomen. Things take a turn for the worse when one threatens the other with a lawsuit for stealing her ideas. A business partner with the accused sister finds an unusual way for the sisters to resolve their conflict.

SITUATION 9: A chronic stutterer dreams of overcoming his affliction and becoming an actor, but continual bullying and inadequate progress in speech therapy dampen his ambitions. Then a wise teacher comes up with a plan that would help him to reach his goal faster than he thinks.

SITUATION 10: Longing to become an actor does not diminish a young woman's stage fright. She has tried therapy, mental tricks that fellow thespians have suggested, and even sedatives, but nothing works. Then she meets an actor who claims to have recovered from stage fright and is convinced he can help her—but his methods are unorthodox.

CATEGORY 3: CONQUERING A DISEASE OR ILLNESS

Illness and disease are often complex, difficult to diagnose, and difficult (if not impossible) to cure—but the efforts of the medical profession are unwavering, along with the efforts of individual sufferers to triumph over their afflictions. As the following scenarios suggest, disease- or illness-themed stories can be suspenseful and inspiring.

SITUATION 1: Despite being diagnosed with a neurological disorder, a teacher is determined to prove that the condition is reversible or at least manageable while continuing a career. The educator's son, a health-care professional, cannot decide whether to help his parent; years ago, they had a falling out.

SITUATION 2: The wife of a hypochondriac tries ingenious methods of helping her husband conquer his affliction, but nothing works until she stumbles upon a possible cure nobody would have expected—a cure that could be worse than the disease.

SITUATION 3: What bizarre disease is causing people's skin to turn blue? As researchers search for an answer, it becomes evident that blue skin is only the tip of the iceberg—people's behaviors are changing, too. Finally, a pathologist offers a theory: The blueness is caused by excessive use of electronic devices.

SITUATION 4: People in an isolated community suffer from a disorder that causes them to turn violent for no apparent reason. Who can one turn to when even the police, the clergy, and medical professionals are also afflicted by this disorder?

SITUATION 5: In the early twenty-second century, a genetically engineered antiviral agent mutates into a lethal virus that other antiviral agents cannot neutralize. A team of microbiologists works feverishly to come up with a new kind of miracle drug.

SITUATION 6: The protagonist suffers from an unknown illness that causes her to lose her sense of time. She does not know if she is talking to someone "now" or years earlier. A neurologist thinks he has determined the cause—but it seems too fantastic to be real.

SITUATION 7: Children in a small town contract a disease that heightens their senses. For example, they begin to hear things miles away. They also begin to hear people's thoughts—the reason the town physician is reluctant to treat them.

SITUATION 8: Bacteria dormant since the last ice age are discovered in Greenland's permafrost and brought to the United States, for study, but a lab accident causes the bacteria to escape quarantine. People quickly become infected with a bizarre illness. The protagonist must find an antidote before the disease spreads.

SITUATION 9: A village is stricken with a sleeping sickness. People fall asleep and do not awaken for forty or more hours and, when they do wake up, their personalities are altered. A specialist in sleep disorders tries to solve the problem. After he falls ill with the disease as well, he gains insight into its nature, but his new personality keeps him from creating an antidote.

SITUATION 10: Should a cure for a deadly disease be adopted if the means by which that cure was obtained is unethical? Or does the end always justify the means? A dying boy's family begs the doctor to use the controversial cure, but the doctor resists.

CATEGORY 4: CONQUERING ENVY OR JEALOUSY

It is said that envy and jealousy are left-handed forms of flattery. These green-eyed monsters can ruin a healthy relationship if not kept in check. In any case, they can fuel powerful tales and have done so since ancient times.

SITUATION 1: A newlywed couple experiences bouts of jealousy triggered by insignificant instances that are blown out of proportion. Aware that their marriage is being threatened over trifles, they both independently search for ways to vanquish their jealousy—but not before the groom demonstrates a serious lapse of judgment.

SITUATION 2: Sick of the public's obsession with appearance, a young woman instigates a revolt against the fashion industry and targets models in particular. The more her efforts gain influence, however, the greater the backlash.

SITUATION 3: A marathoner is driven to win an upcoming race, but her deeper goal is to beat her principal rival. Alas, the rival decides to drop out of the race. How she can persuade him to reinstate himself?

SITUATION 4: A failed businessman becomes jealous of his daughter whose business becomes successful after she resorts to tactics that her father condemned.

Suddenly her business starts to decline, and she discovers that her father has something do with it.

SITUATION 5: Pathologically jealous of her husband, a woman sees a psychiatrist who thinks he can cure her of this fault. His treatment, involving the transference of emotion, backfires when she transfers her jealousy into aggression in her sales job.

SITUATION 6: A struggling singer realizes that her jealousy of the singers she idolizes is interfering with her growth as a performer. She begins composing original songs, but they do not advance her career until she recruits a publicist. The publicist then becomes jealous of the singer.

SITUATION 7: Jealous that his girlfriend is flirting with other men, the narrator asks a friend, an actor, to stage a knife fight with him in front of the girlfriend. The friend complies, and the narrator thinks that the girl will be impressed with his courage. Alas, the friend isn't too skilled with his knife. While the boyfriend recovers, the actor begins to fall for the girl and confesses his role.

SITUATION 8: Envious of her friends who can sing, a high-school student takes voice lessons but makes no progress. A friend tells her she must deal with her envy in other ways. Easier said than done but together they find a new, surprising talent!

SITUATION 9: Mutually envious and fiercely competitive, the narrator and her sister reach a point where their competitiveness interferes with their athletic performance. The narrator communicates this to her sister, but the latter assumes it's just another ploy to get her to drop her guard.

SITUATION 10: The narrator seeks spiritual guidance to rid himself of envy and jealousy at work. But when a rival employee receives a promotion that he, the narrator, expected, he berates his spiritual guide on grounds that envy and jealousy are necessary in the competitive workplace. Is he right?

CATEGORY 5: CONQUERING A PHOBIA

> The toughest obstacles to our mental well-being may very well be ourselves. Phobias have a way of impeding our ambitions and even destroying them altogether. It usually takes professional guidance to help victims break through these psychological obstacles—and the effort to do so can yield compelling stories.

SITUATION 1: Fear of open spaces (agoraphobia) prevents a recluse from enjoying the outdoor activities his wife loves After letting her engage in her activities alone (and consequently feeling like they're drifting apart), he makes a heroic attempt to overcome his phobia.

SITUATION 2: A claustrophobic woman who avoids taking elevators must now use them in a hotel after being given a room at the top floor. Her first elevator ride is uneventful, but on the second, the elevator jams. Those riding the elevator with her try to keep her from panicking.

SITUATION 3: After experiencing an emergency landing, a business executive becomes fearful of flying (aviophobia)—a problem because her profession requires her to fly often. Despite her efforts to vanquish the phobia, it doesn't go away—until she meets someone with a similar affliction.

SITUATION 4: After almost drowning, the protagonist develops a fear of water (aquaphobia), whether swimming or boating or even walking on beaches. While he is at a lake, struggling to overcome his phobia, he witnesses a boat capsizing. He and his friend want to rescue the boaters, but the protagonist's phobia is a formidable obstacle.

SITUATION 5: Certain events have eroded a teacher's self-confidence and he develops a fear of public speaking (glossophobia) after years of being comfortable in social situations. To vanquish his phobia, he analyzes his teaching skills—and makes a startling discovery.

SITUATION 6: Until her fiancé takes her hot-air ballooning, a woman never realized her fear of heights (acrophobia). Caught in a windstorm, they are buffeted severely and the woman panics, endangering the two other couples in the balloon. Clever thinking on everyone's part helps the woman overcome her fear.

SITUATION 7: Plagued by recurring nightmares, a woman develops a fear of sleeping (somniphobia). Sleep therapists have not helped. Home remedies have not helped. When her nightmares become a waking reality, she fears losing her mind altogether. Finally, someone from one of those nightmares steps forward with a possible solution to her crisis.

SITUATION 8: Despite his arachnophobia, a biology student has a scientific interest in spiders, especially tarantulas, and wants to put an end to their poaching (to satisfy the pet-shop market). But the more extensive his research, the more aggravated his phobia becomes.

SITUATION 9: A woman assaulted as a child by someone of a different ethnicity suffers from xenophobia. Even though her rational mind tells her it is illogical

58

to fear people because of their ethnicity, she cannot rid herself of the phobia. Finally, an incident occurs that helps her vanquish her fear.

SITUATION 10: Desperate for work, the narrator takes a job as night watchman even though he suffers from noctiphobia, or a fear of the night. At first he forces himself to concentrate hard enough on his duties to keep the phobia from getting the better of him, but on the second night there's a power outage, followed by strange sounds coming from the elevator shaft.

CATEGORY 6: CONQUERING LAZINESS OR LOSS OF AMBITION

Laziness or lack of ambition is like dead weight on our chests. All it takes is one big push and we're free, but that "big push" is not always easy to muster because the effort seems a lot more difficult than it actually is. The situation is similar to trying to get out of bed as soon as we awaken from a long sleep, and fighting this feeling can make for excellent drama.

SITUATION 1: A gifted athlete keeps missing golden opportunities because she cannot bring herself to practice—or, more precisely, to begin to practice. Once she is in the swing of things, there's no stopping her. But overcoming that sedentary impulse is nearly impossible for her—until she meets someone who shows her a few mental tricks.

SITUATION 2: Following a hand injury, a pianist loses his ambition to become a great performer, convinced that he could never achieve the dexterity needed to become a concert pianist. A physical therapist believes he can bring him to that level—but only with extraordinary effort on the piano player's part.

SITUATION 3: After serving heroically in combat, a veteran falls into depression as soon as he comes home, now that the continuous adrenalin rush of being at war has ceased. He loses all ambition and begins drinking heavily. But then a friend gets him involved with volunteer firefighting, hoping to rekindle his ambition for living and the feeling of brotherhood.

SITUATION 4: Crippled by depression, a laborer is unable to get out of bed one morning. His family and friends help him comb through facets of his life, and though they find various negative things, nothing qualifies as the cause of his depression. But then a friend turns up something unexpected.

SITUATION 5: An artistically talented teen loses her desire to paint after someone she admires criticizes her "poorly executed" drawings. Not even encouragement from teachers and other art experts are able to revive her desire to draw again. But then a psychologist comes up with a clever way to rekindle that desire.

SITUATION 6: Intimidated by fellow students, a journalism major decides to drop out of college, on grounds that she lacks the ability to make journalism her career, though her advisor believes otherwise. Finally an opportunity arises that requires on-the-spot reportage, and the student proves her worth to herself.

SITUATION 7: An aging circus clown is discouraged by his growing inability to do pratfalls and other physical comedy and makes kids laugh. Then a fellow clown comes up with some inventive new acts that are certain to generate laughter. But these new acts will take a lot of practice and daring to master.

SITUATION 8: After his wife leaves him, a country-western singer-composer loses his ambition to create new songs, despite the fact that country music thrives on songs about lost love. But after a female fan catches his eye, he begins composing songs about the conflict between new and old loves, and he finds great success. Hearing of his success, his ex returns, heightening his conflict.

SITUATION 9: Medicated for his attention-deficit disorder, a teen loses his ambition to do anything. When off medication, his ambition returns—but his temperament becomes dangerously erratic. A neurologist searches for a middle ground—but is "middle ground" acceptable for one who would otherwise be highly creative?

SITUATION 10: After months of being bullied about his ballet endeavors, a teen tells his teacher that he has lost his ambition to become a great dancer. Instead of dropping him from the program, she goes after the bullies and not only gets them to apologize but to become active participants in the ballet program.

CATEGORY 7: CONQUEST OF REASON OVER SUPERSTITION

Superstition cannot be brushed off lightly, even in our scientific age. Many people want to believe there are powers in the universe that transcend cause-and-effect rationality. And maybe, just maybe, there are forces that science may never be able to explain. While the jury is still out, we can rest assured that stories about the inexplicable will continue to be welcomed.

60

SITUATION 1: A journalist's superstitious mother is afraid to venture out of the house if her horoscope does not sanction it. Despite frustrating attempts, the journalist creates a clever ruse using a horoscope writer at the local newspaper to force her out of the house ... with unfortunate results.

SITUATION 2: A teacher with a strict evangelical upbringing who also developed a keen interest in science struggles to reconcile her religion with evolution and paleontology. At first swayed by Intelligent Design, she soon realizes that it is simply creationism pretending to be rooted in science. Her fiancé, a progressive theologian, helps her to resolve her dilemma.

SITUATION 3: Obsessed with performing superstitious rituals before playing baseball, a junior-league batter nevertheless keeps striking out. He blames it on not performing the rituals correctly, but the manager is convinced that the rituals themselves are to blame and discovers the underlying causes of the player's obsessions.

SITUATION 4: Once religious, a biology student struggles to maintain her faith despite the skepticism she must sustain to be a good scientist. Her musician boyfriend has the opposite problem: He is struggling to maintain his reasoning skills despite his conviction that the real world is ruled by magic. Together they work to resolve their respective dilemmas.

SITUATION 5: Convinced that faith healing will save their seriously ill daughter, a couple refuses medical treatment and threatens to sue if medical experts attempt to override their authority. When the daughter's fever reaches a critical level, the family lawyer attempts to persuade the couple to relent.

SITUATION 6: It's Friday the 13th, and seeing no hope for recouping her investment loss, a woman gets ready to jump out of her twentieth-floor office window. One of her associates sees her in time and tries to reason with her. Everything he says fails—but then he comes up with an especially persuasive tactic.

SITUATION 7: In this story, a ten-year-old becomes convinced that Santa Claus is some sort of demon or monster, thanks to a friend's father's strict moral lecturing. When his parents take him to the shopping mall (secretly to visit Santa), he panics the instant he sees him. Santa and his parents try to reason with the boy, but that just makes matters worse. And then Santa has a clever idea.

SITUATION 8: In a world where those who ridicule superstitions are suspect, many are enslaved by superstitions. The rationalists in this world are outcasts; they risk their lives trying to free people from their crippling beliefs, despite "evidence" to the contrary.

SITUATION 9: Because it is Friday the 13th, a superstitious guard refuses to unlock a vault reportedly containing a bomb. The others who know the vault code have been abducted. It is up to an FBI agent to reason with the guard so he will open the vault in time.

SITUATION 10: A diplomat uses reason to win the trust of refugee teenagers from an enemy nation. But the children have been indoctrinated by militant extremists and must be considered extremely dangerous.

CATEGORY 8: MILITARY CONQUEST OR RESISTANCE

History is filled with stories of the struggle to conquer. Whether armies or armadas set out to conquer nations or resistance fighters struggle to drive out conquerors, these experiences matter to us because they at least illuminate the human condition, if not improve it. Here are ten scenarios for you to work with.

SITUATION 1: After enjoying tranquility for years, a community is threatened with an invasion of extremists. Even before the threat, a less-than-idealistic member of the community was secretly training a group to use long-forbidden high-tech weaponry. The combat trainer needs recruits for their "army" to stand a chance, but no one wants to volunteer out of fear that the weaponry would bring an end to their peaceful way of life.

SITUATION 2: A high-tech battleship that has mysteriously traveled back five hundred years confronts an armada of sixteenth-century warships on its way to conquer another nation in its lust for world domination. But the battleship crew is determined to dissuade the warmongers of that objective by way of sophisticated technology.

SITUATION 3: During a military coup, the dictator targets the charismatic leader of the resistance to wipe out all that he represents: worker equality, the arts, distribution of wealth. But the resistance leader has more military savvy than the dictator realizes.

SITUATION 4: In the future, women wage war against men—literally. They have formed their own armies. But one of the female generals embarks on a diplomatic mission to resolve their differences, which are largely tied to inherent convictions about the essential nature of each gender.

SITUATION 5: Industrialists have declared war against environmentalists. At stake is the future of the planet, which teeters on the edge of a global-warming and pollution catastrophe. The industrialists insist that their approach to saving the planet is better: Regulate pollutants, and preserve the economy.

SITUATION 6: A highly skilled archer trains soldiers for the Battle of Agincourt (in 1415, part of the Hundred Years' War between England and France), during which the outnumbered English army fights the French army. The challenge: Imbue the men with courage despite the dismal odds. The English win the battle, thanks in part to the longbow and the skills of the archer and his men.

SITUATION 7: In an alternate earth, there are two species of humans: cybernetic nomads and peace-loving city dwellers. The nomads continuously attack the city dwellers in search of a precious substance that imbues the city dwellers with the strength to defeat the nomads.

SITUATION 8: The vampires in this world comprise an army bent on overwhelming the uninfected and corralling them for their sanguine needs. The survivors have found a new weapon and have installed them around their last bastion: huge UV sunlamps. But a traitor lies in their midst.

SITUATION 9: During the Punic Wars in the first and second centuries BCE, Rome conquered Carthage (near present-day Tunis), thereby extending its empire across North Africa. The protagonist is a citizen of Carthage, who witnesses the death of his culture and tries valiantly to preserve some part of it.

SITUATION 10: An antigovernment militia is poised to take over a state government after attacking an office building in the capital city and taking several workers hostage. A retired police chief once knew one of the militia members and thinks he can neutralize the group through that person.

CATEGORY 9: CONQUEST OF MIND OVER MATTER

Some of our toughest conquests are conducted internally. The weapon of choice in this battle is willpower, the ability to resist temptation. Much potential drama can be mined in this universal human struggle. The following situations should get you started writing a compelling mind-over-matter story everyone can identify with.

SITUATION 1: Accused of being timid one time too many, a young woman turns to dangerous, thrill-seeking activities on the weekend to spice up her life. When she sets out to do something seemingly suicidal, her former boyfriend (feeling guilty about initially encouraging her reckless behavior) tries to reason with her.

SITUATION 2: When it comes to quitting the bottle, the protagonist finds that her struggle to put mind over matter is complicated by the physical and psychological effects of alcohol addiction. But the protagonist is determined to quit because she is pregnant and wants to prevent fetal alcohol syndrome. The effects of withdrawal, however, are such that she doubts she can survive the ordeal.

SITUATION 3: After a gay teen has been bullied to the point of wanting to commit suicide, a friend intervenes just in time. Together they will confront the bullies, but before they can do that, the bullied teen must develop his self-esteem.

SITUATION 4: When identical twins display their feats of prodigious memory, their impoverished parents attempt to market their skill. But the twins secretly cultivate their ability to move objects by thought alone (telekinesis), which could bring them a fortune.

SITUATION 5: Because reading minds was getting her into trouble, the protagonist looks for ways to be rid of that power. But nothing makes it go away. Finally, she meets someone trained in eastern spirituality who claims he can help by bestowing some of his mental powers upon her.

SITUATION 6: Able to become invisible whenever he chooses, a scientist chooses to remain invisible after failing to find companionship outside of his work. Before too long, though, he grows tired of being invisible, and when he tries to become visible, nothing happens.

SITUATION 7: A magician discovers she can escape from any confined space, no matter how secure, just by concentrating hard enough. But then she encounters another magician who bets her a million dollars that she cannot escape the room he designed.

SITUATION 8: An innovative teacher at an inner-city school is criticized for introducing unusual creative methods of instruction to enhance her students' motivation for learning. Despite the principal's insistence on retaining traditional methods, the teacher secretly continues her creative methods to demonstrate the students' potential.

SITUATION 9: After a disastrous marriage, the narrator vows never to marry again, even though her lifelong dream was to raise a family and prove she could overcome her own harsh childhood. Finally a close friend helps her to overcome

64

her past and her fear of another failed marriage by way of focused mental exercises in self-determination.

SITUATION 10: An aspiring teacher suffers from severe stage fright. Therapists have not been able to help her. Although she can tutor one-on-one just fine, she longs for classroom teaching. Finally, one of her friends, an actor, comes up with an imaginative idea.

CATEGORY 10: CONQUERING A PHYSICAL DISABILITY

Life is filled with hazards. Accidents happen, and sometimes the injuries are traumatic and life-changing. Good stories about the different ways of coping with physical disability and about the struggle to conquer despair and physical limitations are always in demand in these dangerous times.

SITUATION 1: Can a singer continue his profession after laryngeal surgery? At first it seems hopeless, but a surgeon who has created an artificial larynx thinks she can modify her invention to make it work to meet the high demands of a singing voice. After initial modifications fail, the singer is ready to give up.

SITUATION 2: When she develops arthritis, a pianist fears her career is in jeopardy. She undergoes physical therapy, but the resulting improvements are inadequate. Finally she meets a specialist who takes an inventive but risky approach to treating the condition.

SITUATION 3: A teacher undergoes eye surgery to correct macular degeneration. When the bandages are removed, his vision is better ... yet different: He sees things that are not really there. By the time the surgeon agrees to operate again, the teacher wonders if his altered vision is a special gift.

SITUATION 4: Determined to remain the fastest sprinter ever, an athlete trains for the Olympics despite botched surgery for a severely torn ligament. But during rehab he pushes himself too hard and tears the ligament once again.

SITUATION 5: A marathoner suffers a heart attack during a race. Despite her cardiologist's recommendation to stop running, she hires a physical therapist to help her get into top shape. Just before the next marathon, however, her pulse becomes erratic.

SITUATION 6: Various maimed animals come together to tell stories of how they overcame their injuries—being struck by a car, losing a leg in a trap, escaping a fire, etc. Together the animals learn not only to cope but to capitalize on their ordeals.

SITUATION 7: Repeatedly told that he could never play professional basketball because he is too short, the narrator defies all odds with his court skills during college. Even so, no professional team is willing to recruit him. Then he achieves something truly extraordinary.

SITUATION 8: Badly scarred from an accident, the narrator becomes reclusive, convinced that her appearance is revolting. But one day she encounters a severely scarred war veteran whom people admire, calling his scarred face "noble" and "heroic."

SITUATION 9: Several war veterans form a support group. They are all amputees. All have gone through stages of despair; all have had to change their lives to accommodate their disabilities. Each shares his or her particular strategy of learning to enjoy life again by overcoming the traditional obstacles associated with the loss of limbs.

SITUATION 10: Paralyzed from the neck down (although his spinal cord was not severed) a veteran scoffs at anyone who claims he can regain partial use of his arms and legs through mental discipline alone. But then he meets a guru who teaches him mental powers he didn't know he had.

CHAPTER 5

COMMUNICATING WITH X

CATEGORY 1: COMMUNICATING WITH AN ANIMAL OR INSECT

Scientists have long tried to find ways to communicate with other species and have had very limited success with primates, such as chimpanzees and gorillas. But what if we found a way to greatly improve communication? What might we discover? The following story situations can help you generate some possibilities.

SITUATION 1: Unlike most chimpanzees that have been taught simple sign language, a chimp trained by a visionary animal psychologist can convey abstract ideas on a special computer; some of these ideas are astonishing. Unfortunately the sponsor plans to cut off funding because of the controversy brewing over these experiments.

SITUATION 2: A biologist discovers dolphins with amazing communication skills. But as she establishes two-way communication with them, the dolphins seem to have an agenda of their own and it involves the restriction of ocean exploitation.

SITUATION 3: While studying how a particularly aggressive species of ants communicates, an entomologist makes a disturbing discovery regarding their collective intentions—something to do with transforming their natural habitat into one that is dangerous to humans.

SITUATION 4: Bees bred to produce more honey are also developing advanced communication skills—not just with other hives and species of bees but other animals. Suspecting hostile intentions, one scientist tries to communicate with the bees—with unfortunate consequences.

SITUATION 5: In this world, horses speak but do not care to communicate with humans. The narrator, who shares her horse's love of magic, convinces the horse to lead her to a land of equestrian enchantment.

SITUATION 6: A Native-American child can communicate with wolves that are being driven out of their territory by hunters. The child tries in vain to help them, but some don't want his help. Meanwhile a group discovers the boy's activities and plans to use him to kill off all of the wolves.

SITUATION 7: In the future, bioengineers enhance the intelligence of various animals to get them to help save remaining habitats on a ravaged earth. Some of the animals turn against the humans and create their own sanctuaries.

SITUATION 8: Elephants are critically endangered in this world of the near future. Scientists in an African sanctuary are trying to communicate with genetically enhanced elephants. Their goal: Get the elephants to attack ivory poachers.

SITUATION 9: Scientists examining bizarre creatures on a distant world discover that they possess a complex language. They also discover that they can manipulate reality with language.

SITUATION 10: An ornithologist's research leads her to establish amazing human-to-crow communication. Once aware of this new communication channel, however, the crows deliver rather frightening warnings to the researcher.

CATEGORY 2: COMMUNICATING WITH THE SENSORY IMPAIRED

The story of how Anne Sullivan helped blind and deaf Helen Keller triumph over her disability has inspired millions. Today neurologists the world over are experimenting with ways to help the sensory impaired. Here are ten story scenarios to help you build dramatic tales of characters who overcome sensory handicaps to live happy and productive lives.

68

SITUATION 1: An operation enables a congenitally blind man to see—but what he sees is so incomprehensible that he fears losing his sanity. A friend finds a way for him not only to maintain his sanity but to use his new visual perception in a unique way.

SITUATION 2: Deaf since infancy, a boy hears voices that seem to be coming from space. Doctors conclude that his brain is compensating for his deafness, but one scientist discovers that the boy has made contact with aliens.

SITUATION 3: A rare disease causes a woman, who aspires to be a chef, to lose her ability to taste. A mentor teaches her to compensate by discerning how things taste by their smell and appearance. Alas, few restaurant employers are willing to give her a chance to prove herself.

SITUATION 4: Forbidden to leave the house, a precocious girl is homeschooled by her parents. An outside counselor tries to circumvent the parents, but the parents claim to have a valid reason for keeping their daughter apart from other young people.

SITUATION 5: Identical twins, separated at birth, maintain a mysterious psychic connection until one of the twins has an accident that leaves him mentally impaired. The other twin is determined to restore his mental ability.

SITUATION 6: Unable to feel pain because of a congenital disorder, a boy learns to live with the dangers involved. But where does he draw the line between living an insular existence and enjoying life? An acquaintance with her own disability becomes his guide—and he hers.

SITUATION 7: His short-term memory damaged by a head injury, a former chess champion struggles to regain his talent. A neurologist whose specialty is memory loss tries a new memory drug on him ... with astonishing results.

SITUATION 8: The narrator's platoon has been ambushed. Shell-shocked, the leader struggles to keep himself and his men alive, but the enemy is bearing down on them. Facing doom, one of the soldiers has a plan, but it requires the shell-shocked leader to assist him in what may be a suicidal maneuver.

SITUATION 9: Suffering from aphasia, a woman loses her ability to process and understand language. Ignoring her colleagues' conviction that no cure is possible, a neurologist tries a radical new form of therapy that may enable the protagonist to continue using language to communicate.

SITUATION 10: Sensory overload is this person's affliction, which keeps him from processing stimuli properly. The condition is ruining his life, but a neurologist figures out a risky strategy for how he might cope—and cope he does, but in a way that endangers those around them man and creates new problems.

CATEGORY 3: COMMUNICATING WITH THE COMATOSE OR HYPNOTIZED

The mind has been compared to a giant iceberg: While consciousness pokes above the surface the subconscious occupies the greater portion below the surface, and much of it is a mystery. Long before Freud's revelations, writers and artists created psychodramas rooted in the mysteriousness of the subconscious. The scenarios that follow will help you create your own.

SITUATION 1: A man displaying a demonic "second personality" is hypnotized in an effort to exorcise that evil second self—but instead of being exorcised, the demonic self becomes the dominant personality.

SITUATION 2: An important diplomat lies unconscious as a result of a serious accident. It is imperative that the top-secret information she was supposed to deliver—information so sensitive that her government would not risk putting it in writing or in digital format—gets delivered in person. But an enemy double agent gets to her first and tries to extract the information using hypnosis.

SITUATION 3: After being brought back to a former life via hypnosis, a woman reconnects with her long-suppressed alter-ego so that when she is awakened, she assumes that persona. The problem is that this persona is criminally insane.

SITUATION 4: An esteemed diplomat falls into a coma but her subconscious mind remains active, and the omniscient narrator relates her visions, which play out various versions of a current and dangerous diplomatic issue. After experiencing an array of decisions and consequences, the diplomat discovers a way to communicate with his caretakers and tries to resolve the issue.

SITUATION 5: A psychiatrist establishes communication with a woman who has entered a perpetual state of hypnosis. Nothing has been able to awaken her. At the same time, she is capable of conversing, although very slowly, and some of the things she says seem to come from an unknown plane of reality.

SITUATION 6: A hired killer is given posthypnotic suggestions that will cause her, at the confluence of certain circumstances, to assassinate government individuals as part of a scheme to overthrow the government. The protagonist must find a way to neutralize the hired killer's posthypnotic suggestions before it's too late.

SITUATION 7: Scientists tap into a subject's genetic memory—to a life lived in Biblical times. The patient's revelations about those times are neither in the historical record nor in Scripture. The scientists want to prolong the patient's hypnotic state, despite the danger of him permanently losing his waking self.

SITUATION 8: Spurned by the woman he idolizes, an infatuated young man plans to hypnotize the woman and influence her to love him. He manages to hypnotize her, but under hypnosis she discloses a facet of herself far from what he expected.

SITUATION 9: A time traveler from the distant future is trapped inside the body of a homeless person. When he persuades a psychologist to hypnotize him, the psychologist discovers how dangerous the time traveler could be.

SITUATION 10: A diplomat is injured in a car accident, and the doctor must induce a coma to keep him alive. But the secrets he carries in his mind must be conveyed several days before the surgeon can safely remove him from the coma. The only way out of the dilemma is to communicate with the diplomat while he is comatose.

CATEGORY 4: COMMUNICATING WITH THE DEAD OR UNDEAD

Death may be that "undiscovered country from which no traveler returns," as Hamlet memorably stated, but that does not prevent some people from trying to communicate with those who have crossed to the other side. Try your hand at developing one of the following scenarios involving reaching out to the dead.

SITUATION 1: A medium, knowing full well she's a fake, is astonished when during a séance she actually conjures up the spirit of a patron's dead grandfather, who subsequently refuses to return to the land of the dead when the medium orders him back.

SITUATION 2: After a plague transforms several of her friends and relatives into zombies, a biologist experiments with a way to restore some of their human attributes—but her methods yield unexpected side effects.

SITUATION 3: Vampire hunters discover that several of the emperors of ancient Rome became vampires and are still wandering the earth and searching for opportunities to infiltrate politics in various countries.

SITUATION 4: The narrator finds a way to communicate with Jesus Christ through a medium whose séances with other Biblical figures had driven him insane. The narrator must grapple with the medium's insanity in order to establish contact with Jesus.

SITUATION 5: A paranormal researcher establishes a communication link with a zombie who is part of an entire community of zombies living deep inside a cavern. Despite being warned to stay away, the researcher manages to locate the zombie colony—and puts himself in danger as a result.

SITUATION 6: Having learned to communicate with deceased persons by establishing contact with them immediately after they're pronounced dead, a sorcerer manages to bring one of these persons back to life, with unexpected consequences.

SITUATION 7: Determined to prove that Heaven exists, a researcher hypnotizes a woman and converses with her about her experiences after having been declared dead. What the researcher discovers is evidence of a realm no one has ever anticipated.

SITUATION 8: A hypnotist keeps his dying patient's consciousness alive after he physically dies so that he can describe the land of the dead in all its grotesque detail. When the narrator brings this man back to life, the patient has been horrifically transformed.

SITUATION 9: A carnival medium, pretending to establish communication with deceased loved ones, actually does establish such a link. At first she suspects that she has fallen for one of her own deceptions—but the spirit persists in speaking to her after she closes up for the day.

SITUATION 10: When a biochemist discovers a way to transform vampires back into humans, dozens of vampires storm his laboratory in hopes of receiving the treatment, but the treatment involves communicating with demonic forces that could destroy the vampires.

72

CATEGORY 5: COMMUNICATING WITH THE ENEMY

It is more likely that countries with widely differing cultural, political, and religious views will be enemies rather than allies; peace takes work. And even despite extraordinary efforts to achieve peace, those efforts can be in vain. Use the following scenarios to spark developing stories that illuminate a fresh approach to making peace.

SITUATION 1: The protagonist breaks a family rule by establishing communication with members of a family long considered a bitter enemy. He wondered why they should stay enemies forever, but his family has a reason: The enemy may be in possession of one of their precious heirlooms.

SITUATION 2: The leaders of two countries, enemies for decades, find common ground in their mutual respect for the natural world. Together they design a plan for lasting peace—but other members of their respective governments will do anything to stop them.

SITUATION 3: Who is the enemy, and who is the ally? In this scenario, enemy forces infiltrating areas thought to be in allied hands have disguised themselves as allies. The platoon leader, however, has devised subtle communication clues that will give them away ... or so he hopes.

SITUATION 4: Due to a dispute over territory, two formerly friendly nations become enemies. Despite the efforts of the ambassador of one nation to make amends, the other ambassador suspects a hidden agenda.

SITUATION 5: The United States has lost diplomatic relations with an ally that is rapidly becoming a paranoid enemy and secretly stockpiling nuclear weapons. The narrator must find a way to reestablish communication before the Premier follows through on his threat to launch missiles, but the Premier may be in the throes of a mental breakdown.

SITUATION 6: A brutal enemy threatens a peaceful kingdom, one lacking a strong military but harboring a wizard. The king warns the enemy that their military cannot stand up to wizard magic, but the enemy laughs it off. The king does not know that the enemy forces include an evil sorcerer.

SITUATION 7: Can one's best friend also be one's worst enemy? A musician considers this question, as his best friend (a rival musician who owes his success to this friend) secretly wants to destroy his reputation. Alas, both musicians at one time were in love with the same woman—the same one who now strives to find a way for both musicians to reconcile.

SITUATION 8: One of this European nation's most influential diplomats communicates misinformation to an enemy in the hopes of triggering a war that his country would surely lose—in retribution for a past injustice.

SITUATION 9: An enemy nation pretending to be an ally communicates misinformation to U.S. agents about a terrorist cell. The agents discover the ruse by intercepting coded communication to the terrorists. Hopefully the agents are not too late to prevent an attack.

SITUATION 10: As soon as an ally communicates vital information about high-tech military equipment, that nation breaks off relations with the United States. It is up to a top diplomat to learn the ally's reason for severing relations. Her discoveries draw her into a web of top secret operations in reaction to an unforeseen threat.

CATEGORY 6: COMMUNICATING WITH AN ESTRANGED FRIEND OR RELATIVE

> Friends and relatives often drift apart, sometimes for no justifiable reason. But friendship and close family ties are beneficial in so many ways that make the efforts to preserve those ties worthwhile. Stories drawing from this category can prove to be illuminating and healing.

SITUATION 1: Two women, once close friends, have become bitter enemies as a result of a love triangle. One of the women tries to make amends after her breakup with the man in question, but the other woman is still bent on revenge.

SITUATION 2: When her father divorces her mother, the daughter tells her father she never wants to see him again, assuming the breakup was entirely his fault. No matter how hard he tries to convince her otherwise, she refuses to see him. But then he comes to her mother's aid after she falls ill, and the daughter has second thoughts.

SITUATION 3: The narrator is warned by the father of his closest friend never to associate with his son again because the narrator is homeless. In a moment of solidarity, the friend runs away with the narrator to experience life on the street and later tries to reconcile with his father. The friend attempts to convince his family to take in the narrator, who is hopeful but afraid the plan will backfire.

SITUATION 4: Once the closest of friends, two college students become estranged over differing political views. Their views clash dramatically during a political rally. The rally's organizer is a moderate who knows both of the students and tries to get them to reconcile their friendship.

SITUATION 5: A mother leaves a small fortune to three of her four surviving children, but the fourth child is left with a tiny amount because of her life-long rebellion against the rest of the family. That estranged daughter does all she can to ingratiate herself to her siblings, in the hopes that they will share their inheritance.

SITUATION 6: Two close friends become estranged after one of them is diagnosed with bipolar disorder and becomes dangerous. Despite his illness, he believes that their long friendship will persist. One day, the bipolar friend loses control and nearly kills his good friend.

SITUATION 7: After being chastised for becoming romantically involved, the narrator and his cousin, both teenagers related through marriage, not blood, cave under the pressure and become estranged. But when his cousin is assaulted, the narrator fights back and resumes their relationship despite threats from bullies.

SITUATION 8: A modern-day Hamlet (narrator) is raised by his uncle after his father dies. But when the uncle makes advances toward his mother, the narrator feels alienated by him and tries to prevent their marriage.

SITUATION 9: Two religious friends drift apart when one loses her faith. The other tries to keep her in the fold, but she declines. She then experiences an epiphany that rekindles her spirituality, but it is nothing like her former church-oriented spirituality. When she conveys her spiritual epiphany to her friend, the latter is torn between her traditional beliefs and her friend's revelations.

SITUATION 10: When Siamese twins have a serious falling out, they decide to become surgically separated even though their chances of surviving the operation are slim. But while they await the operation, the fear of dying gives them renewed incentive to work out their differences.

CATEGORY 7: COMMUNICATING WITH HUMAN COLONISTS AND ALIENS

Despite a fifty-year search using radio telescopes, no extraterrestrial signals have been detected. But it's a big universe, and the possibilities are tantalizing. In the future, however, human beings will be colonizing space and developing into independent cultures, and maybe we'll even change physically.

SITUATION 1: A SETI (Search for Extraterrestrial Intelligence) researcher detects an artificial signal emanating from Triton, Neptune's largest moon—which doesn't make sense because that moon seems incapable of sustaining life of any kind, let alone intelligent life. Perhaps ETs from the stars have colonized Triton, probably with robot emissaries. NASA sends astronauts there to make physical contact.

SITUATION 2: Turning his ESP gifts heavenward, the narrator establishes contact with ETs who have been searching for a planet to colonize. The narrator, an undergraduate majoring in astronomy, becomes earth's first ambassador to the stars.

SITUATION 3: Astronomers intercept signals that may have originate in deep space. One of the transmissions, after being partially decoded, appears to be a response to an old television show. Other transmissions suggest something more ominous. Astronomers then debate about whether to respond to the transmissions.

SITUATION 4: In the twenty-second century, lunar colonists revolt against Earth rule in an effort to achieve independence, now that they are technologically self-sufficient. But Earth fears that the colony is too militant to be independent. The narrator must negotiate a treaty that will satisfy both parties.

SITUATION 5: The narrator discovers that an alternative reality exists, which is accessible by falling asleep in a specific room in her grandmother's home. She discovers her mirror self, as well as mirror friends and relatives. Things seem almost identical in this alternative reality, but there are subtle differences that can prove deadly.

SITUATION 6: Spacefarers in the future encounter beings whose religion is based on a deity that actually exists in their world and with whom the aliens communicate. When the astronauts try to communicate with the deity, their minds are transformed.

SITUATION 7: It is the twenty-eighth century. Human colonists on Mars and the moons of the outer planets have developed their own cultures and their own technologies. One colony wants no further interaction with Earth; however, the natural resources of their world make it too valuable a colony to give up. To prevent a war, the narrator struggles to negotiate with the colonists.

SITUATION 8: An expedition to Jupiter's ice moon Europa, with its subsurface ocean, leads to a discovery of intelligent sharklike creatures that possess limbs and have built dwellings inside vast sea caves. Once they manage to communicate with the creatures, the scientists are shocked by what they learn.

SITUATION 9: Something inexplicable has happened to the astronauts who journeyed to Venus to examine what appears to be an alien artifact orbiting the planet. Their brains seem to have become linked with an alien computer system. The narrator's job is to tap into that link and sever it.

SITUATION 10: Shape-shifting aliens infiltrate human populations on Earth and disguise themselves as preachers to win everyone's trust. Once they do, they try to convert people to their own religious views, which include learning distinctly inhuman skills.

CATEGORY 8: COMMUNICATION WITH A FUGITIVE

Fugitives from justice often have second thoughts about living in self-imposed exile. The clash between love of country and commitment to one's beliefs can be a powerful one that results in memorable stories. See what you can do with one or more of the following situations.

SITUATION 1: A fugitive from justice wishes to return to the United States after long ago abandoning her citizenship. Despite multiple governments accusing the fugitive of having revolutionary ties, the State Department agrees. The fugitive disappears once she enters the US, and only one FBI agent, long obsessed with her activities abroad, knows how to communicate with her.

SITUATION 2: A computer programmer in an enemy nation wants to defect to the United States. Intelligence officials insist that before she can be given asylum, she must agree to decode classified information from her country's military intelligence. The would-be defector quickly agrees—which leads the narrator to suspect that she may be a double agent.

SITUATION 3: The protagonist is innocent of the crime she's been accused of but guilty of a crime she has not been accused of, so she changes her appearance and tries to evade capture. An old friend learns of her whereabouts and establishes communication with her but then becomes torn between wanting to keep her safe and wanting her to face justice.

SITUATION 4: Angry that he has been falsely accused of being anti-American because he is a Muslim, the narrator confronts a neighbor. When the neighbor reports him, describing him as a terrorist, he runs away. An investigator for Homeland Security searches for a way to communicate with the fugitive and resolve the injustice.

SITUATION 5: Living abroad as a fugitive from justice, a playwright wishes to return to the United States—but he must face obscenity charges if he does. He wishes to communicate the fact that his plays, and the way they are staged, are not obscene.

SITUATION 6: Leading a group in designing a sting operation to flush out a dangerous fugitive, an espionage agent poses as a fellow conspirator to assassinate a major political figure. But to be convincing, the agent must learn an obscure language and become skilled at several other tasks.

SITUATION 7: A wealthy video-game designer goes into hiding after her jealous ex-husband accuses her of having plagiarized one of his ideas. The charge is false, but the inventor wants to avoid her ex's wrath. A clever mediator resolves the issue.

SITUATION 8: An Iraq War hero becomes a fugitive from justice after he and the militia he organizes fail to occupy a federal office building and hold its employees hostage. A fellow combatant in the War serves as mediator between the fugitive and the FBI.

SITUATION 9: Once a charismatic spiritual leader, the focal character has become a fugitive from justice after being accused of embezzling funds from a charity he helped establish. He is not the embezzler—but he fled the country to avoid the possibility of being charged with an even worse crime.

SITUATION 10: An engineer creates a robot that undermines his hopes for harmonious relationships between humans and intelligent machines. Disgusted, he destroys the factory where the robots are manufactured and goes into hiding. But one of the surviving robots, ironically, convinces him that not all is lost.

CATEGORY 9: COMMUNICATING WITH ONESELF

The word *communication* implies transmitting thoughts to others, but sometimes people need to communicate with themselves because they experience conflicting impulses, as the expression "being of two minds" suggests. Inner conflicts, like external ones, can generate powerful stories.

SITUATION 1: In this fantasy (rooted firmly in reality), a man whose inner nature is very conflicted literally splits into three persons. Only when they figure out a way to integrate their conflicting demands are they able to become one person again—but it takes a little outside help, namely a woman.

SITUATION 2: A person with bipolar disorder struggles with his conflicting selves: One self is a preacher; the other self is a vicious assailant. The preacher's efforts to vanquish the assailant self seem hopeless until a colleague suggests that vanquishing is not the solution; assimilating is.

SITUATION 3: The protagonist likes to talk to himself, despite the fact that everyone thinks he is mentally ill for doing so. He isn't schizophrenic; he simply acknowledges that three individuals comprise his psyche. Lately the arguments among the three selves have turned acrimonious, and something must be done to prevent all-out war among them.

SITUATION 4: The narrator's alter ego has become a separate person and is terrorizing her other half. No matter what the narrator does to reconcile their differences, her other self becomes increasingly menacing: She sneaks into her house and steals things; she sabotages plans with friends. Finally, the narrator figures out a way to bring her two selves back together.

SITUATION 5: After years of floundering and some jail time, an "at risk" adolescent catches the interest of a counselor who notices the teen possesses musical ability. Once she wins the teen's trust, she hypnotizes him to get him in touch with his artistic self. The result is a tempestuous outpouring of musical expression.

SITUATION 6: A painter with a split personality tries to reconcile his two warring selves—the self who paints serene landscapes and the self who paints violent scenes of war and destruction. Alas, the conversations turn into diatribes—until the violence-loving self threatens to annihilate the peace-loving self forever.

SITUATION 7: Conflicted over whether to pursue a lucrative career by training in her father's business or devoting herself to helping the poor, the protagonist tries to resolve her dilemma with therapy. Meanwhile her husband insists she pursue the lucrative career and give a percentage of her earnings to charity. But that, to her, seems a cop-out.

SITUATION 8: The protagonist and her alter ego (who emerges as a separate entity because she cannot abide living inside the other's skull) argue constantly over what constitutes the ideal man. They each agree to test out the other's preferences, using two dates as test subjects. The results are not at all what either self expects.

SITUATION 9: The spirit of a warrior from a lost kingdom partially takes over a woman's consciousness. When the woman begins to acquire her ancestor's views and habits, the situation wreaks havoc with the woman's daily life—especially when the warrior urges her to challenge an adversary to a swordfight.

SITUATION 10: Dissatisfied with his life as a custodian, a middle-aged man travels back in time to persuade his younger self to avoid the obstacles that kept him from pursuing his dream job. After convincing his younger self that he is his future counterpart, the former heeds the latter's advice—but his actions seem to be leading to the same outcome.

CATEGORY 10: COMMUNICATING WITH A SPIRITUAL ENTITY

What would it be like to communicate with entities from the heavenly or nether realms? Humans have invoked supernatural beings since prehistoric times, and countless tales have been written. Try your hand at some of the following otherworldly scenarios.

SITUATION 1: It is one thing to see a ghost but quite another to sit down and have a sustained conversation with one—which is what the focal character does. The ghost he has made contact with has been trapped in a hotel room in an obscure country and wants to recruit the narrator for a long-overdue mission.

80

SITUATION 2: Two archaeologists explore an ancient cliff dwelling inhabited by Anasazi ghosts, some of whom tell the explorers terrifying stories about their demise many centuries ago. Two of the ghosts decide to inhabit the bodies of the archaeologists in order to carry out an ancient dream.

SITUATION 3: In this world, mortals and angels interact, not always harmoniously. Some mortals want to dupe angels into giving them divine favors, but some angels have a dark side and want to dupe mortals into doing outrageous things. Sometimes it isn't easy to distinguish between good and bad mortals, good and bad angels—but the protagonist must try.

SITUATION 4: An unsuccessful artist encounters, through a medium, the spirits of three of the great Renaissance masters, each of whom advise her on how to succeed as a painter. But her artistic tastes are distinctly modern, which the Renaissance masters find repugnant ... with one exception.

SITUATION 5: An aspiring escape artist manages to evoke the spirit of Harry Houdini. When he asks Houdini to teach him some of his tricks, the master refuses, telling him that they weren't tricks. When the young magician persists, Houdini teaches him an important lesson, a "secret" that is not about performing an escape but developing a state of mind.

SITUATION 6: In this world, spirits openly coexist with mortals because each provides something the other lacks. Spirits continue to hunger for sensory experiences; mortals long to transcend physical limitations. One mortal, however, wants to exploit the spiritual entities for experiences they do not want to share.

SITUATION 7: The ghost that has inhabited the narrator's home tries to converse with him, but neither understands the other's language. The narrator tries a few words in modern languages and then he tries Latin and ancient Greek, but the ghost's language seems to be even older. With the help of a linguist, the narrator finally connects, and the ghost divulges strange secrets.

SITUATION 8: An Inuit woman who is fully assimilated into Anglo culture and has no desire to be regarded in the context of her ethnicity (indeed she avoids anything having to do with Inuit culture), is visited by several ancestors who slowly bring her back to her roots.

SITUATION 9: When two siblings discover an abandoned cemetery near an English village, they are overtaken by resident ghosts. The ghosts want to communicate warnings to anyone who will listen. The siblings are so unnerved by the encounter that they do not heed the ghosts' warnings. The ghosts search for them after they leave the cemetery.

SITUATION 10: As she is examining a mummy, an Egyptologist is astonished to discover that the mummy has telepathically established communication with her. When she recovers from the shock, she realizes the mummy has many extraordinary stories to tell about a long-vanished age.

CHAPTER 6

THE CURSE OR PROPHECY OF X

CATEGORY 1: A CURSE FROM THE DEPTHS

The horror factor in Gothic fiction typically stems from its settings: dungeons, cellars, laboratories, caves, grottos, secret passageways—wherever darkness and mystery reign. Similarly there are non-supernatural tales to be told about curses and prophecies. The story premises that follow should help you conjure up your own Gothic chillers or real-life psychodramas stemming from curses or prophecies passed from generation to generation.

SITUATION 1: A rowboat containing a skull washes onto the coast of Spain. Accompanying the skull is a parchment containing a prophecy: Whoever finds the skull must return it to the family of the deceased, or the finders will suffer calamity. Alas, the curse is not taken seriously.

SITUATION 2: While exploring her parents' private documents, the adolescent narrator discovers a letter from a relative leveling a curse on the firstborn of the parents' children (which would mean the narrator) in retribution for a terrible misdeed. When the narrator confronts his mother with the letter, she begs him not to tell his father.

SITUATION 3: Prospectors inspecting a cave find an urn containing relics and a prophecy on calfskin: Whoever finds this urn will be imbued with the power to perform miraculous changes in the world. Alas, the prophecy has a hidden dark side.

SITUATION 4: In an effort to determine why his newly purchased Victorian home is haunted, the owner digs up the cellar (following clues found in the previous owner's diary) and unearths an amulet that's under a vile curse.

SITUATION 5: Archaeologists disturb a burial site and awaken a primeval demon that targets the violators. Nothing anyone can think to do stops the demon … until one of the archaeologists discovers an ancient secret.

SITUATION 6: Strange curses emanate from an abandoned well, but efforts to find the source have been futile. Finally, excavators dig a tunnel parallel to the well that breaks into a chamber where outcasts were sent to die—except that they didn't die. They mutated into creatures that utter lethal curses.

SITUATION 7: A demolition crew bulldozing an old house exposes a passageway leading from the cellar to … where? No one has any idea. The team follows the passageway to a dwelling place of humanoids that warn of a doomsday prophecy about to come true.

SITUATION 8: A document describing an Indian burial ground underneath an old Washington, DC office building is discovered—along with a curse against anyone who would disturb it. This presents a dilemma to the company that wants to tear down the old structure to build a restaurant.

SITUATION 9: Three miners inspecting a long-abandoned shaft uncover signs of a secret cult that had settled there; they also uncover a curse with the warning that deeper penetration into the chamber will result in disaster. But the miners continue exploring.

SITUATION 10: A curse uncovered from a crypt buried underneath a church warns of demons that will invade the surface unless their demands are met—demands involving reparations for abuses going back several centuries.

CATEGORY 2: ANCIENT OR MEDIEVAL CURSES OR PROPHECIES

The ancient and medieval worlds have been an ongoing inspiration for writers of Gothic, fantasy, and historical fiction. The civilizations of the ancient Middle East, Egypt, Greece, Rome, and the Far East (together with the so-called Dark Ages) are an unending source of ideas for stories of treachery and sorcery propelled by curses and prophecies.

SITUATION 1: Looters in a medieval cemetery plunder a grave, the marker on which is engraved: *Disturb this grave, and evil will be unleashed.* The looters assume the curse is merely a deterrent to protect the treasure that had been placed inside the crypt with the deceased—but they assume wrong.

SITUATION 2: Egyptologists inspecting a tomb try to lift the curse that is preventing them from opening the tomb's sarcophagus, but no matter what incantations they use, the curse remains, in the form of a demon that appears and reappears—each time more menacing than before.

SITUATION 3: Monks have hidden a book of magic for centuries because anyone attempting to practice its magic has suffered misfortune. A visiting historian persuades the monks to ignore the curse on the grounds that the misfortunes were caused by disease and natural disasters; but they insist the curses are real and set out to prove it.

SITUATION 4: The child of a Babylonian slave has the gift of prophecy, and her life is in danger because of it. Rival heirs to the throne either want to kidnap her (and keep her prophecies secret) or kill her so she will not disrupt the status quo.

SITUATION 5: Genghis Khan returns in the body of a villager to fulfill a prophecy that his descendents will one day re-conquer the regions of his domain. But to accomplish this, he must summon his army back to earth, using the people in the village as hosts.

SITUATION 6: A stranger gives a magician a book of incantations that had been in his family for generations: Most of the incantations are indecipherable. But when the magician deciphers some of them, he realizes they are dangerous—so potent that reading them silently to oneself is enough to activate them.

SITUATION 7: Archaeologists working in Alexandria, Egypt, discover ancient scrolls that turn out to be prophecies. One scroll describes events that have taken place in the twentieth century; another scroll describes catastrophic events that haven't yet taken place. Most of the scientists do not take the prophecies seriously, but those who do fear them for compelling reasons.

SITUATION 8: An ancient Chinese prophecy is discovered carved on an ivory tusk—but it is incomplete. Another tusk contains the rest of the prophecy, and the clues disclosing its location are given on the first tusk. Because the prophecy alludes to an extraordinary celestial event, finding the second tusk becomes a high priority.

SITUATION 9: Curses are found embedded in shrunken heads belonging to an Amazonian tribe that had vanished centuries ago. Linguists are brought in to decipher the curses; what they discover is relevant to the tribe occupying the site today.

SITUATION 10: In India, a prophecy uttered by the god Kali triggers pandemonium after a shaman reinterprets it. It is up to the village's more progressive disciples of Kali to bring things back to order—but they are fighting an uphill battle against the orthodox set.

CATEGORY 3: CURSES OR PROPHECIES OF THE CONQUERED

It is said that history is written by the victors. That may be true, but the vanquished also manage to make themselves heard, sometimes in less obvious ways such as in secret writings, in paintings or sculptures, and in curses. What sorts of stories might such curses generate?

SITUATION 1: A gypsy fortune-teller placed in a concentration camp conjures up curses against the guards, transforming some of them into wolves which (it is hoped) the other guards will kill. The risk is that the wolves will be more dangerous to the prisoners than the guards.

SITUATION 2: A manuscript written in an unknown language is found in an ancient tomb. Only partially deciphered, it prophesies the awakening of beings placed under a curse by their conquerors. The rest of the manuscript needs to be deciphered to learn when the beings are supposed to awaken and what their purpose may be.

SITUATION 3: In an isolated Southwestern town, normally placid people become violent. Some show signs of being possessed. It seems that the avenging spirits of a tribe of conquered Native Americans are responsible.

SITUATION 4: Invaders underestimate the inhabitants of the city they conquer: Each member of the invading army is tormented by the ghost of the person he or she slew in battle. The ghosts will not lift the curse against the invaders until the latter atone for their misdeeds.

SITUATION 5: Conquered and forced into slavery, members of a religious sect learn through a sympathizer among the conquerors that they possess a rare talent—but it is dormant and can only be conjured up with an incantation now lost. However, the sympathizer thinks he can locate that lost incantation by way of a certain prophecy.

SITUATION 6: Fearing a prophecy that someone among the youngest generation in their community will bring an end to that community's secure but sterile way of life, the village elders incarcerate every young person who expresses dissident ideas. One of the incarcerated adolescents, however, escapes confinement and initiates a rebellion.

SITUATION 7: The natives who live in a toxic world conquer human colonists—not militarily but through mind control. The natives want to use the female colonists to produce offspring, as the native females are no longer fertile due to the toxic environment.

SITUATION 8: For years a clan of alchemists lived peacefully among their militaristic overseers, but then one of the overseers uncovers a prophecy warning that the alchemists are demons who plan to wipe out the overseers with magic potions.

SITUATION 9: An obscure Christian sect with formidable powers (their curses work; their prophecies come true) flourishes underground. The Romans discover them and, knowing their powers, attempt to destroy them.

SITUATION 10: A colony of mice enslaved by cats acquires supernatural strength after a small solar storm enhances their growth. The mice overpower the cats and enslave them, just as they had been enslaved. But the cats have been affected by the solar radiation too ...

CATEGORY 4: CURSES OR PROPHECIES OF MONSTERS OR THE MONSTROUS

Monsters (or the monstrous) are generally a vindictive lot—vengeful and demonic and eager to curse "normal" people or prophesy terrible fates for them. Keep in mind, too, that monsters need not be limited to supernatural beings. The following scenarios give you the opportunity to dramatize the conflict arising between these wrathful monsters and the more-or-less innocent bystanders who get in their way.

SITUATION 1: Because of her vanity, a beautiful heiress is cursed by her jealous sister (who seems to possess satanic powers) to become visibly older every time she looks at herself in the mirror. She implores her sister to counteract the curse, but the sister refuses because of the way the heiress abused her when they were growing up.

SITUATION 2: Cursed by the gods to be hideous because of a transgression, a mortal pleads to Zeus to lift the curse. Zeus agrees, but the mortal must accomplish several extraordinary tasks before his wish can be granted. The last task seems impossible.

SITUATION 3: In this world, curses are immediately heeded by demons; but the demons have grown weary of them. They warn the mortals to curse more discriminately. But when several of the mortals ignore the warnings, their curses backfire and they themselves turn into demons.

SITUATION 4: A monster cursed by an avenging god begs that god to make him normal again. The god agrees, provided the monster performs several tasks—tasks so distasteful that the monster refuses. When the god, incensed, aggravates the monster's condition, the monster turns to other supernatural beings to help him wreak revenge on the god.

SITUATION 5: In this alternate earth, radiation-deformed humans are condemned by a prophecy from a sacred text to live in squalor. But one of them refuses to take any more abuse and launches an attack on the oppressors. The oppressors in turn launch a disastrous counterattack.

SITUATION 6: A child cursed and then exiled into the wilderness grows up to be a savage. This woman returns to the kingdom that exiled her, seeking not only revenge against the evil Queen but to recover her humanity. All of the townspeople drive her away except one who dares to give her sanctuary and help her reach her goal.

SITUATION 7: Deformed for daring to control her own destiny, a woman who possesses the gift of prophecy devotes her life to helping other similarly afflicted persons resist or counteract the curses of their oppressors—especially the one who had deformed her. But that oppressor is not to be avenged.

SITUATION 8: The result of a genetic experiment gone horribly wrong, the narrator has become an amphibious creature who possesses enough of his original intelligence to find a way, despite being unable to spend much time out of water, to take revenge on the geneticist.

SITUATION 9: Several ghosts exact vengeance on the living with curses that, if heard in their entirety, transmute living persons into ghosts. The protagonist, who has studied these curses, tries to find a way to stop the ghosts from uttering a complete curse.

SITUATION 10: A scientist is possessed by some monstrous entity that is taking over her consciousness. She struggles to communicate with it before it takes her completely. She also searches for the reason it has targeted her in particular—and comes across an ancient inscription she deciphered years before that offers a clue.

CATEGORY 5: A CURSE OR PROPHECY FROM A RELIGIOUS ARTIFACT

Sacred treasures tend to be associated with prophecies involving human destiny. And because they are vulnerable to exploitation or destruction, they are often protected by a curse. These are ideal ingredients for suspense and adventure tales.

SITUATION 1: A woman receives a prayer book from her dying grandmother—a book that has been in the family for many generations. When she inspects the book, she discovers an inscription written in the margin, in a language she cannot identify. The inscription turns out to be a curse that has bearing on the narrator's life.

SITUATION 2: While a modern-day monk is praying, Christ speaks to him from the crucifix, as was the case with St. Francis. Christ makes an astonishing prophecy, but in order for the prophecy to come true, the monk and his colleagues must perform several tasks.

SITUATION 3: An ancient object recently excavated seems to be a carving of a starlike emblem—quite likely a religious symbol—but of what religion? Tests reveal that it predates the origins of the major known religions. The narrator thinks she has found evidence of an unknown religion, the roots of which may still exist in obscure parts of the world.

SITUATION 4: A Hopi tribal leader gives the narrator, an anthropologist, a kachina doll which has an ominous prophecy stitched to it, saying the Hopi people will, at a specific time, rise from their graves to re-conquer their land.

SITUATION 5: A divinity student hears strange voices every time she opens her Bible, a family heirloom. The more carefully she listens, the more she realizes that they speak an ancient language. Working with a language expert, she learns that the voices utter curses stemming from an injustice her forebears perpetrated.

SITUATION 6: The burial shroud of an Apostle is discovered in an ancient tomb, and it seems to possess supernatural properties. The narrator, a specialist in early Christianity, becomes entranced by the artifact, which reveals an astonishing secret: a apostolic prophecy.

SITUATION 7: A collector of African art acquires from the Congo a grigri fetish doll that comes to life late at night and utters strange words in an ancient African language, which the collector captures on tape. The utterances detail a fearful curse ... and what must be done to nullify it.

SITUATION 8: Rummaging through a trunk left to him by his grandfather, the narrator uncovers a seven-branched menorah. One evening, as he lights each candle, the menorah utters a prophecy related to each of the seven days of Creation. The prophecies have a chilling relevance to modern-day events.

SITUATION 9: A strange, intricate object lands on earth. Exhaustive probing yields nothing. Everyone is baffled. Eventually people who have laid eyes on the object begin to act strangely. Before long, people are worshiping the object.

SITUATION 10: The narrator purchases a statuette of an Egyptian deity from a pawnbroker. He soon experiences prophetic dreams, and the prophecies come true. Finally, in one of the dreams, the deity identifies itself: It is the one represented by the statuette. When he tries to sell the statuette, the deity materializes.

CATEGORY 6: PROPHECIES, VISIONS, AND HALLUCINATIONS OF THE DRUGGED

Trance-inducing drugs have been used since ancient times. When ingested or inhaled, the subject enters a kind of hypnotic state and is then capable of receiving visions and experiencing spiritual epiphanies—the raw material for fascinating tales.

SITUATION 1: Under the influence of a psychedelic drug, a homeless street musician foretells events that will occur a few hours afterward. Insisting either that the connections are mere coincidences or that the street musician is somehow responsible for them, investigators refuse to administer illegal substances to see if they're the cause.

SITUATION 2: A new kind of psychedelic drug has become the rage on college campuses: It enables the user to make highly specific near-future prophecies, such as who will pass or fail, who will get jobs, and so on. Professors and administrators try to put a stop to this drug use—but then some of them take the drug and become hooked.

SITUATION 3: Sailors on shore leave are introduced to a tobacco-like narcotic that puts them in a trance in which they overhear frightening prophecies. When they emerge from their drugged state, the sailors must persuade their commanding officers to act on the prophecies they've received.

SITUATION 4: Terrorists contaminate a city's water supply with a psychotropic drug that causes people to see reality differently. The chief investigator luckily drinks only bottled or filtered water, but halfway through his investigation, he is given contaminated water disguised as Perrier.

SITUATION 5: Someone has been contaminating food with a drug that causes people to see everything as funny and to laugh uncontrollably. Before long, mass delirium spreads throughout the community. Scientists struggle to solve the problem; however, one group does not want the problem solved.

SITUATION 6: An anti-smoking drug proves to have an unforeseen side effect: It causes users to speak uncontrollably, similar to the effects of Tourette's syndrome but more coherently—and what they spout reflexively are visions of the future.

SITUATION 7: In this alternate universe, drugs enable people to live outside their bodies. Several overenthusiastic users, however, forget to protect their bodies from culprits with the requisite curses, and so the bodies are stolen. The frantic, disembodied individuals launch a hunt to find their bodies before they are transformed beyond recognition.

SITUATION 8: Drugs have been invented that wiped out belligerence. People become more peaceful and friendly. Crime disappears. However, it is dangerous to stop taking the drug. Those who do experience hallucinogenic visions that lead to extreme violence.

SITUATION 9: Artists taking a drug to experience visions (which they translate into paintings and sculptures) also start to experience a disturbing side effect: an impulse to destroy the artwork they've created. However, they feel that the dangers are worth the risk.

SITUATION 10: A new drug enables users to experience visions of the immediate future. Law enforcement and the military scramble to get control of the drug's distribution and make immediate use of it. People start using it (once it's on the black market) without considering its side effects, which include becoming severely paranoid due to the user's inability to block out horrifying visions.

CATEGORY 7: PROPHECIES OF THE HYPNOTIZED

Hypnosis, a tool of psychoanalysis, is used to release buried or suppressed memories, but hypnosis may also be a pathway to supernatural visions and prophecies. Such a possibility can generate spooky tales.

SITUATION 1: Under hypnosis, a mystic relates a prophecy conveyed to him (he insists) by God, that Earth will experience devastation as a result of radical changes in weather systems. The only way to prevent an apocalypse is to follow His steps, which the mystic conveys as a kind of new Ten Commandments. Nobody takes the mystic seriously until a divine demonstration occurs.

SITUATION 2: A stranger in town is hypnotizing people—and when he does, they utter prophecies, most of them trivial, though they turn out to be true. One of the villagers makes a truly frightening prophecy under hypnosis, and townspeople wonder if the hypnotist is partly responsible for making the prophecies come true.

SITUATION 3: When a psychologist hypnotizes his brother, he awakens an entity who utters a terrible prophecy: Their family is the conduit of long-dormant demons who will, on a certain date, turn everyone in the city into an evil enclave. The psychologist must find a way to destroy the entity without destroying his brother.

SITUATION 4: A psychology student who is also fascinated by the occult returns home after college and agrees to hypnoize a friend after a party. The friend soon has a series of violent nightmares and seems to be able to see into the future. The student tries to help end the nightmares, but one day the friend disappears.

SITUATION 5: A man with multiple personalities is hypnotized to retrieve an astonishingly prescient personality that surfaced just once and then disappeared.

Experts think that the lost personality can shed light on a crucial scientific experiment that the hypnotized man had been working on.

SITUATION 6: Mistreated one time too many, a woman hypnotizes her husband and attempts to modify his abusive personality by giving him post-hypnotic suggestions that would cause him to behave with civility. Although her scheme works, her husband also utters ominous prophecies while in a hypnotic state.

SITUATION 7: In this future world, robots practice psychiatry and often hypnotize their patients. One of the psychiatrist robots, however, hypnotizes its patients to get them to accept the prophecy that robots are destined to become their masters. Before long, other robot psychiatrists implant this prophecy in their patients as well.

SITUATION 8: The protagonist is a psychologist who has discovered that his sister's children, twins, can see into the future when hypnotized. One day when he hypnotizes one of the twins to elaborate on a frightening vision of the future, he is not able to bring her out of the trance.

SITUATION 9: A teacher uses hypnosis to convince her underachieving students that they are brilliant, with grand visions of the future to share with the world. Their prophecies enchant the community, who had given up on them. But some of the prophecies are disturbing, and several members of the community want to put a stop to the teacher's tactics.

SITUATION 10: Disgusted by his team's losing streak, the coach hypnotizes several of his players into striving beyond their usual capacity. Implanted with future visions of victory, the players overexert themselves and teeter on the edge of mental breakdowns.

CATEGORY 8: PROPHECIES AND CURSES OF MAGICIANS AND CLAIRVOYANTS

Magicians, shamans, and even ordinary dabblers in the supernatural interested in incantations and other rituals usually hover in that gray zone between benevolence and malevolence. Their ambiguous moral intentions make for suspenseful stories.

SITUATION 1: A carnival clairvoyant tells a young woman that the home she had just moved into with her new husband is haunted—and that her husband knows about it. "Look inside the chest he keeps locked," the clairvoyant instructs.

SITUATION 2: A gypsy occultist whom everyone has assumed to be a fake pleads with the police investigating a string of baffling murders to heed her latest vision, in which she can deduce the identity of the murderer by his clothing (but cannot envision his face).

SITUATION 3: Because of his demonstrated ability to determine a suspect's guilt or innocence of a crime, a former stage magician is recruited by a law enforcement agency. The clairvoyant's skill, however, turns into a curse when one of the criminals is himself a clairvoyant capable of manipulating people's minds.

SITUATION 4: In her recurring nightmares, the narrator receives ominous prophecies about the immediate future—prophecies too strange to be taken seriously. For instance, a deceased relative tells her that an evil spirit is dwelling in her bedroom closet—but after one of the prophecies comes true, she searches for an occultist who can help her.

SITUATION 5: Before his sister died, the protagonist tried to nullify their father's curse, whereby the sister would bear a demon child. The sister died giving birth to such a child. Now the brother learns that he must nullify the curse before the demon child learns to walk.

SITUATION 6: Imprisoned in a haunted dungeon, the protagonist is inhabited by the tormented spirits of former prisoners who died there. First they share their agonies; then they share their visions of the future. Soon they utter curses that function under certain conditions that the protagonist must work to provide.

SITUATION 7: Once a loyal subordinate of Satan, a demon forsakes the dark side and tries to redeem himself by using his ability to see into the future to guide the poor and the outcast. However, he must persuade the villagers to believe he is sincere—no easy task for a demon.

SITUATION 8: A cynical stage magician, weary of his routine bag of tricks, makes contact (via a medium) with a great magician of the past who shares dire prophecies about the future and how he, a practicing magician, can help shape the future for the better.

SITUATION 9: A schoolboy, sick of being bullied, begins studying magic and discovers that he can curse people ... for real. He tries his magic on one of the bullies, but he does not utter the proper incantation and the trick goes terribly wrong.

SITUATION 10: The wife of an abusive husband studies the dark arts and discovers that she has a special ability to wield curses and bizarre visions. When the husband discovers her magic books, he burns them. Although the wife has already memorized how to cast a devastating curse on him, she hesitates.

CATEGORY 9: PROPHECIES, CURSES, AND DELUSIONS OF THE MENTALLY DISABLED

A thin line may exist between the delusional and the visionary, between incoherent babbling and lucid prophesying. That's because the human mind is slow to reveal its mysteries. Perhaps some people possess the gift of prophecy despite seeming mentally unstable.

SITUATION 1: An extremely shy boy, who never speaks and may or may not be autistic or mentally disabled, has the gift of prophecy, but like Cassandra (who possessed the gift of prophecy but was cursed never to be believed), his prophecies (which he writes down), are never believed because they sound so outrageous.

SITUATION 2: The protagonist is thought to be mentally disabled, but she merely has difficulty processing reality because she sees things either hours before they happen or years before. To complicate matters, she prophesies in a strange and complex language that takes so long to decode that the prophecy could occur first!

SITUATION 3: An epileptic experiences otherworldly visions every time he has a seizure—but his seizures are so intense that he can only remember mere fragments of the visions. Finally, a neurologist helps him to piece together one of the visions, and it is frightening.

SITUATION 4: Traumatized by her combat experiences, a veteran discovers that her curses against aggressors are so venomous that they actually come to pass. But then, she loses control and begins cursing anyone who shows any sign of aggression whatsoever.

SITUATION 5: The focal character suffers from delusions of grandeur: She thinks she is the avatar of a powerful goddess. Of course, everyone considers her mentally ill, but she methodically takes steps to transform her delusion into reality.

SITUATION 6: Locked into submissive behavior by her voodoo-priest husband, the narrator executes bizarre crimes that her husband orders her to commit. Just before she attempts to murder a man the husband suspects is a romantic rival, the latter finds a way to snap the wife out of her voodoo-induced spell.

SITUATION 7: A man receives coded prophecies in his sleep but cannot remember them when he wakes. He contacts a therapist who is open to the possibility of supernatural agencies. Together they figure out a way for the man to remember his dreams enough to write down the prophecies and then decode them.

SITUATION 8: Assumed to be mentally disabled, a mute girl receives visions and prophecies from unknown sources, which she stores in her photographic memory. Unbeknownst to her brother or her parents, she shares these visions with her doll, which is inhabited by a goddess who has been assigned to look after the girl's welfare ... until a friend steals the doll.

SITUATION 9: A so-called idiot savant examines the minute fluctuations of highly complex systems like weather, the stock market, solar flares, etc., to make startling predictions about the near future—but few people take him seriously because his behavior is so eccentric. One person who does take him seriously warns experts that ignoring the savant would be a serious mistake.

SITUATION 10: Suffering from post-traumatic stress disorder, a veteran cannot distinguish between mundane, innocuous conflicts and combat situations. Despite being warned not to interfere in others' business, the vet leaps into action when he sees a woman being assaulted.

CATEGORY 10: PROPHECIES AND INCANTATIONS OF SORCERERS

Those who wield mystical powers and observe mysterious visions can be the source of many magical, strange adventures. These kinds of tales can take place in fantasy worlds or our own, but all allow the writer a chance to conjure up astounding stories that can take the commonplace into a whole new realm.

SITUATION 1: Learning that destruction will befall his city because of certain transgressions, a pilgrim from the city tries to reverse Apollo's prophecy via the Sibyl, who transmits to visitors the oracles of Apollo at Delphi and serves as an intermediary between mortals and the powerful sun god, who is also the god of the arts and medicine. Even though the Sibyl warns him that nothing can be done, the pilgrim begs Apollo (again via the Sibyl) to consider a means of redemption.

SITUATION 2: A priest communicates his prophecies through the music he plays on his flute. Because some of his prophecies include grave dangers one needs to understand the "language" of his music—but only one individual in the realm has that ability—and she is insane.

SITUATION 3: As filmmakers arrive in a Caribbean community to make a movie about zombies, voodoo priestesses ask to be part of the team, promising authenticity. Their authenticity exceeds the filmmakers' expectations, as actors become enslaved by the voodoo curses.

SITUATION 4: A homeless man, who also happens to be a soothsayer, utters wild prophecies about the ancient gods returning to settle their affairs with humankind. When he is not being ridiculed, he is arrested for vagrancy. One person (the narrator) decides to take his prophecies seriously and asks the soothsayer how to combat the vindictive gods.

SITUATION 5: Exiled from her homeland after being accused of sorcery, a woman who sees the future wanders the land sharing her visions with the people she befriends. Most dismiss her as a kook, but one takes her prophecies seriously and tries to prevent them from coming true, an adventure that leads them both to the woman's homeland.

SITUATION 6: Soothsayers visit a beleaguered village. Most of them are charlatans trying to sell their prophecies at exorbitant prices. A genuine soothsayer offers his prophecies for free—but they're a combination of bad news and good news—and no one believes them.

SITUATION 7: Having offended one of the gods, a priestess with an extraordinary gift of prophecy is transformed into a hideously deformed creature. She still possesses her prophetic gifts, but no one dares approach her. When she envisions a catastrophe, she searches desperately for a way to disguise her hideousness so others will listen to her.

SITUATION 8: A witch searches for an incantation that would rid her and her fellow witches of their deformities. The first tentative spells backfire, and the witches become uglier. Eventually they come up with an effective spell, and their hideousness vanishes—but other liabilities arise.

SITUATION 9: A dying woman confesses to her son that she is a sorceress and that he must continue her work of propagating spells, incantations, prophecies so as to ward off evil forces threatening to destroy them. The son vows to obey, but naively falls prey to those evil forces before he can fully deploy his adopted sorcery.

SITUATION 10: Despite announcing her retirement from the soothsaying business, a sorceress is besieged by villagers who demand to know what their future holds. When she refuses to cooperate, they try to burn her at the stake, but an old admirer (whom she once rejected) comes to her rescue.

CHAPTER 7

DESCENT INTO X

CATEGORY 1: DESCENT INTO CONFUSION OR UNCERTAINTY

We live in a universe governed by laws, both physical and man-made. When order and rationality break down, it can be frightening and disorienting. But it can also be the basis for gripping psychological stories. Any of the ten situations that follow should enable you to get a psychodrama of your own underway.

SITUATION 1: Convinced by her husband and his parents that homemaking is her wisest career choice, the protagonist remains frustrated by missing out on her childhood dream of becoming an archeologist. Should she still pursue that dream? Everyone dissuades her ... except her brilliant sister.

SITUATION 2: Facing the responsibilities of fatherhood, the narrator experiences anxiety about his new role in life. How can he succeed as a father when he, an orphan raised by an alcoholic uncle, has no role model to draw from?

SITUATION 3: A woman struggling with a life-threatening illness searches for reasons to keep going. She refuses traditional spiritual or religious comforts but still searches for evidence that life is not just sound and fury signifying nothing. A revelation comes from a child.

SITUATION 4: Attempting to reconcile her religion with her scientific training, a physicist grapples with the uncertainties built into nature: pi, irrational numbers, logical paradoxes, and quantum mechanics. Finally, she discovers a basis for reconciliation during a pilgrimage.

SITUATION 5: As a result of a sleep experiment gone terribly wrong, the narrator finds himself increasingly incapable of distinguishing reality from dream. As his life descends into chaos, his sleep therapist (who performed the experiment) does all she can to undo the damage—but only makes matters worse.

SITUATION 6: An enemy nation launches a cyber attack against the CIA, resulting in the Agency's collapse into chaos. In desperation, they solicit the help of a former agent turned outlaw hacker before all of their secrets are stolen and shared with the world. But maybe this hacker wants that to happen, too.

SITUATION 7: Some people tolerate uncertainty more than others; some cannot tolerate it at all—as is the case with a business owner who uses every promotional strategy he can think of—yet his business still languishes. Finally, he turns to a rival who offers an offbeat solution.

SITUATION 8: The heir to the throne enacts edicts that cause the society to fall into chaos. The harder his advisors struggle to restore order, the more chaotic things become. As a last resort, the heir asks a former rival for help; she agrees but still harbors resentment toward the new monarch for past abuses.

SITUATION 9: In this world where magic rules, one can move from one reality to another as easily as walking from one room to another. But an evil magician has been tampering with one of the junctures, and the narrator pops into a strange reality instead of the one she meant to visit.

SITUATION 10: The narrator slips into despair when he discovers that his grandfather, a WWII physician, had secretly collaborated with the Nazis. To find out why, he probes his grandfather's activities during the war years—and makes a startling discovery.

CATEGORY 2: DESCENT INTO DESPAIR

Despair is as far as one can descend internally—deeper than grief (which generally is short-lived), despair persists, consuming the sufferer with hopelessness. Convincingly told stories about people who are rescued from despair can be extremely inspirational.

SITUATION 1: Thomas Paine writes in *The Age of Reason* that to be happy one must be faithful to oneself. Feeling herself on the brink of despair for having compromised too much in her love life and in her career, the narrator makes a pledge to herself: no more compromises.

100

SITUATION 2: Having lost his ability to sing following an operation on his larynx, a singer slips into despair, and no one can pull him out of it. After a surgeon restores 50 percent of his voice, the singer's hopes temporarily rise, but soon the despair returns—until he meets a woman who comes up with an ingenious way of using his semi-restored voice.

SITUATION 3: With her memory deteriorating, an elderly woman seeks to end her despair. She befriends a man suffering from a similar memory loss. Together, with the help of a psychologist, they struggle to save themselves from their crippling disorder.

SITUATION 4: Professional athletes thrive on intense competition, but some, like the protagonist, are so competitive that they despair if they lose, especially when they go from a winning situation to a losing team. How to maintain reasonable sanity while being sufficiently competitive to win is the dilemma here.

SITUATION 5: In the old west, a Nevada sheriff reputed to be a deadly shot loses his skill due to an accident. When outlaws hear about this, they set out to kill him. Sensing that his days are numbered, the sheriff slips into despair—but a stranger with a gift for restoring lost skills offers to help him—for a price.

SITUATION 6: A vampire lapses into despair after all of her fellow vampires have been destroyed. She cannot bear to be isolated in the world of the living. When a young man befriends her, the vampire considers asking him to find a way to destroy her.

SITUATION 7: Stripped of her powers, a disobedient angel is sentenced to a year of life as a mortal. Living without the ability to fly, to read minds, or to be invisible, she despairs until a human friend comes to her rescue by showing her the strengths she possesses as a mortal.

SITUATION 8: After an evil magician strips his benevolent counterpart of his magic, the benevolent magician falls into despair. None of his colleagues know enough magic to retrieve the lost magic until a stranger with unusual powers appears. But this stranger has a secret agenda of her own.

SITUATION 9: A circus clown who struggles with violent mood swings looks for ways to keep from falling into despair. Whenever he encounters a child who reminds him of his younger self, flashbacks of abuse are triggered. He must find a way to overcome his past and seeks out long-estranged friends and siblings.

SITUATION 10: Always cracking up her audience, a stand-up comedienne grieves when her lover leaves her. How will she be able to perform? An annoying admirer suddenly seems like a promising antidote—except that he may be emotionally unstable.

CATEGORY 3: DESCENT OR TRESPASS INTO A DANGER ZONE

Few things are as irresistible as defying a NO TRESPASSING warning. What secrets are being protected? What dangers are involved? Are the warnings to protect outsiders from something within or to prevent them from learning precious secrets? Stories that take us into forbidden regions make for exciting reading.

SITUATION 1: Mountain dwellers in an imaginary land have long been forbidden by their religion to descend into the lower regions. Curious to understand why, an explorer discovers records that describe biological experiments gone awry. However, this frightening revelation only increases her desire to explore the region.

SITUATION 2: For this explorer, the sealed accesses to underground passageways are major incentives to find out where these tunnels lead. Even after she finds a way into the passages, she encounters several unusual obstacles. What she and her team finally discover is astonishing.

SITUATION 3: A popular municipal park is sealed off from the rest of the town. Officials forbid the townspeople from entering it but do not explain their reasons despite media pressure. The narrator and other investigators try to solve the mystery.

SITUATION 4: Explorers in this fantasy realm penetrate a land that has been forbidden for ages. No one venturing in has ever emerged. The explorers rightly assume that the land is ruled by demonic beings wielding powerful magic—but they are confident they can overpower the demons' magic with their own.

SITUATION 5: An accident has caused the region surrounding a nuclear facility to become irradiated. After the region is sealed off, the narrator sneaks in because of an extremely valuable object that he must retrieve—even though he could suffer radiation poisoning.

SITUATION 6: For ages, no one has been allowed to enter the Forbidden Zone—yet long-lost records reveal that it was once a sanctuary, following the Robot Wars of the twenty-second century. An explorer and a few brave friends find a way to enter the zone, even though it is heavily guarded.

SITUATION 7: Genetic mutants, lepers of the twenty-second century, have isolated themselves in a Nevada desert where they have been secretly working on a doomsday weapon. A military officer leads a team into this dangerous area to destroy the weapon.

SITUATION 8: A brutal gang has claimed two city blocks as its sovereign territory, allowing only gang members into the area. The mayor dispatches police, SWAT teams, and even the National Guard, but all are repelled by a force field. An engineer and gang expert tries to find a way to break through.

SITUATION 9: Two realities, one ordinary, and one supernatural, have intersected; officials in the ordinary reality have blocked access to the supernatural one, fearing mass migration from the former to the latter. But the lure of the supernatural is too compelling despite its dangers.

SITUATION 10: Anarchists have been planting bombs in churches, rendering them danger zones. Efforts to find the perpetrators have been futile. Finally, the protagonist pieces together clues to come up with a possible motive for the attacks.

CATEGORY 4: DESCENT INTO HADES

Descending into anything breeds fear and nightmares or at least anxiety; it also promises a good read if the storyteller handles the nether journey skillfully. The following scenarios of descent into the mythic land of the dead should stir your darker imagination.

SITUATION 1: Hades, one of the three deities lording over creation—the others being Zeus (heaven) and Poseidon (the sea)—feels that he and his fellow underworld inhabitants do not get enough respect. He thus recruits his human captives to stage an event that would make his brothers change their minds about him. Now Hades must persuade Zeus and Poseidon to descend to his realm to see the show.

SITUATION 2: Persephone demands that her abductor, Hades, allows her to return to the surface whenever she pleases, not just to usher in springtime.

When he refuses, she plans a clever escape—with surreal consequences to Earth's climate.

SITUATION 3: The story of Orpheus, who descends to the underworld to rescue his beloved Eurydice, is well known. What no one knows, though, is that before finding Eurydice, Orpheus encountered a temptress being punished for seducing warriors and causing them to lose their respective battles. Orpheus falls under her spell as well, despite his longing for Eurydice.

SITUATION 4: Sophocles is invited by Hades to visit the underworld as his special guest. All Hades asks for in return is that Sophocles write a play embodying his experiences in the underworld, with Hades himself as the star of the show. Sophocles complies but not in a way Hades would like.

SITUATION 5: The dwellers of Hades yearn for life and for sunlight—and will cajole visitors from the surface to find some way to help them escape. Of course, no one can return to life ... but one of the visitors is a sorcerer who wishes to recruit some of the residents of Hades to participate in a special task back on the surface.

SITUATION 6: No longer willing to bear their mean parents' harsh discipline, two siblings run away from home and evade capture by escaping through the Gates of Hades. Finding themselves in the frightful underworld, they try to go back, but it's not going to be that easy.

SITUATION 7: Curious to see what Hades is like and what secrets she can learn there, a young woman sneaks through the Forbidden Gates. But the beings she encounters are unlike anything she ever expected. She finds them so fascinating that she fails to see that they are seeping away her soul.

SITUATION 8: An interview with Hades yields new insights into the land of the dead. Hades even discloses little-known facts about his own life, his pursuit of Persephone, his relationships with other gods, and so on. The interviewer becomes so intrigued that he wishes to linger ... or is that just Hades playing mind games with him?

SITUATION 9: Hades conducts an open house of his domain, giving tours for the still living to see how pleasant and diverse the underworld can be. But his hidden goal is to lure certain individuals to participate so he can set a trap for them.

SITUATION 10: Before Hades abducted Persephone, she was wooed by a mortal. Now that Persephone is Hades' bride in the underworld, the former suitor longs for her so deeply that he devises a plan to rescue her from Hades' clutches.

CATEGORY 5: DESCENT INTO PURGATORY

Purgatory is the realm of neither here nor there—neither Heaven nor Earth nor the Underworld but in between. It's a place where souls are to be purified (purged of sin) through penance. Stories set in Purgatory offer a drama of transition that can be just as riveting as more overt types of drama.

SITUATION 1: Because of their insolence, three angels are sent to Purgatory as they await their ultimate fate. They express their outrage against the powers of Heaven and search the dark, forbidding landscape for a way out as they submit themselves to the required purification process, and discover things about themselves they never realized.

SITUATION 2: A modern-day poet embarks on a self-guided tour through Purgatory, using Dante's experience with Virgil as a touchstone. However, things have changed in Purgatory since Dante envisioned it in the early fourteenth century, and the poet will be fortunate if he can reemerge in one piece.

SITUATION 3: An appeals court in Purgatory listens to the arguments of those who wish to enter Heaven. Each makes an impassioned case, highlighting his or her contributions (artistic, scientific, religious, humanitarian, etc.) and sidestepping the faults (disorderly conduct, vanity, indolence, etc.).

SITUATION 4: In a section of Purgatory dwell individuals who drifted aimlessly through life, unable to commit to a goal or adhere to a credo. Now one of the longtime residents of Purgatory shares with newcomers the wisdom she has acquired—wisdom that, if applied wisely, might give them a second chance.

SITUATION 5: The narrator enters Purgatory and meets Plato and Socrates. He becomes embroiled in their philosophical discussions. When the debate turns to spirituality, the narrator asks them how they wound up in Purgatory, a realm conceived of by Christians. This sets off a heated debate regarding the relevance of Christianity to pre-Christian pagan beliefs.

SITUATION 6: Purgatory is filled with the disobedient, the unrepentant, and the sacrilegious; they will remain there until they learn to obey, desire forgiveness, or become faithful. When a newcomer enters Purgatory, she urges these resisters to continue resisting—that there is more to goodness than those ideals, which she finds antithetical to humanity.

SITUATION 7: A court hearing is held in Purgatory to decide the fates of individuals whose actions while alive were questionable at best. How does one judge whether certain kinds of behavior may be good in some context and yet contemptible in others? Who establishes the context for good and evil when deciding whether—or how—a soul in Purgatory should be purged?

SITUATION 8: The Purgatory in this world is a concrete place and functions as a kind of detainment center. Persons whose behavior or ideas are questioned by the status quo are brought here, and their cases are tried by a jury who represent the standards necessary for maintaining a harmonious society.

SITUATION 9: When he learns of the luminaries in Purgatory, a poet opts to go there rather than to Heaven (which to him sounds boring). When he is brought to Purgatory, he delights in meeting his idols—ancient Greek dramatists, philosophers, writers, and painters—but soon discovers how unhappy they all are, the causes of which gradually become apparent.

SITUATION 10: Rescuers search Purgatory for a physicist who died before she could perfect her fusion generator. But the Guardian of the souls in Purgatory proves to be a formidable obstacle for the rescuers to get around.

CATEGORY 6: DESCENT INTO MADNESS

> Where does the boundary between sanity and insanity lie? Is there even a boundary? What may pass as madness to one person may be a perfect illustration of creative genius to another. At the same time, mental illness, difficult as it may be to diagnose, is a reality that must be heeded. Fiction can do much to illustrate this important issue.

SITUATION 1: Obsessed with visions that are both frightening and astonishing, a painter wonders whether she is going insane. At first she is grateful for her visions—they result in breathtaking paintings. But then the visions threaten to overwhelm her, and she fears tumbling into the abyss of madness.

SITUATION 2: Kept in a locked room by her abductors, a woman struggles to keep her sanity—and loses. But her madness illuminates a daring method for breaking free of her captors. The only problem is that the captors are themselves murderously insane.

SITUATION 3: An avant-garde sculptor walks a tightrope between creative visions (which she strives to translate artistically) and madness. Her neighbors are eager to accuse her of the latter and do all they can to have her arrested for terrifying them with her creations.

SITUATION 4: Because his parents fight continuously, a teenager worries that he is on the brink of madness and looks for ways to get his parents to become more civil, if not more affectionate with each other. When these plans fail, he tries one more drastic measure.

SITUATION 5: Psychologists test astronauts who have volunteered for long-term flights to Mars and beyond. Brought to the brink of madness, one astronaut experiences uncanny hallucinations; another experiences extraordinary visions that, ironically, could prove valuable for a long space flight.

SITUATION 6: Afraid that he is slowly being driven insane by his domineering father, a young teen plans an escape but is caught and confined to the basement. There the teen does go mad—diabolically mad.

SITUATION 7: After being confined to a single room for two years, a kidnapped teen descends into madness, which ironically gives her enough strength and cunning to escape. But the madness worsens after she is free: She is now obsessed with exacting vengeance on the abductors her own way.

SITUATION 8: The narrator is cursed with the ability to read minds—cursed because she cannot block the flood of garbled, bizarre, ugly thoughts. Her therapist offers several techniques, but nothing works. Finally, she visits a spiritual leader who suggests a powerful but risky antidote.

SITUATION 9: After years in space, an astronaut returns home to a world in which everyone seems to have gone insane. People scramble about directionless, unable to control their emotions. Nobody can speak or act coherently. Society has fallen to pieces. What could have caused such a global catastrophe?

SITUATION 10: When a telepath falls in love with a mentally disturbed woman, he delves into her psyche and also becomes mentally disturbed when the woman begins manipulating his telepathic ability.

CATEGORY 7: DESCENT INTO POVERTY AND SQUALOR

More poor people exist than shelters to provide for them. To survive, many of them resort to living inside sewers, drainage pipes, subways, and such, visiting the streets only to beg. These underground realms, where the poor live in almost total darkness, are a kind of Purgatory. Situations like these can make for gritty, realistic stories.

SITUATION 1: A Jewish family in a Nazi-occupied country joins an underground sanctuary, but the inhabitants fear that informers will turn them in or Nazis will find them. The narrator must come up with a way to make their discovery less likely while still being able to secure food and water.

SITUATION 2: Disgusted with the complacency of the rich, a nobleman gives up his possessions, joins a group of homeless people living in the sewers, and helps them become self-sufficient. Ironically, they resist his efforts.

SITUATION 3: His home and possessions destroyed by a fire, a once-successful craftsman, unable to recoup his losses, becomes homeless. His experiences on the streets provide him with ideas for starting anew—but he needs to break his drug addiction and find someone willing to back him.

SITUATION 4: After surveying the poverty in his country, a prince gives up his privileges and lives among impoverished laborers, intending to help them improve their condition. But the plan backfires when he is recognized and attacked as an emblem of evil royalty.

SITUATION 5: When his girlfriend disappears, the narrator (a criminal investigator) follows clues that lead her to a slum where she once lived. Why did she return? As he continues to investigate, he discovers that his friend, also trained in criminal investigation, has been tracking the person who murdered her brother.

SITUATION 6: A billionaire spends a month on the streets to experience homelessness firsthand. His findings differ radically from his previous assumptions about the poor. He is also disgusted by many of the people's lack of drive—and is determined to kindle their ambitions.

SITUATION 7: Following the example of Francis and Clare of Assisi, an affluent brother and sister give up their possessions to live among the poor and help them improve their lot. But one of the poor people learns of the siblings' secret and accuses them of being phonies because they still have some resources to fall back on.

SITUATION 8: After losing his entire savings in a casino, the narrator looks for a way to redeem himself by volunteering to help compulsive gamblers. At a group meeting, he meets a woman whose gambling addiction is complicated by the fact that she can read minds and knows instantly who is bluffing at the poker table. However, this skill comes and goes.

SITUATION 9: Assuming she has inherited a nest egg from her father, the protagonist (who has been living in poverty) discovers that her father left her nothing. Instead he willed his entire estate to an organization which his daughter used to ridicule. The daughter now devotes her life to wreaking vengeance on the organization and her father's legacy.

SITUATION 10: Humanitarians enter an African village in an effort to save hundreds of people from starvation—but the militaristic regime threatens to murder anyone who tries to administer aid to these people.

CATEGORY 8: DESCENT INTO THE SUBCONSCIOUS

One might compare the subconscious mind to a vast subterranean chamber that has been only partially explored. Ever since Freud opened the door, psychologists have been exploring this terra incognita. Who knows what dark recesses remain to be uncovered?

SITUATION 1: A scientist investigating paranormal phenomena undergoes a radical change in personality. The psychiatrist who hypnotizes him encounters an alien entity that has overtaken him. When the psychiatrist tries to exorcise the alien, she finds herself being influenced by the alien as well.

SITUATION 2: An artist suffers from a psychosomatic disorder: Some entity in his subconscious is causing him to do outlandish things against his will—some of them illegal. Worried he might break the law, he sees a psychiatrist who thinks she can coax forth the entity.

SITUATION 3: Forensic psychologists probe the subconscious of a serial killer and are horrified by what they uncover: grotesque fantasies, sadistic obsessions, etc. The deeper they probe the serial killer's psyche, the greater that psyche's hold on them becomes.

SITUATION 4: Enemy agents abduct a diplomat and give her a post-hypnotic suggestion to obtain secret information. Another agent probes the diplomat's subconscious to determine her assignment. But the agent discovers two conflicting assignments and suspects that both could be false leads.

SITUATION 5: A radio host suffers a psychic breakdown and begins inserting apocalyptic visions from her subconscious into her commentary. When she is taken off the air, her fans demand her return. The execs comply, and she soon creates a new religious movement that could endanger the lives of listeners.

SITUATION 6: The leader of a cult, who openly admires Charles Manson, is said to control his followers through psychological manipulation. After eluding police, a forensic psychologist posing as a runaway manages to join the group and tries to neutralize the effect of the leader's psychic powers on certain members— but the effort backfires.

SITUATION 7: An artist uses her canvas to probe deeply into her subconscious in a sustained effort to bring long-buried experiences to the surface ... not just for the sake of her art but because she suspects that her repressed memories may help solve a crime.

SITUATION 8: Brain researchers exploring the subconscious discover a new area related to dreaming, which could greatly enhance the dream state. Their efforts to keep their research secret, however, backfire; profiteers begin selling dream-state access to the public.

SITUATION 9: A neurologist probes the subconscious minds of adolescent offenders. She searches for root causes of criminal behavior. Some of her findings are so unexpected that her superiors threaten to stop funding. Her goal: to get her peers to take her seriously.

SITUATION 10: Terrorists use mind control to carry out their attacks. They use a high-tech device to establish brain links with guards, soldiers, etc., and then manipulate these victims' subconscious minds to make them commit self-destructive acts. But the protagonist risks her life to devise an antidote that disables the brain links.

CATEGORY 9: DESCENT INTO SUBTERRANEAN REALMS

Based on what anthropologists and archaeologists discover as they explore caves and subterranean chambers, historians regularly revise history. We often wonder, too, about the possible existence of hidden cities, underground or underwater, that await our discovery. Descent into dark and mysterious underground realms makes for engrossing tales.

SITUATION 1: The narrator gets on an elevator an presses "Lower Level." The elevator descends ... and descends. After two minutes, he presses all the buttons in an attempt to stop the elevator, but it will not stop. When it finally reaches the bottom, he finds himself in an incomprehensible place.

SITUATION 2: A family on vacation drives into a tunnel that doesn't seem to end. In fact, the road begins descending. Every time the narrator tries to turn back, the car stalls. Resigned, they follow the tunnel into an underground city inhabited by dwarf humans. The dwarves built the tunnel to gain access to surface resources and the vacationing family will prove a most useful ally.

SITUATION 3: Astronauts exploring an Earthlike planet enter a deep cavern. There they discover exotic life forms in streams and thermal pools and collect samples from them. Despite taking precautions to keep the organisms from escaping confinement, the spacecraft becomes contaminated.

SITUATION 4: Upon entering her usual New York City subway station as she heads for work, the narrator notices slight changes—the Metro Card dispenser, the color of the subway line, the texture of the walls, etc. Even the train seems different. She gets on anyway ...

SITUATION 5: Explorers discover a sealed underground city on one of Saturn's moons—evidence of alien explorers. When they penetrate the seal, they discover a hibernation chamber filled with grotesque-looking creatures. They debate whether or not they should try to revive them, but during the process one slowly wakes from its deep sleep.

SITUATION 6: Underwater explorers discover a sea cave in which species of fish thought to be extinct are flourishing. But there are even stranger things about the cave that don't seem to be connected to any other life forms in the ocean—or anywhere else on earth.

SITUATION 7: In the future, a plague of unknown origin decimates the inhabitants of an underground lunar city. When a medical team investigates, they become infected by a deadly alien virus. The narrator and her team, searching for an antidote, come upon a group of survivors who seem immune to the virus.

SITUATION 8: Vampires have built an underground city. The narrator, a vampire hunter, and his team sneak into the underground city intending to destroy it—but what they discover changes their minds.

SITUATION 9: The search for missing persons takes three detectives into the bowels of a large city, where they follow tunnels into forgotten chambers used as bomb shelters during the world wars. There they find a colony of mutant humans—some of whom might be the missing persons.

SITUATION 10: While excavating an Egyptian necropolis, archaeologists locate a tunnel leading to subterranean living quarters, apparently used by escaped slaves. More astonishing, these quarters still show signs of being occupied.

CATEGORY 10: DESCENT INTO WONDERLAND

Alice falling down the rabbit hole is the archetypal descent into a realm where logic no longer holds say and magic reigns—but also lunacy. Most of us yearn to escape, through the power of story, from the mundane to the mysterious and enchanting.

SITUATION 1: When his elderly neighbor fails to answer the doorbell, the narrator ventures inside. When he checks the basement, he discovers the entrance to another world, full of strange delights. But where is the neighbor?

SITUATION 2: A descendent of Alice (of Wonderland fame) discovers the journal that her great-great grandmother kept of her adventures, including the secret location of the entrance. When she descends, she finds Wonderland in ruins. About to return, she encounters a survivor, who explains what happened. Together they set out to rebuild the enchanted realm.

SITUATION 3: The white rabbit possesses magical powers that he's kept secret until now. Alas, because his magic keeps getting him into trouble, he needs a friend—a modern-day Alice Liddell—to guide him. Unfortunately he is difficult to befriend.

SITUATION 4: Alice's brother descends into Wonderland, intending to bring some of the enchantment back with him to the real world. When one of the Red Queen's guards discovers what he is up to, he chases the brother back to the surface and gets caught up in an aboveground adventure.

SITUATION 5: Many obscure places in Wonderland await exploration by curious types, like two teenage siblings who stumble upon the entrance. But instead of embarking on an adventure, they plan to abduct the strange creatures (the Caterpillar, the Cheshire Cat, etc.) and turn them into circus attractions.

SITUATION 6: Wonderland is under siege by realists. Their goal: Shut it down, for it keeps kids from learning about the real world. But the residents of Wonderland have a surprise in store for these realists.

SITUATION 7: Entrepreneurs attempt to turn Wonderland into a theme park. They dazzle some inhabitants with promises of fame and fortune—but the entrepreneurs get greedy and write up contracts that put the inhabitants at a disadvantage. The Mad Hatter enters the fray to expose the swindle.

SITUATION 8: Alice discovers an alternate Wonderland inhabited by creatures only superficially similar to those in the original. Some are shape-shifters with the ability to turn into beasts. One of the characters tells Alice that the transformations are due to a curse—and with Alice's help they can neutralize the monsters and restore harmony.

SITUATION 9: Now a teenager and nostalgic for Wonderland, Alice returns and meets a sorcerer with whom she falls in love. But the sorcerer is unprincipled—he turns animals into people and vice versa. When Alice protests, he turns her into a witch.

SITUATION 10: A resident in an assisted-living community is a magus who opens a portal into Wonderland. He persuades other residents to join him in an Alice-like adventure. When they arrive, they discover that Wonderland is not hospitable to the elderly. Undeterred, the magus takes steps to change that.

CHAPTER 8

THE DISCOVERY OR CREATION OF X

CATEGORY 1: THE CREATION OF ARTIFICIAL LIFE

Ever since Mary Shelley electrified the world with *Frankenstein; Or, The Modern Prometheus*, writers and scientists alike have not stopped fantasizing about creating living beings out of nonliving matter (or, in the case of Shelley's novel, reanimating cadavers). Possible story situations abound; here are ten of them.

SITUATION 1: A scientist uses her supercomputer to redesign the human genome so that the so-called "junk" DNA (comprising 90 percent of human DNA) dramatically advances human nature. But she fails to anticipate a latent lethal element in that DNA.

SITUATION 2: Engineers create a robot with artificial intelligence capable of reproducing itself. When the robotic being it creates commits a crime, a debate is triggered: Is that robot offspring a "person," and how should justice be served?

SITUATION 3: Cats are on the verge of extinction because of a lethal artificial virus that escaped confinement. To compensate, a scientist creates a robotic cat that looks and feels exactly like the real thing—but there are dangerous differences.

SITUATION 4: After announcing that she has created a living organism out of nonliving matter, a biochemist is harassed and her laboratory sabotaged. A detective assigned to the case is brutally beaten. Meanwhile the organism grows rapidly into a creature that behaves in ways utterly unlike existing life forms.

SITUATION 5: In this alternate world, magicians routinely create artificial life-forms for amusement: The creatures do not live longer than the length of the demonstration. But one of the lifeforms not only continues to exist after his creator's performance but escapes confinement.

SITUATION 6: Consulting a medieval book of sorcery, a rabbi creates a golem out of raw earth to protect the members of his family, for they are being persecuted by the villagers. The golem, however, uses radical ways of fulfilling his duty and soon places the rabbi's family in even greater danger.

SITUATION 7: Engineers develop a workforce of robots capable of building a colony on Mars. The robots not only build the colony; they populate it with their offspring and prevent the human colonists from moving in.

SITUATION 8: Astronauts journey to a "rogue planet" (a planet not orbiting a star) just beyond our solar system. They discover the remnants of a city that apparently flourished eons ago. The city is filled with disassembled robots. The astronauts' first question: What happened to the inhabitants?

SITUATION 9: Doubt exists about whether the organism biologists have created is technically "alive." The boundary between living and nonliving is ambiguous. The artificial organism exhibits fascinating behavior, but the lab administrator still threatens to destroy the organism.

SITUATION 10: No one can decide whether the latest cyborg is artificial or natural since it consists of both organic and inorganic systems. When the cyborg runs for office, this traditionally philosophical issue becomes a political and legal one.

CATEGORY 2: THE CREATION OF MARVELOUS MACHINES

Machines have shaped civilization since the beginning, with inventions like the wheel, the pulley, the plow, the windmill, and the loom. These machines are certainly marvelous, but since the industrial revolution, clever machines like automatons (the precursors of robots) have expanded mechanical possibility—and make for great reading.

SITUATION 1: Everyone is raving about the new nanomachines that zap tumors and repair defective heart valves, but when a technician is treated for a brain tumor, her personality changes radically. Scientists suspect that only another micromachine can reverse the outcome.

SITUATION 2: An inventor of Rube-Goldberg machines, according to her neighbors, is simply a village eccentric. Her new invention, however, seems to border on the miraculous. Should she be praised or is the machine dangerous?

SITUATION 3: The human/machine boundary becomes blurred when prosthetics researchers create a cyborg capable of feats like smashing through concrete bunkers and destroying weapons. It's a phenomenal new invention, but the cyborg is difficult to control in extreme situations.

SITUATION 4: Aliens introduce humanity to machines that compose music, that establish communications links between the user and other life forms, and perform other marvelous feats. One of these machines enables humans to engage in reality-shifting activities.

SITUATION 5: It is 2050, and people visit robot physicians for routine physicals. These robots function well ... until someone interferes with their functions—which is what the narrator's mischievous friend does, with unsettling results.

SITUATION 6: A robotics engineer creates a brain implant that accelerates learning. The only drawback is that prolonged use can cause erratic behavior.

SITUATION 7: Sigmund II is a robot psychiatrist who is reputed to be far more successful in healing its patients than human psychiatrists are. But when the narrator begins a treatment regimen under Sigmund II, strange things happen to both doctor and patient.

SITUATION 8: A machine has been designed to help people control their emotions. However, the machine overregulates the brain's neurochemical balance, which causes the user to undergo extreme psychotic episodes.

SITUATION 9: In this near-future society, one can purchase courage from a machine: The more money you insert, the longer your courage will last. The narrator opts for an extra-lengthy episode to see how effective machine-bought courage can be.

SITUATION 10: SOULMATE, a compatibility machine, determines whether couples are compatible. When the narrator and his fiancé hook up to SOULMATE, the machine determines that they are incompatible. "A machine shouldn't determine our fate," he protests, but his fiancé disagrees.

CATEGORY 3: THE CREATION OF MIRACLE DRUGS

One of the greatest achievements of the twentieth century was the creation of "miracle drugs"—antibiotics, antidepressants, cholesterol medications, etc. But sometimes drawbacks occur, especially when the drugs are misused. Good stories can raise awareness of these limitations.

SITUATION 1: In this world, medications for experiencing intense, vivid dreams become available—different meds for different kinds of dreams. Soon a black market springs up for meds that produce erotic dreams. But these meds have an unpleasant side effect.

SITUATION 2: In the future, people take an immunity pill to protect themselves from disease, but they grow less concerned about maintaining healthy lifestyles. Mutations of bacteria and viruses soon evolve that are resistant to the immunity pill.

SITUATION 3: Women can take a pill that prevents birth defects but doing so dulls the infant's pain receptors. The mother of such a child searches, ironically, for a treatment that will enable her child to experience pain normally.

SITUATION 4: Employers in this future scenario require their employees to take drugs that ensure optimal job performance: better eyesight, quicker reflexes, accurate decision-making, etc. But as the protagonist discovers, these pills have negative side effects.

SITUATION 5: It is the year 2100, the average human life span is 125, and drug companies compete to produce drugs that ensure that a person's youth spans his or her lifetime. But some people are too zealous in using these drugs, which have unpredictable side effects.

SITUATION 6: A new drug makes people taller. One user, who has always longed to be tall, eagerly takes the drug, which does indeed work beyond the user's expectations, and now it won't stop. He is desperate to find an antidote.

SITUATION 7: People in the future take "brain pills"—specific drugs for learning specific tasks. Education has become so medication-dependent that no one can do much of anything without taking a pill for the task.

117

SITUATION 8: Dissatisfied with his personality (or lack thereof), the protagonist, like others in this future society, can take a personality drug, which comes in a wide spectrum of enhancers or modifiers: serene, aggressive, adventurous, contemplative, wild, etc. However, the drug is addictive.

SITUATION 9: Imagine a drug that enables the user to see supernatural beings: angels, ancient deities, even God. A pharmacologist has created such a drug, and the demand for it is extreme. Atheists insist the drug is a hallucinogen ... until they try it themselves. Alas, the side effects should make people to think twice about taking the drug.

SITUATION 10: Equipped with antibiotics, the narrator travels back in time to save his great grandmother (said to be a genius) from tuberculosis. He also brought enough antibiotics with him to save others. However, his supply is stolen.

CATEGORY 4: THE CREATION OR DISCOVERY OF NEW SOCIAL STRUCTURES

Societies are organized in many different ways, and for the past century and a half, anthropologists have studied these social structures and have drawn correlations between structures, ethics, and individual behavior. Writers tap into these insights for in-depth stories about people in complex social contexts.

SITUATION 1: The appointed guardians of this utopian society prove to be the enemy—they become so obsessed with protecting the society that they disregard people's need for autonomy and basic freedoms.

SITUATION 2: A future society is plagued by segregation: People are separated by skin color—not just black-brown-white but by numerous shades of each color. Interbreeding between people from different categories is forbidden and results in exile. The exiled inhabitants form an insurgency against the status quo.

SITUATION 3: Angels govern this society. Although the angels are revered and slavishly obeyed, the society is no utopia as secret sects exist that consider the angels to be soulless aliens aiming to neutralize the human souls and take over their bodies.

SITUATION 4: Weary of techno-industrial culture, several nature lovers establish a commune devoted to ecological and contemplative ideals. However, inhabitants near the site of their commune regard them as dangerous radicals and try to sabotage their plans.

SITUATION 5: A future utopian society living on a remote island is organized according to artistic interest: Poets live with poets, painters with painters, etc. The protagonist feels isolated because she believes in integrating the disciplines. But her attempts to integrate the existing groups is met with fierce opposition.

SITUATION 6: What if the slave army led by Spartacus had escaped their Roman pursuers and formed their own society far from Italy? In this alternate-history scenario, the new slave society forbids any kind of servitude except one: the subordinate role of women. Several of the slave women plot a revolt.

SITUATION 7: This society of the future is a matriarchy in which men, considered genetically unstable, are second-class citizens by law and no longer needed for reproduction now that semen can be produced artificially.

SITUATION 8: Explorers discover, deep in the Himalayas, mystics who seem to interact with supernatural beings. The explorers observe their rituals with much skepticism ... until one of the beings materializes before them.

SITUATION 9: In this fantasy world, governance is based on the capacity to perform magic. Those who can perform the most important magic are appointed to the highest posts. The problem is that some of the most powerful magicians perform dark magic.

SITUATION 10: In the future, human diversity is more prevalent than it is today; all races, genders, sexual orientations, and religious views are fully integrated. However, isolated gangs of racists spread their hate to sympathizers who want to return to "the good old days."

CATEGORY 5: THE DISCOVERY OF ANCIENT DWELLINGS AND BURIAL SITES

Archaeology changes history to some degree with each new find. That fact alone makes archaeological discoveries a rich source of story ideas. With the discovery of ancient dwellings and burial sites, we gain new knowledge about the everyday lives of ancient peoples.

SITUATION 1: Outside Giza, an Egyptologist discovers a necropolis unlike any seen before. It antedates the known necropolises by several centuries and contains evidence of interaction with alien technology.

SITUATION 2: Inhabitants of a lost dwelling discovered inside the crater of an extinct volcano on a remote island that is cut off from the rest of the world have cultivated magic to help them survive. The narrator and his team, however, have detected signs that the volcano is awakening.

SITUATION 3: In a recently unearthed prehistoric dwelling, scientists discover evidence of a cross-species of human previously unknown. Astonishingly strange pictographic carvings are found that suggest an extraterrestrial influence. Before further examination can be done, the artifacts disappear.

SITUATION 4: When a dwelling on an island off the northern coast of Scotland is excavated, scientists find what seem to be fragments of a map. Once enough pieces are gathered, the assembled map indicates an offshore atoll that no longer exists. Divers explore the area and discover an incredible treasure.

SITUATION 5: Remnants of a dwelling dating 25,000 BCE are uncovered inside a cave; they are too recent to belong to Neanderthals and too old for modern humans. Bones showing attributes of both species, plus those of an unknown species, are then discovered, suggesting that modern humans have more pre-human DNA than previously suspected. Could that DNA again become dominant?

SITUATION 6: When a mall developer has a Native-American burial mound excavated (a state mandate before building can proceed), blueprint programs somehow become corrupted; fires break out in the developer's offices, etc. The developer ignores these incidents and proceeds with his plans.

SITUATION 7: Workers in England clearing a path for a new highway uncover an ancient Druid temple containing maps etched in stone that appear to indicate alien visitation. But one of the bulldozers has already accidentally shoveled away a stone block bearing part of the inscription.

SITUATION 8: Treasure seekers unearth a site filled with religious artifacts embedded with jewels. Ignoring the warning that profaning these artifacts could lead to terrible consequences, the treasure seekers realize too late that the artifacts are laced with natural toxins that drive humans insane.

SITUATION 9: Antarctic scientists uncover a city buried under hundreds of feet of ice. They also discover frozen bodies that do not resemble any known species of hominid, past or present. When an excavator, disobeying orders, secretly thaws one of the bodies, chaos follows.

SITUATION 10: Originally assumed to be a burial site, a cave on a remote island proves to be an ancient suspended animation chamber. The aliens are still asleep. Should they be revived? Some say yes; others insist that they need to search for clues about why they're in suspended animation.

CATEGORY 6: THE DISCOVERY OF EXOTIC/ENDANGERED LIFE FORMS

It may be hard to believe, but scientists continue to discover new species of plants and animals, especially in remote rain forests and deep underwater (where extremely high pressures make exploration difficult). A newly discovered species can lead to a rewriting of the biological record. There is also the potential for fascinating stories to be told.

SITUATION 1: Primatologists in the near future struggle to keep gorillas from going extinct, but the poachers are ruthless and armed and the scientists are losing the battle. Scientists attempt to lead gorillas into a remote, unexplored part of the jungle, where an even more rare and previously undiscovered species of gorilla appears, one that may be able to help endangered gorillas outsmart the poachers.

SITUATION 2: Intelligent jellyfish? Marine biologists encounter (and subsequently examine) an unknown species that seems to possess self-awareness. But only when one of the scientists is stung does the truth of these jellyfish finally emerge.

SITUATION 3: Ornithologists in a little-known patch of South American rain forest are amazed by parrots that seem to be trying to communicate with them. Perhaps they are reacting to the clear-cutting that has been going on around them. Or perhaps they are warning the humans that their exploitation of the forest has to end.

SITUATION 4: A diver encounters an octopus with very special powers, such as the ability to conjure up images in the diver's mind—images that reveal an enchanted world from which the octopus has been exiled ... and longs to return. Would the diver help? A great reward would be in store.

SITUATION 5: Antlike species encountered on a distant world surpass human intelligence but only collectively. Their queen integrates the separate inputs from each "ant" and makes decisions based on that input. Humans try to establish a cooperative, but the "ants" become disenchanted with the humans and resist further contact with them.

SITUATION 6: When a search party locates the lost explorers they'd set out to find, they also find snakelike creatures sharing the forest dwellings with them. As the search party helps the explorers get ready to leave their encampment, the explorers insist that the creatures come along—that they need to come along.

SITUATION 7: While exploring an African lagoon, the narrator and her party discover a species of reptile thought to have gone extinct; they also discover the reptile's nest of eggs. One night, the eggs hatch and the progeny escape confinement.

SITUATION 8: Scientists explore an alternate Earth in which giant birds—some beautiful and majestic, some ugly and powerful—are the dominant species. It turns out that some of these species are highly intelligent—especially the powerful ones, which see the humans as easy prey.

SITUATION 9: Although their numbers have grown as a result of government protection, wolves continue to be endangered because of unregulated hunting. The narrator tries to make a case for the wolves, but a vigilante group of farmers and ranchers are determined to sabotage his cause.

SITUATION 10: After an alligator nearly kills a child, authorities launch an effort to wipe out all alligators from a popular tourist county in Florida. It is up to the protagonist to persuade the authorities to desist, but her alligator-protection measures are putting her cause—and even her life—at risk.

CATEGORY 7: THE DISCOVERY OF GATEWAYS TO THE PAST

Time travel is likely to remain the stuff of fantasy. That does not stop writers from weaving fascinating tales of going back in time to stop awful events from happening—either in history or in one's own life. It is human nature to want to undo mistakes.

SITUATION 1: Two siblings discover a way to travel back to the time of Christ's ministry and get involved with the politics of the day—too involved, as one of the brothers is pursued as a heretic. The other brother becomes a secret follower of Jesus. When the heretic tries to get his brother to return to the present, he refuses.

SITUATION 2: Time travelers journey back to Europe circa 1930 to stop the rise of Nazi power; however, the deeper they probe, the more difficult it becomes to pinpoint the causes. They travel even further back in time on time in a quest to find the root cause.

SITUATION 3: A teenager finds a magic stopwatch in her grandmother's attic and travels back to when her grandparents were courting. Her mission: Stop her grandmother from conceiving her aunt (her mother's sister), whose son has caused so much grief in the teen's life.

SITUATION 4: The focal character's greatest wish is to contact the great Queen Nefertiti and acquire some of her magical powers—especially the one that enabled her, a beautiful woman, to become ruler of Egypt. But when she finally encounters the Queen, she is nothing at all like the woman portrayed in the history books.

SITUATION 5: Regretting the terrible mistakes she made, a corporate vice president, finds a way to return to her undergraduate years to follow the career path she really wanted to take. Despite this opportunity, she encounters a major distraction that she must resist.

SITUATION 6: Having discovered a gateway to his past, a laid-off blue-collar worker returns to earlier years who has never been satisfied with his interactions with others. In those days, whenever he tried to improve something, the opposite occurred. He now realizes that he was focusing on the wrong things.

SITUATION 7: When a lonely woman goes back in time to relive a special moment in her past, something goes wrong and she winds up in someone else's past ... and in someone else's body. To get back to her own body and time, she must use the stranger whose body she now inhabits to help her find her past self.

SITUATION 8: Unhappy with the modern world, a teacher travels back to his favorite period, mid-nineteenth-century Vienna. As he loses himself in the orchestral and operatic scene, he unwittingly becomes mixed up in the political struggles of the time.

SITUATION 9: Seeking to undo the past, in which she had been abused by her husband, a woman travels back to when she first met her husband and persuades her younger self to drop him—which she does, only to result in an even rockier train of events.

SITUATION 10: The protagonist finds a gateway to ancient Jerusalem, where her involvement there causes a cascade of events that lead to a very different kind of religion than Christianity. Horrified, she returns to ancient Jerusalem to set things straight—but with mixed results

CATEGORY 8: THE DISCOVERY OR INVENTION OF MAGICAL REALITIES

Imagine what it would be like if other realities really existed—worlds or entire universes in which the laws of physics operated differently, where the distinction between magic and reality does not exist. Imagine the things you could write about if you were allowed to make your own rules ... this is your chance.

SITUATION 1: In an alternate-reality Earth, trees have the power to move objects at will and gain psychological control of people. This results in a bizarre symbiotic cooperation between people and trees—including situations in which people become virtually enslaved to the whims of some trees ... but not all.

SITUATION 2: To save endangered frogs from extinction, a biologist with a mystical bent establishes communion with one of the frogs, which in turn introduces the biologist to a hitherto unknown dimension of frog culture in an obscure rain forest.

SITUATION 3: On this world, people are transformed by rain: Their personalities, thoughts, and even their appearances change. Rain cults are everywhere. But then something happens to the planet's climate, and rainfall becomes torrential and damaging.

SITUATION 4: A maverick scientist discovers a way to cross into different dimensions; each reality differs substantially from the others because of one key difference. For example, in one dimension, the earth has two moons instead of one; in another dimension, dinosaurs never became extinct, and so on.

SITUATION 5: Not only butterflies undergo metamorphosis in the future. People do as well, now that it's possible for humans to regenerate at the end of their natural lives. There is one catch: Memories do not transfer. However, scientists are working to change that.

SITUATION 6: A computer programmer invents a virtual world filled with magical possibilities such as the ability to walk through walls or levitate. But he gets carried away and some of the magic he programs into his virtual universe becomes impossible to negate.

SITUATION 7: In this magical realm, people have the ability to change into flying creatures. However, flying is dangerous because of invisible predators. The protagonist thinks she has found a way to make the predators visible.

SITUATION 8: A reclusive couple living deep in a forest has been cultivating a magic garden containing plants that can heighten consciousness and even transform people's appearances. When hikers in the forest discover the couple's residence, they are lured by aromatic smells from the garden.

SITUATION 9: The focal character is repeatedly bullied because he always appears to be talking to himself. Actually he is in contact with a wizard from another dimension who explains how to neutralize bullies.

SITUATION 10: After a CAT scan, the narrator finds herself in an alternate reality—but the differences between realities are hard to spot. She suspects that something is wrong during a conversation with her husband. She notices other differences and panics. How is she going to return to her true reality?

CATEGORY 9: THE DISCOVERY OF NEW WORLDS

> Ours is an age of planetary discovery, thanks to powerful space telescopes like Kepler. Over a thousand extrasolar planets have been detected thus far, including a few that seem Earthlike. It is possible, too, that the satellites of planets may be more Earthlike than the planets themselves. What marvelous planetary discoveries will continue to be made? What secrets will we learn about them? What stories might they generate?

SITUATION 1: A newly discovered asteroid heading toward Earth is small enough not to threaten mass extinction but large enough to do widespread damage. But closer inspection reveals that the asteroid is artificial and it is able to manipulate its own trajectory.

SITUATION 2: A multigeneration starship has arrived, after one hundred years, at the inhabited, earthlike planet that had been discovered in the system of a neighboring star, but since the discovery, the beings were invaded by a hostile force, which the crew must now confront.

SITUATION 3: Spacefarers discover a garden world orbiting sun that emits lethal bursts of radiation every few centuries. When they learn that the sun is overdue for another lethal burst, they try to salvage as much of the exotic flora as they can, even though they risk becoming exposed to the lethal radiation.

SITUATION 4: Interstellar explorers land on a planet whose surface is a frozen wasteland. To their amazement, they come upon a domed city in which strange machines are everywhere. All of them are defunct except for one ...

SITUATION 5: Astronauts get pulled into a spatio-temporal rift and emerge in orbit around a parallel earth—in this one, gigantic craters cover most of North America. When the astronauts land, they encounter militaristic societies engulfed in war.

SITUATION 6: When scientists find a portal leading to a mirror universe, they encounter their duplicate selves just about to enter the portal from the other end. One scientist interrogates her other self—and discovers a shocking difference between their two realities.

SITUATION 7: Embedded in a meteorite is a videodisc similar to the one attached to Voyager in the 1970s. The disc depicts a world dozens of light-years distant inhabited by strange creatures, several of whose minds have been uploaded onto the disc.

SITUATION 8: An autistic child appears to inhabit her own world. Psychologists try to enter that world by hypnotizing her but fail—possibly because they have difficulty understanding the nature of her autism. But then a psychologist finds a new way to enter her world, and it's extraordinarily beautiful and intricate.

SITUATION 9: Physicists produce an electromagnetically generated portal into another dimension of the existing universe. When scientists venture into it, they encounter weird anatomical differences in people, including themselves. While they are superficial similarities, their behaviors are drastically different.

SITUATION 10: When astronauts visit an asteroid that has been behaving erratically, they discover a city deep in its interior, one that seems to have been dormant for thousands of years. There are no clues to its origin until an ancient computer is discovered ... and awakened.

CATEGORY 10: SCIENTIFIC AND TECHNOLOGICAL DISCOVERIES

Science and technology continue to transform the world and our understanding of it, just as they have been doing since the seventeenth century. And while there is a mechanistic, soulless aspect to science and technology, the wonders and insights into nature (and ourselves) far outshine those negative aspects. In either case, stories abound.

SITUATION 1: Suspended animation has been perfected, and thousands of people—especially those with incurable illnesses—sign up to sleep for fifty years and (they hope) awaken to a time when their maladies can be cured. The narrator has done exactly that. He wakes to a world that not only can cure his illness but is required by law to modify him in other ways.

SITUATION 2: Scientists generate a wormhole—a shortcut through space-time that enables passage across vast interstellar distances. They also learn to keep the wormhole stable for a sufficient amount of time to send large numbers of people and vehicles through. What they haven't figured out is how to "aim" it. When they emerge on the other side, they have no idea where they are … or what is waiting for them.

SITUATION 3: Computer chips are implanted in newborns in this future world, and the miraculous benefits of a healthier life, greater strength, and mental agility are tempered by unpredictable side effects. In one instance, the protagonist begins to realize that the implants give him directives to perform certain tasks he finds immoral and that he is aware of what is happening because his implants are malfunctioning. He tries to convince others of the truth, but finds himself hunted and alone.

SITUATION 4: A movement is afoot to create "in vitro" meat: Cloning cow cells in the lab and developing them into steaks, etc., thereby alleviating global warming by reducing methane gas. Of course the cattle industry is outraged by this idea and fights back every way it can.

SITUATION 5: Computer wizards have discovered a way to link people to the Internet via their brains. All one has to do is blink to access the Internet and to vocalize commands for surfing or sending messages. But, as the focal character observes, people are changing in disturbing ways.

SITUATION 6: Scientists have discovered a way to transmit radio signals through warps in space. The signals can reach inhabited worlds hundreds of light-years away in minutes rather than years. The scientists soon contact alien beings—but they're not friendly.

SITUATION 7: When a team of researchers develops a new kind of gene therapy derived from embryonic stem cells (and which restores cancerous cells to normal function), Stockholm is ready to bestow the Nobel Prize on them. But radical pro-life groups demand that the researchers be arrested for destruction of embryos, tantamount (they insist) to first-degree murder.

SITUATION 8: A team of biologists wants to clone a mammoth using DNA from a mammoth carcass discovered in Arctic ice. A bioethicist protests: Would it be ethical? The biologists in favor of cloning argue that the protestor lacks the credentials to make that judgment.

SITUATION 9: Neurologists find a way to accelerate learning, enabling young and old to master any subject in a fraction of the time normally expected. There is a risk factor, though: The brain's synapses tend to overload, triggering some bizarre side effects.

SITUATION 10: In this world, people learn in their sleep. Students take "sleep courses" for college credit; travelers learn a new language while asleep. But this seemingly ideal way to learn has serious drawbacks, not the least of which is its addictive quality.

CHAPTER 9

ESCAPE FROM X

CATEGORY 1: ESCAPE FROM ABDUCTORS

Abductions demand the most skilled criminal investigators. The safety and lives of the persons abducted are not only threatened, but the status of their condition is usually kept secret. Whether the victims will survive unharmed is always unpredictable. All of this makes for high-voltage suspense storytelling.

SITUATION 1: The billionaire CEO of a genetic engineering company is abducted. The abductors' demand is not for money but for a change in the company's policies regarding the patenting of certain genetically engineered substances. Refusing to comply, the CEO plans a risky escape with the help of an unlikely ally.

SITUATION 2: A TV celebrity who plays a villain is kidnapped. The ransom is excessive, but the kidnappers are unwavering and will kill the celebrity unless the ransom is paid. However, the celebrity is craftier than they think and uses skills devised by his fictional persona to escape.

SITUATION 3: While crossing a park, a Navy vet returning home is abducted and taken to a house where he is interrogated. It soon becomes clear that he has been mistaken for someone else. When the correct man is also kidnapped, they devise a way to escape.

SITUATION 4: A wealthy industrialist's cat is stolen, and a search is launched to find it because it is wearing a collar with something valuable hidden within. Its abductors cannot figure out how to extract the item from the collar without destroying both. Meanwhile the cat manages to escape and is found by a young girl who heard about the reward on the news.

SITUATION 5: A remote island becomes the site of a prison for saboteurs who have been destroying oil refineries and other enterprises they consider unhealthy for the environment. One of the saboteurs uses his experiences to attempt an escape.

SITUATION 6: Astronauts exploring a derelict spaceship orbiting Jupiter become trapped inside the ship. The aliens responsible need the astronauts for some urgent purpose; the astronauts' only hope for escape is to figure out what that purpose is and either accomplish the goal or sabotage the aliens' plan.

SITUATION 7: A popular television newscaster is abducted by a stalker who wants the newscaster to tape a segment featuring himself as an expert on stalking. As the taping gets underway, the celebrity escapes confinement—but the stalker anticipated the move.

SITUATION 8: The wife and children of a bank president are abducted by terrorists who demand the access codes to all of the banks' customers. If the bank president doesn't comply by the imposed deadline, one hostage will be killed every hour.

SITUATION 9: In the future, prisons are maintained and guarded by robots. When a robotics engineer is wrongly convicted, he tries to escape, thinking he can outsmart the very robots he helped invent. But the robots have another reason for keeping him imprisoned.

SITUATION 10: A billionaire's daughter is abducted by militants who demand $100 million. They intend to use the money to stage a coup. While the police work to foil the plan, the daughter comes up with a clever way to escape: She expresses enthusiasm for the militants' cause.

CATEGORY 2: ESCAPE FROM AN ABUSIVE PARENT, SPOUSE, OR PARTNER

> Even before Huck Finn escaped from his abusive father, stories had been written about children or teens escaping from tyrannical or abusive parents. The theme has universal appeal: All of us, at one time or another, have dreamt of escape from parental control.

SITUATION 1: A single mother tries to keep her rebellious and musically gifted daughter from making the same mistakes she did. Finally, the daughter escapes by running off with an older man who promises to get her a job as a nightclub singer. Unfortunately the nightclub is a front for a prostitution ring.

SITUATION 2: When his father ridicules him for wanting to become an astronaut, a teenager escapes from home and bonds with a friend who has escaped his domineering parents. Both of them want to invent marvelous machines. But because they are seventeen, their parents order them home.

SITUATION 3: After months of abuse from her stepfather, a teenager escapes and seeks refuge with her natural father—but her natural father is emotionally unstable. With no one else to turn to, she plans an assault on her stepfather.

SITUATION 4: Two brothers escape their abusive parents by using their supernatural powers to open a portal into an alternate universe. The parents discover the portal while they're escaping through it and follow them into the alternate world. The boys consider trapping their parents in the alternate world and escaping, but one doesn't want to go back.

SITUATION 5: A "control freak" prevents his girlfriend from visiting friends and family or doing anything without his permission. She plans an escape, but he gets wind of it and resorts to terror tactics to keep her from running away.

SITUATION 6: Successful as a child star, the protagonist resists his actor-parents' efforts to keep him in the movies. He rejects Hollywood and wants to pursue a career in science, especially astronomy. At age sixteen, however, he has difficulty overriding his parents' insistence on furthering the family's acting legacy.

SITUATION 7: Lacking self-worth, a possessive young man begs his live-in girlfriend not to leave. She is torn between escaping from his suffocating hold on her and protecting him from his own inner torment.

SITUATION 8: Despite following all the "rules" of ideal parenting—applying discipline lovingly, imparting values, etc.—the focal character's family, to his confusion, is breaking apart. His pre-teen son, in particular, wants to escape, to be as far away from him as possible.

SITUATION 9: The protagonist tries to reconcile with her husband, who had been abusing her before she left. But after she experiences another abusive incident, her ten-year-old son convinces her to escape with him for good.

SITUATION 10: Mistreated by his father, a teenage boy runs away from home and spends a year on the streets. Meanwhile his contrite father searches everywhere and finally locates him in a hospital where he is dying of a drug overdose.

131

CATEGORY 3: ESCAPE FROM SLAVERY OR BONDAGE

Slavery has been eradicated from the world, although not totally, as holding innocent people against their will exists in many forms: via dictatorships, sex trafficking, kidnapping, and hostage situations. Another form of slavery is found in psychological bondage such as intimidation, blackmail, and extortion.

SITUATION 1: In the pre-Civil War South, bounty hunters capture an escaped slave, but the slave has a plan that could make them all rich. However, it would be easier to collect the bounty, so the slave must make his plan compelling.

SITUATION 2: Just before a young slave is to be auctioned, he escapes, steals a firearm, and returns to the plantation to rescue his parents. The plantation owner anticipated that move and has already sold his parents. He must now decide between saving himself and venturing deeper into the slave-owning South.

SITUATION 3: In seventeenth-century Salem, an adolescent whom no one suspects to be a witch actually is one, and she uses her powers to help those falsely imprisoned for sorcery by the governor. One of the clergymen learns about the deception and attempts to hunt them all down.

SITUATION 4: An indentured servant with a gift for scientific reasoning asks for her freedom in the newly independent United States—but the farm owner and chemist refuses. The servant secretly conducts experiments in chemistry.

SITUATION 5: Imprisoned in her own home, the wife of a once-loving man, now insanely jealous over false information of her promiscuity, refuses to let her out of his sight. She is torn between the person he used to be and the possessive monster he has become, but soon she must choose to stay or leave for good.

SITUATION 6: The slave owned by a prominent politician in early nineteenth-century America petitions for her freedom after secretly educating herself with the help of the politician's wife, who taught her to read, and by devouring books in the library when the family was asleep.

SITUATION 7: Punished by her owner for stealing his wife's journal, a slave plots her escape—but first she must retrieve the journal from wherever the slave owner has hidden it because it contains information about where her children now live.

SITUATION 8: In this alternate America, slavery persists into the twenty-first century, despite abolitionist movements. The KKK and other racist groups are more powerful here and terrorize anyone who tries to undermine the economic juggernaut powered by the slave trade.

SITUATION 9: Workers in a sweatshop are abused by bosses who force them to work ungodly hours in wretched, unsafe conditions. Finally three of the workers secretly plan to revolt by sabotaging the equipment. Unfortunately, the plan could trigger a fire and the factory doesn't have a fire escape.

SITUATION 10: A woman forced into prostitution escapes her captor and demands that the police chief break up the prostitution ring. When the chief refuses (he is being bribed by the ringleader), the woman takes matters into her own hands.

CATEGORY 4: ESCAPE FROM DEATH— ACTUAL OR IMMINENT

The ultimate escape is from the clutches of death. Of course any such escape is temporary, unless we're in a science fiction or fantasy universe. In any case, escaping from or defying death lies at the heart of a thriller.

SITUATION 1: Trapped in a hotel about to collapse from an earthquake, a family struggles to dig through rubble and make their way down twenty floors. The power is out and gas lines have been ruptured. And the building keeps shaking.

SITUATION 2: Faced with a terminal illness, an engineer in this near-future scenario searches for a way to transform her doomed body into an artificially constructed one. Her desperation stems not just from her will to live but from an experiment she must complete. However, one of her enemies wants to sabotage her replacement body.

SITUATION 3: With a tornado about to bear down on them, teens on a hiking trip must find a way to survive. Their options are few, but one of the hikers has been through a tornado before and knows what must be done.

SITUATION 4: After being in suspended animation for a hundred years, hoping to awaken in an age when a cure is available for their genetic disease, siblings find themslves in an overpopulated world that not only does not try to prolong life, but searches for ways to shorten it.

SITUATION 5: A social misfit joins a religious group with a hidden agenda: to escape the world's woes by dying. But breaking free of the group's influence is difficult, especially when (as a consequence of their brainwashing strategies) the misfit wants to remain with them.

SITUATION 6: First responders to a volcano-ravaged town struggle to rescue people trapped inside their homes before the next imminent eruption, which experts warn could well be greater than the first. The matter is complicated by torrential rain, a lack of supplies, and an impending order to evacuate before the next eruption.

SITUATION 7: Two adventurous teens stow away on a freight train that turns out to be a ghost train heading for the Land of the Dead. They don't realize this, alas, until it is too late: The box-car doors will not open ... until they arrive at the destination—at which time they attempt to escape.

SITUATION 8: While oceanographers are conducting underwater research, an earthquake strikes, trapping the researchers inside their diving bell. There seems to be no means of escape.

SITUATION 9: Facing imminent execution, a spy offers an unusual deal: In exchange for his life, he will provide access to top-secret military files. The executioners agree—but they secretly plan to kill him anyway after obtaining access to the files.

SITUATION 10: A physicist volunteers for an experiment designed to take her into death's very domain—with the expectation, of course, that she will be retrieved with full recall of what transpired, but something goes wrong and she is trapped.

CATEGORY 5: ESCAPE FROM DIVINE WRATH

How does one escape from the inescapable? Enterprising mortals can find clever ways through ritual sacrifice, repentance, appeasement—or even by garnering the sympathies of rival gods or demigods. Mortals have always dared to rebel against divine forces.

SITUATION 1: Prometheus is rescued from his horrible fate (being chained to a rock so that birds peck away at him) by a former rival mortal who dared defy divine laws. He then asks Prometheus to work with him to steal more secrets from the gods.

SITUATION 2: Once beloved by Athena, a poet-singer has inflamed the goddess's wrath by becoming infatuated with a woman whom the goddess once punished. He and the woman try to escape the goddess's wrath with the help of a sorcerer.

SITUATION 3: After the focal character preaches that the gods are part of a mass delusion, one of the gods robs him of speech. When he prays for forgiveness, the god punishes him even more. Enraged, he seeks revenge against the spiteful god.

SITUATION 4: In this world, the monarch is a supernatural being whose divine powers and endless wrath have alienated her subjects to the point of avoidance rather than worship. To remedy this, she recruits a revered philosopher to teach her how to be admired.

SITUATION 5: No longer will Job bear God's tests in this variation of the Biblical story. Job seeks vengeance against those he feels have made his life torturous and specifically turns away from God, who now fights to win Job back.

SITUATION 6: A lone adventurer suffers the wrath of Aphrodite after he defeats one of the goddess's favorite warriors in a battle over the right to pass through a sacred land dedicated to her. The warrior attempts to evade and then appease the goddess. Nothing works. Finally, he promises he will do anything to win back her good graces—and she accepts the offer.

SITUATION 7: After having terrorized his people for ages, a "god" is suddenly shown to be a fraud who recruits magicians to create impressive pyrotechnics to convince his minions of his power. But now, with chaos imminent, the community needs a leader and even another false god will do.

SITUATION 8: Sisyphus, desperate to escape his rock-pushing punishment, plots a way of escaping Zeus's wrath. Although trapped in the Underworld, he persuades Pluto to help him escape his punishment. Pluto, however, makes his own stringent demands in return for the favor.

SITUATION 9: Defrocked for his transgressions, a priest suffers further from God's wrath. When asked what he must do for forgiveness, God tells him he must figure that out for himself; meanwhile the priest is desperate to escape God's wrath.

SITUATION 10: Transformed into a hideous beast by an avenging goddess, the narrator strives to make amends for his wrongdoing and thereby placate the goddess. Nothing works; finally he approaches a sorcerer who claims to know what must be done. Meanwhile the beast he has become is taking over his human will.

CATEGORY 6: ESCAPE FROM INCARCERATION

Who can resist stories of escape from jail or prison? Whether the protagonist has been justly or unjustly incarcerated, we still root for him to defy the grim odds and figure out a way to elude the detection of heavily armed guards, electronic detection, and the like. This is edge-of-the-seat reading, to be sure.

SITUATION 1: During World War II, two POWs plan to escape from a German prison camp, but they need to recruit one of the German guards to pull it off. One of the guards seems to be on their side—but before they launch the escape, the POWs must be certain.

SITUATION 2: Terrorists booby-trap a skyscraper with a bomb while thousands of people are working inside. Unless their demands are met, they will detonate the bomb. If anyone attempts to leave the building before the demands are met, the bomb will go off. Anyone attempting to enter the building will also set off the explosion.

SITUATION 3: Imprisoned for a crime she did not commit, the narrator befriends a guard who believes her story about who actually committed the crime—someone dangerous to the State. Later that person is imprisoned, yet the narrator is denied release and is forced to confront the new prisoner.

SITUATION 4: Forced to remain indentured even after serving his term, a servant demands his freedom, but the farm owner has him in a moral quandary because the owner once saved the servant's life.

SITUATION 5: A prostitute wants to escape the brothel despite the brothel owner's threats to harm her if she tries to escape. Her escape is complicated by the fact that she had committed a felony and the brothel owner covered up for her.

SITUATION 6: During the French Revolution, a loyalist about to face the guillotine befriends a guard. One day he even persuades the guard to enter his cell to deliver a manuscript he'd been writing—at which time the prisoner begins his harrowing escape.

SITUATION 7: Incarcerated by sadists and about to be tortured until he confesses to a crime or dies, the prisoner formulates a convincing enough excuse to grant him the opportunity to be taken outside. He cleverly manages to unshackle himself, but now he must find a way to escape the sadists.

SITUATION 8: In a future war between humans and robots, a group of human resistance fighters is captured and imprisoned by the robots. Chances of escape are nil, but the lead resistance fighter befriends one of the robots and it helps the group plan an escape.

SITUATION 9: When a killer escapes from a maximum-security prison, several inmates are accused of helping him. The warden makes a deal: "Show us how he did it, and I'll reduce your sentences." But when the prisoners reveal the escapee's secrets, the warden extends their sentences instead. The inmates then plan a revolt.

SITUATION 10: A prisoner studies the dark arts and uses what he learns to plan a prison break. The warden finds out, but instead of punishing the one prisoner, he masters the magic himself—and uses it to torment all of the prisoners.

CATEGORY 7: ESCAPE FROM SELF (FROM ONE'S OWN DEMONS)

Some people imprison themselves—with drugs, with crippling superstitions, with childhood fears that don't go away. The profession of psychiatry exists to help such people overcome these elusive kinds of illnesses. Good stories can also help us to understand the complexities of mental illness.

SITUATION 1: A physicist is tormented by an alter ego who disagrees with his basic views of nature and wants to discredit those views. Ironically, just when the physicist (with the help of a psychiatrist) is on the verge of exorcising that hostile self, the narrator suddenly realizes that some of its views hold important insights after all.

SITUATION 2: An actor harbors a demon that wants him to commit suicide. On several occasions the demon almost succeeds, but the actor resists fiercely every time. But when the actor is discouraged or depressed, the demon has the upper hand. When his fiancée (the director) learns about the demon, she makes a valiant effort to exorcise it.

SITUATION 3: A film actress suffers from a volatile temper. Even little things send her into a rage. Her partner helps her battle this inner demon but lately that demon has been gaining ferocity. Her last outburst may cause her to lose her role in the film she is making.

SITUATION 4: An unrepentant kleptomaniac gets caught again. Knowing that another conviction will result in a long prison term does not stay her hand. She then meets someone who persuades her to give up petty theft for grand larceny.

SITUATION 5: Despite their misdeeds while raising their children, the protagonist's parents struggle to win his siblings' affections now that they are grown up and successful, but nothing the parents do or say has any effect. The protagonist is willing to forgive, but first the parents must own up to their past abuses.

SITUATION 6: A demon is trying to persuade the narrator to commit suicide. At first she resists, but then the demon's urgings become more compelling. She seeks the help of a priest—but he turns out to be just another demon in disguise. In desperation she turns to an eccentric and much derided local spiritualist, who nonetheless seems to possess strange powers.

SITUATION 7: After several years in full control of her gambling compulsion (she had spent a year in rehab), the protagonist suffers a lapse. During a convention held in Las Vegas, her current boyfriend, who was secretly jealous of her professional skills, encourages her to gamble. But another friend rescues her just in time.

SITUATION 8: A newly ordained female Episcopalian priest not only struggles against old prejudices about women in the clergy but also against the residue of her former self—a free-spirited nonbeliever. Just when she seems to have succeeded, she encounters a man from that free-spirited past who is determined not to let her forget it.

SITUATION 9: Abusive and self-centered, the focal character vows to his estranged wife that he has escaped his inner demons and is a new man, but she refuses to believe it. He tries to persuade her through his children, but they refuse to believe it as well. As a last resort, he tries one last scheme.

SITUATION 10: Realizing that her long-suppressed murderous alter ego has returned, a woman entrusted to the care of elderly people struggles to exorcise this hostile other self. She tries prescription drugs and spiritual meditation, but they only make things worse. In desperation, she turns to a mystic for help.

CATEGORY 8: ESCAPE FROM TIME CONSTRAINTS

Time is the ultimate jailer. Everyone dreams of escaping the relentless and invariable unfolding of hours, days, and years. Of course there is subjective time and relative time; there is also the near-timelessness of sleep, but actual deliverance from the flow of time remains in the realm of science fiction and fantasy.

SITUATION 1: Frustrated that she will not be able to complete her all-important experiment before a terminal illness claims her life, a scientist makes a deal with the devil to give her more time. The devil agrees; however, the more time she requires, the stiffer the price.

SITUATION 2: Weary of living by the clock, a teacher quits her job and heads into the woods—a female Thoreau. She soon discovers that such self-sufficiency is tougher than it seems. Still she struggles "to live deliberately" in her chosen peaceful setting.

SITUATION 3: In this future society, a drug is available that causes people to experience time passing at a much slower rate. The higher the dosage, the slower time seems to pass. When the focal character overdoses on the drug, time nearly stops for him and causes unexpected alterations in his brain chemistry.

SITUATION 4: The narrator and her husband join a group devoted to mind control. One of their missions is to experience life free of all time constraints and still be able to accomplish important goals. No drugs are involved—only mental discipline. However, some of these disciplinary tactics generate hallucinations that become increasingly invasive.

SITUATION 5: Seeking escape from schedules and deadlines, a journalist quits her newspaper job and lives in Jerusalem, where she steeps herself in the cultures that come together there. Ironically, she becomes involved in projects that compel her to work harder than ever, one of which involves keeping the peace after a terrorist attack.

SITUATION 6: An engineer invents a skullcap that gives the wearer a sense of timelessness. One is thus able to read, concentrate on difficult problems, or create without any sense of time passing—a physical state that's similar to being asleep. But she overlooked a serious side effect—which she'd better address quickly.

SITUATION 7: In this universe, people's biological clocks are slowed down or sped up according to the whims of a cosmic Time Master, to whom the people owe allegiance. When transgressions occur, the Time Master makes them age faster. When they do something pleasing, their aging slows. But the protagonist has had enough of this kind of manipulation.

SITUATION 8: Burnt out from their jobs, several freethinkers plan a utopian rural community where they can enjoy self-sufficiency and release from time constraints. However, the realities of day-to-day subsistence undermine their ideal goal. But the leader of the group has another somewhat controversial idea.

SITUATION 9: Knowing that she and her engineering team must complete a huge project on time or pay a crippling fine and lose future contracts, the protagonist looks for a way to justify an extension. One of her team members, at the eleventh hour, suggests one compelling way, but it would be unethical.

SITUATION 10: Entering a dream state, an elderly woman relives a special moment from her life. On the verge of awakening, she encounters an angel who suspends time and takes her back and forth through other special moments ... until it is time to wake up. But the woman begs the angel to let her remain in the dream state.

CATEGORY 9: ESCAPE FROM WARTIME CONDITIONS

> War dehumanizes and shortens lives in more ways than one: Shortages of food, shelter, and medical care and rampant crime often lead to despair and death. The struggle to escape such bleak conditions makes for grim but gripping survival stories.

SITUATION 1: A brother and sister struggle to escape a war-torn European city toward the end of World War II. Their parents are missing or dead; their lives are in constant danger from looters and other criminals. Knowing there is safety in numbers, they forge friendships with other survivors.

SITUATION 2: When a drunken enemy guard on a prison island dozes off, two prisoners on work duty grab his pistol and tie him up. But before they can escape the island prison, they must tackle two or three more guards in the same fashion while also making their way to the marina. It seems hopeless—until one of the guards, teased by the others and recently unfairly demoted, decides to help them.

SITUATION 3: Imprisoned as a POW, an American correspondent works out an escape, but he needs the help of one of the guards whose life he once saved on the battlefield. However, that guard has been reassigned to another POW camp.

SITUATION 4: After enduring a year of hard labor in a Siberian gulag, a literary dissident during the Stalinist era plots an escape ... with the subversive manuscript he'd been working on. His escape depends upon the cooperation of one of the guards, a secret sympathizer to his cause.

SITUATION 5: In this future dystopia that claims to be a utopia, it is required for citizens to own a mobile device and to keep it on at all times. Ostensibly an entertainment device, it is also a GPS locator used for tracking each citizen's movements. The focal character and his family look for a way to escape to another place.

SITUATION 6: Police using high-tech surveillance devices have seized control of the State. Inspection stations are everywhere, not just in airports. One police officer is secretly using her surveillance training against the system.

SITUATION 7: A new Cold War has developed between Russia and the United States as a result of the Russians selling weapons of mass destruction to Middle-Eastern countries harboring terrorists or those susceptible to being infiltrated by them. The narrator, a diplomat, searches for a way to defuse a growing crisis.

SITUATION 8: In an effort to stop a war before it begins, tech-savvy pacifists plan a cyberattack on their country's plan to deploy drones into the enemy's capital and assassinate the president. The attack not only fails; it causes all the drones in the installation to deploy haphazardly.

SITUATION 9: A general loyal to the dictator has a sudden change of heart after learning about the dictator's genocidal plans. Torn between escaping the country and disobeying orders, the general seeks out an accomplice to help him decide.

SITUATION 10: Targeted for extermination, a brother and sister escape their captors and beg to be taken in by a peasant family. The family complies, but when the captors offer a huge reward for the escaped siblings, the family decides to betray them—until one of the siblings makes a startling offer.

CATEGORY 10: RESCUE FROM BEING LOST OR MAROONED

We have all been lost at one time or another, and so we can easily empathize with characters who struggle to find their way back from whatever has gotten them off course or has trapped them. How they manage to do so makes for exciting reading.

SITUATION 1: A malfunction occurs while oceanographers are conducting a top-secret experiment on the sea floor. They cannot survive without being rescued, but the nature of the malfunction is such that a successful rescue would be extremely difficult.

SITUATION 2: Sailors are trapped in a storm, and their boat capsizes against the rocks of an uncharted atoll. Their radio and computer are damaged, so they must find a way to repair the equipment and figure out where they are.

SITUATION 3: When a detective investigating a bomb threat is ambushed and hidden inside the building in question, his rescuers rush to find him before the bomb he was about to defuse detonates.

SITUATION 4: Mountain climbers stranded on a peak in the Andes await rescue, but their food and water are running out and they are trapped inside a crevasse where it would be nearly impossible for a rescue crew to lift them to safety.

SITUATION 5: The queen is abducted and taken to a forest outside the kingdom. When the king learns of her whereabouts, he sends a rescue party—only to discover that the queen has escaped her captors. But she must have gotten lost, for no one can find her.

SITUATION 6: A famous physicist disappears during a hike in a mountain wilderness, and it is imperative that he be found at once and returned to his lab, where a crucial experiment he had designed has gone terribly wrong.

SITUATION 7: Fatigued, an elderly woman gets on a subway train late at night without checking to see that it is the right one. She dozes off almost immediately in her seat and awakens in an unknown place. Disoriented, she wanders through a labyrinthine chamber where she encounters someone who agrees to help her—except that he is also disoriented.

SITUATION 8: After an underwater ogre traps a goddess's favorite mortals and holds them for ransom, the goddess agrees to the ogre's terms but recruits her most talented sorcerer to cast a spell on the ogre without endangering the captives.

SITUATION 9: A cruise ship vanishes into a temporal rift and is trapped in the distant past. Scientists eventually figure out what happened to the ship and plan a rescue, but meanwhile, the ship must deal with Jurassic sea creatures.

SITUATION 10: A distraught son searches for his father after the latter, an investigative journalist, disappears in a politically unstable country. The son manages to get access to places otherwise off-limits to tourists and suspects that the father's integrity has been compromised.

CHAPTER 10

EXAMINATION OR EXPLORATION OF X

CATEGORY 1: THE EXAMINATION OF A COLD-CASE FILE

We are all analysts and explorers to some degree—analysis and exploration being basic skills in making sense out of life's complexities and mysteries. We champion investigators who pursue even the least promising clues after a criminal case officially turns "cold"; we take pleasure in exploring natural phenomena. Such pursuits, too, offer an abundance of story material.

SITUATION 1: A detective uncovers clues to a cold-case homicide overlooked or ignored by others. The clues lead her to other cold-case crimes with similar characteristics that were committed over the years, including one that involved her mother before the detective was born.

SITUATION 2: After years of following leads in search of a missing child, police detectives have turned up nothing, but a private detective hired by a concerned aunt follows leads that the police considered unreliable or preposterous—and makes a disturbing discovery.

SITUATION 3: Investigators tried for years to solve the murder of a violinist. The murderer left no clues, no weapon was found, and no motive surfaced. But then a member of the orchestra comes forward with information sufficient to reopen the case.

SITUATION 4: Unable to catch a sniper who terrorized a community for a month, police close the case, but when a controversial celebrity pays a visit, the sniper shootings resume and a new detective reopens the case.

SITUATION 5: Several professors vanish from a well-respected small college. After much sleuthing neither campus police nor municipal police find any leads and the case is closed. Then one of the colleagues of the missing professors comes forward with a possible lead.

SITUATION 6: A case concerning threatening graffiti on bridges and buildings was never solved. But then one of the threats about detonating a bomb in an empty building is carried out. The case is re-opened with the fear that the other threats will now come true.

SITUATION 7: After closing the case of a theft of several sculptures, one of the pieces shows up in a private gallery. Police are reluctant to reopen the case because the sculpture was judged a fake. But a new appraisal affirms it to be genuine, worth millions. However, the gallery's purchase records are missing.

SITUATION 8: When the clues gathered during the investigation of a number of small-town murders dead-ended, the case was closed. Detectives found no commonalities, no motives. But then a new detective reviews the case and sees similarities where others did not.

SITUATION 9: For years, detectives tried to solve the murders of several lawyers based on clues that the murderer deliberately left, but they closed the case after deciding that the clues were faked. An expert reopens the case when she is convinced that the clues can help solve the murders.

SITUATION 10: Someone is threatening medical researchers who conduct stem-cell experiments, but the case is closed after detectives fail to trace the letters. Now new threats against the researchers have surfaced, and one of the researchers has vanished.

CATEGORY 2: EXAMINATION OF A COVER-UP

Anyone familiar with Watergate knows about cover-ups and how they can occur in the highest echelons of government or private industry. Of course, conspiracy theorists routinely look for signs of cover-ups—the result of reading too many thrillers or simply knowing that cover-ups are always a possibility.

SITUATION 1: After a sex scandal threatens to expose the incompetent management of a charity organization, the manager opts for a cover-up. But when a journalist exposes the scandal, the manager accuses the journalist of launching a personal vendetta against him for spurning her supposed advances.

SITUATION 2: Corrupt investment consultants skillfully cover their tracks as they pocket clients' investments. But one of the consultants has second thoughts and assists a watchdog group.

SITUATION 3: Residents of a small town fear that their police department is covering up a sinister extortion ring. When the protagonist, a former police detective, investigates, he is assaulted and warned to stop snooping.

SITUATION 4: Burglars secretly employed by an extreme right-wing congressperson break into women's health-care clinics and sabotage equipment. The congressperson and her assistants devise a clever cover-up, but one of the seemingly loyal members of her team blows the whistle.

SITUATION 5: After a biotech company covers up illegally conducted embryonic research considered a dead-end, a former researcher for the company learns that the old research is vital and he tries to retrieve it—but the biotech company refuses to share.

SITUATION 6: Burglars hired by a biotech company steal secret formulas from a competitor and then plant false "evidence" to make it look as though the competitor had stolen those formulas from them and tried to cover it up. In any event, the formulas were derived from illegal research.

SITUATION 7: A conspiracy to overthrow a European government is brewing within that country's secret service, but the conspirators cover their tracks. The narrator, an outsider who had fallen out of favor with the organization, finds a way to expose the conspiracy.

SITUATION 8: A successful hotelier has always played by the rules—but she succumbs to an offer from the Mob she cannot resist. She manages a clever cover-up. Even so, the narrator, a private investigator, smells a rat.

SITUATION 9: When a mayor realizes she may lose her seat to a rival, she hires burglars to break into the rival's home to dig up dirt—and then to cover up the burglary. Dirt is indeed uncovered, but then the rival does some digging of his own and finds clues that implicate the burglars and the mayor.

SITUATION 10: After hacking into a secret government surveillance operation, the narrator covers her tracks and then pretends that someone in the operation leaked the information to her. She then blackmails the officials, but one of the officials suspects her because she had once been an object of surveillance.

CATEGORY 3: EXPLORATION OF A DANGER OR FORBIDDEN ZONE

Places become dangerous or forbidden for many reasons: pollution, radioactivity, geologic instability, environmental sensitivity, military neutral zones, religious or occult taboos. Of course, restrictions against trespassing often arouse curiosity and daredevilry—and therein lies the opportunity for suspenseful stories.

SITUATION 1: The queen has forbidden anyone to enter a tract of land she has designated the Forbidden Zone. She is the only one who knows why it is forbidden, and she isn't telling. The protagonist, however, cannot resist learning the secret, even when threatened with execution.

SITUATION 2: Once upon a time, a thriving village fell under a terrible curse, and one by one the inhabitants died. The village was declared a forbidden zone. The protagonist dares to violate the "no-trespassing" edict to learn the secret of the cursed village.

SITUATION 3: The Forbidden Zone is so designated because of a parasitic organism that has infected everyone there, including the emperor's brother, a bitter rival who is planning an invasion. The protagonist searches for the brother despite the danger of being infected by the parasite.

SITUATION 4: Exposed to radiation from an experiment, scientists from a top-secret operation are forced into quarantine miles from any community. Years later, the quarantined area is a forbidden zone. But a group of scientists ignore the restriction, enter the isolated community, and are shocked by what they discover.

SITUATION 5: Geologic instability has rendered a rare earth mine off-limits, but the narrator is too tempted by the possibility that the mine still holds a fortune in ore. She and her team indeed locate a vein of precious ore—but drilling triggers a cave-in.

SITUATION 6: Scientists examine the massive impact site of a meteorite that has been restricted and surrounded by the military for several years. The scientists are perplexed by an energy source emanating from it. The mystery deepens when one of the scientists who inspected the meteorite experiences strange changes in his vision.

SITUATION 7: Extreme pressure is building up underneath Yellowstone—signs that a super-volcano may erupt there. Should that occur, much of the United States would be in grave danger. A geologist wonders if she should request a mass evacuation or risk spending more time to investigate.

SITUATION 8: Archaeologists in search of a lost civilization must enter a region reputed to harbor evil spirits. Everyone doubts their presence, but evidence exists that the evil spirits are there. Still, the scientists are confident that they can deal with those spirits.

SITUATION 9: When the military declares a stretch of Arizona desert off-limits to the public, conspiracy theorists immediately suspect a cover-up. But the reason for the declaration has to do with a failed top-secret project, one too strange even for conspiracy theorists to imagine.

SITUATION 10: Soldiers have learned via codebreaking that the enemy is holding kidnapped children hostage. To reach the village where the children are held, soldiers must travel down a road riddled with land mines and ambush pinch-points. A small group of soldiers volunteer, but the biggest problem remains: How will they get the children to safety?

CATEGORY 4: EXPLORATION OF A GHOST TOWN OR ABANDONED DWELLING

Gothic fiction originated in the eighteenth century and has been popular ever since. Today, in addition to haunting medieval castles and dungeons, vampires, zombies, ghosts, ghouls, and other super-natural creatures take up residence in villages, abandoned towns, and even metropolitan areas. Lots of story possibilities here!

SITUATION 1: Ghost hunters explore a village where ghouls are rumored to have taken up residence and have inhabited the bodies of some of the townspeople. When one of the ghost hunters is possessed, the others must figure out a way to resist before they, too, are compromised.

SITUATION 2: A mysterious accident causes city officials to evacuate a section of the city. No one is allowed inside, and a wall is built to seal off the section. But that does not stop the narrator, a reporter, from sneaking inside to learn the secret.

SITUATION 3: An electrified fence surrounds a long-deserted mountain villa. The narrator, a historian, seeks to learn its secret and to gain access. He tries to get through via legitimate means, but the harder he tries, the more resistance (including threats) he encounters. Finally, he decides to penetrate the barriers on his own.

SITUATION 4: Anthropologists discover a cave dwelling in the Pyrenees, but they cannot identify the dwellers: The bone fragments are unlike any previously discovered. And then they find signs that the cave may still be inhabited.

SITUATION 5: A pair of detectives searching an abandoned motel encounter squatters who may have been involved in a rash of crimes committed in that area years earlier. Pretending to be cooperative, the squatters manage to entrap the detectives and hold them hostage.

SITUATION 6: A library is haunted by the ghosts of forgotten authors. They hypnotically lure patrons away from their video games and into the stacks, where the ghosts introduce them to great books. But one librarian decides to rid the library of its ghosts.

SITUATION 7: A creature has taken residence inside an abandoned house. The city inspector investigates but finds nothing except a giant lizard. He suspects the lizard may be an alien lifeform and takes it to a lab for analysis. Meanwhile neighboring residents are experiencing strange symptoms.

SITUATION 8: No one is aboard a yacht drifting off the coast. No bodies have been discovered nor any sign or record of ship distress. The protagonist inspects the ship and encounters an apparition that eerily resembles a famous movie star.

SITUATION 9: For years no one dared enter the haunted house at the edge of town. The last person who did so was never seen again. Now two detectives who do not believe in ghosts will enter the house and put an end to the townspeople's fears.

SITUATION 10: A popular amusement park is shut down after a rash of strange accidents. Investors reopen the park—and are confronted by a shape-shifting demon lurking within.

CATEGORY 5: INVESTIGATION OF MISSING PERSONS, ANIMALS, OR PROPERTY

People and pets go missing nearly every day; possessions get lost or stolen, but when "missing" means "kidnapped" or when "stolen" means "grand larceny," harrowing stories are waiting to be told.

SITUATION 1: Pets have been vanishing. At first police make the case a low priority, but then a celebrity trainer's prized dog vanishes. As soon as the case is given higher priority, the celebrity trainer vanishes as well.

SITUATION 2: A dog wearing a collar emblazoned with stolen gemstones has gone missing, and it is up to the protagonist to find the dog. She finds it ... without the collar. However, she also finds clues that point to where the collar, with its jewels, might be.

SITUATION 3: An exhibitor abducts several show cats worth a fortune and demands a ransom, threatening the cats' lives. When the catnapper tries to sell the cats to unsuspecting breeders as well as collect a ransom, one of the breeders realizes what is happening and turns the tables.

SITUATION 4: Detectives are searching for a scientist's daughter who has disappeared—apparently kidnapped for ransom (her father was working on a secret military project). One person suspects she may have become an enemy spy.

SITUATION 5: The owner of a prized coin collection is murdered, but none of the coins are missing. A detective with numismatic knowledge is hired to investigate, and she suspects that the murderer has replaced the most valuable coins with fakes.

SITUATION 6: After a circus acrobat is abducted, the circus owner receives a ransom note demanding an outrageous sum. The kidnappers apparently assume the acrobat possesses a fortune—but no one has any knowledge of his finances.

SITUATION 7: Soon after a genetics researcher discovers a way to replicate human organs (using lab mice as hosts of the reengineered cells until mature enough for transplanting), the scientist is kidnapped. The kidnappers warn that if these experiments do not cease, the scientist will die.

SITUATION 8: Someone has abducted a loquacious parrot. Not only is the parrot capable of amazing oratory feats, it can also communicate the whereabouts of buried treasure. The narrator must find the abductors before the parrot discloses the secret.

SITUATION 9: Several animals trained for military purposes have been stolen. When no ransom note materializes, investigators suspect animal rights activists.

SITUATION 10: A Washington official on a commuter train finds a briefcase filled with top secret documents. When the finder visits the Pentagon to turn in the briefcase, he is arrested and charged with theft and espionage.

CATEGORY 6: EXPLORATION OR EXPLOITATION OF SPACE

Humans are insatiably curious about nature, including the unimaginably vast and mysterious universe beyond our home world. No longer exclusive to science fiction, space exploration has been underway for decades. Once-inexplicable cosmic mysteries are now understood; new mysteries, however, are steadily being revealed.

SITUATION 1: The sun has been behaving strangely: Solar flares and magnetic fluctuations have been increasing. Scientists believe a major solar storm is developing and could wreak havoc on communications satellites. When they recommend the country return to older communication systems, they are ridiculed.

SITUATION 2: An expedition to a wormhole discovered near the orbit of Jupiter aims to study the wormhole's nature and determine whether it can be used as a shortcut through interstellar space. But the phenomenon is more mysterious—and dangerous—than anyone realized.

SITUATION 3: Astronauts detect a tiny black hole formed just beyond the orbit of the moon. As they approach it, it sucks them in despite their precautions. They reemerge in an unknown place.

SITUATION 4: A mother lode of minerals, rare on earth and urgently needed for advancing technologies, is discovered on the moon, near one of the Apollo landing sites. But mining the minerals would lead to rapid degradation of that historical site. The clash between preservationists and industrialists leads to political chicanery and violence.

SITUATION 5: Scientists discover primitive life forms inside a comet's nucleus, a rare type of meteorite known as a carbonaceous chondrite, and place it under tight quarantine. But the organisms escape confinement and begin interacting with earthly life in bizarre ways.

SITUATION 6: A gravitational anomaly causes a rift in space. When explorers enter it, they wind up in another dimension in which reality has changed: Choices that were rejected are now the ones that have been accepted. The narrator is delighted at first but then discovers a formerly rejected option that should have stayed rejected.

SITUATION 7: Seeking a better life on another world, pacifists establish a colony on the moon—but by this time exploitation of lunar minerals is already in progress. The miners see the colonists as obstacles and make every effort to get rid of them ... or persuade them to become mineral merchants.

SITUATION 8: An enormous asteroid is heading for Mars, and astronomers fear that the impact could jettison so much material into space that it would, after a decade or so, endanger Earth. It might be possible to deflect the largest chunks, but the cost would be enormous.

SITUATION 9: In the far future, rogue robots cause the sun to emit lethal doses of radiation, thereby threatening all life on Earth. But guardian robots are sent out to destroy the rogues—hopefully before it is too late.

SITUATION 10: Martian explorers discover a transport device that opens up an alternate Martian reality in which the Red Planet is seething with life, including very dangerous life forms. By activating the device, they unwittingly enable the dangerous creatures to cross over.

CATEGORY 7: EXPLORATION OR INVESTI-GATION OF UNUSUAL PHENOMENA

No matter how deeply scientists investigate the mysteries of nature, it seems unlikely that they will ever explain all the mysteries since new ones continually arise. And that's a good thing, for it reminds us that science alone can never fully explain life.

SITUATION 1: Strange lights begin to appear in the night sky—multicolored luminescence that forms weird shapes. Some think they're a phenomenon like the northern lights, but they're not and scientists have no idea what is causing them. A weather expert tests an outlandish theory and reaches an astonishing conclusion: The atmosphere may be changing to suit a rapidly evolving organism.

SITUATION 2: A farmer swears that a UFO has landed and buried itself in his field, but no one believes him. Then a friend agrees to investigate the strange noises emanating from the purported landing site. When he cannot locate anything, this friend asks a scientist to take a look.

SITUATION 3: Fruits that have been genetically engineered to grow larger and more flavorful have an unanticipated side effect: They alter people's skin pigmentation and eye color. While scientists work to develop an antidote, societal dynamics begin to change dramatically.

SITUATION 4: Animals of all kinds have inexplicably begun to grow larger. Biologists suspect that an experimental growth hormone has entered the environment. The problem is urgent, and there doesn't seem to be a limit on how large the animals can grow.

SITUATION 5: The mutant offspring of animals that had been irradiated during the era of atomic testing have been smuggled off a quarantined zone for analysis, but then an earthquake occurs and the animals escape into a heavily populated area.

SITUATION 6: Geologists investigating thermal vents in Yellowstone discover a new organism that seems to thrive on sulfur. Both the thermal vents and the organisms are proliferating, and the lead geologist worries that these organisms might pose a health threat.

SITUATION 7: Rumblings in the earth lead scientists to suspect an imminent earthquake, even though no faults are nearby. Further investigation leads to another possibility—that a magma chamber may rupture—and cause more damage than a conventional volcanic eruption would. Residents aren't persuaded.

SITUATION 8: A fishing community panics when tens of thousands of fish float to the surface dead. Biologists work around the clock to determine the cause. It turns out that the villagers are responsible since they dumped chemicals that no one had thought were toxic into the water.

SITUATION 9: Something is hiding in the sewers of this European city; it regularly sneaks to the surface and goes unnoticed, except by a homeless person, who describes the creature as serpent-like. A team goes down to investigate and discovers an entire nest of the creatures.

SITUATION 10: Uncanny weather systems plague the country: Floods in arid regions, snowstorms in tropical regions, etc. Something besides global warming may be responsible: possibly a change in the earth's magnetic field. A geophysicist investigates.

CATEGORY 8: EXAMINATION OF STRANGE BODILY PHENOMENA

A fine line sometimes separates the known from the unknown. We may think we know all there is to know about human and animal physiology, but nature continues to elude us, even in the scientific age. Many stories are waiting to be told that explore these unknown regions.

SITUATION 1: A fringe physician explores the possibility of male pregnancy. When he alters a male subject's abdominal physiology without his knowledge, enabling him to unwittingly carry a child, there is public outrage—and also celebration.

SITUATION 2: When a dermatologist explores the possibility of keeping hair from turning gray, he triggers a fierce debate between those who want to preserve graying as a natural and dignified facet of aging and those who regard graying as a curse.

SITUATION 3: Astronauts examining a lifeform they discovered in one of Titan's methane lakes fail to exercise sufficient precautions. The creature jettisons hundreds of microtendrils into the examiners.

SITUATION 4: A neurologist examining the brain functions of an Alzheimer's patient thinks she can reverse the patient's memory loss with a new combination of drugs, but when the patient suffers from unexpected side effects, the hospital administrator insists that the neurologist end the treatment.

SITUATION 5: While studying the remains of a body that had been perfectly preserved in an Arctic glacier for millennia, a paleoanthropologist soon realizes that the body is neither human nor part of the hominid family tree. This leads to further searches of the site, and what they discover is astonishing.

SITUATION 6: A medical researcher exploring the properties of HIV in an effort to wipe it out is threatened by a homophobic doctor who orders him to stop his research. If the researcher continues his work, the doctor will expose his past transgressions.

SITUATION 7: Dogs in a suburban neighborhood begin behaving viciously—attacking their owners, passersby, etc. When a vet conducts an autopsy on a dog that had been struck by a car, she is shocked to discover a strangely altered brain.

SITUATION 8: A children's theater producer recruits children to act in plays about demons. All in good fun, so they think. But then the characters they portray take over the children's lives. A psychologist hypnotizes the children in an effort to recover their identities, but in so doing he winds up battling with the demons. Meanwhile the search is on for the producer.

SITUATION 9: Angels are infiltrating the population, and the narrator, a neurologist, is able to detect them. Not all of the angels are benevolent, however, and she cannot distinguish good angels from bad ones. One of the angels agrees to assist her by allowing her to study his brain functions.

SITUATION 10: Airborne parasites of unknown origin have infected the inhabitants of a remote village. When scientists examine the parasites, they are shocked to discover human DNA intermingled with the parasites' DNA.

CATEGORY 9: UNDERWATER EXPLORATION OR EXPLOITATION

Two-thirds of the earth is covered by water, and much of it remains unexplored. Great depths make exploration difficult if not impossible. Rare and exotic life forms exist in these depths, and scientists speculate that humans may someday colonize these undersea domains. Here are ten story possibilities set under the sea.

SITUATION 1: Coral reefs have begun dying rapidly, and a scientist searches for a way to combat what seems like an irreversible trend because of warming ocean temperature and increased pollution. Working with oceanographers, climatologists, environmentalists, and biologists, she arrives at a radical solution—but encounters fierce opposition.

SITUATION 2: Deep-sea explorers encounter a strange life form on the ocean floor. It has characteristics of both plants and animals. It has tendrils and eyes. The eyes seem to be focused keenly on the scientists inside the bell.

SITUATION 3: Terrorists seize control of an underwater "bubble city" in this future earth. Unless their demands are met, they will rupture the bubble, and everyone in the city of one-hundred thousand will perish. The focal character works feverishly with the terrorists to reach a settlement.

SITUATION 4: Young scuba divers discover an underwater cave filled with exotic sea creatures. Most are friendly and enchanting, but one of them lures the divers into the deepest regions of the cave, where it reveals its true menacing nature.

SITUATION 5: When a UFO crashes into the sea, a diving expedition sets out to locate it. When they do, they find it surrounded by a bubble. The captain of the expeditions decides to penetrate the bubble and examine the UFO up close.

SITUATION 6: Divers exploring an ancient ship at the bottom of the Mediterranean are amazed to discover a sealed compartment filled with artifacts that belong to an unknown civilization. Among the artifacts is a papyrus map that indicates the whereabouts of a treasure, which the ancient ship's crew probably set out to find.

SITUATION 7: Marine archaeologists locate fragments of a statue just beyond the harbor, buried under sediment. After they bring the fragments ashore, they discover inscriptions on the pedestal that detail secret compartments in the statue.

SITUATION 8: Underwater explorers in the Mediterranean monitor an ominous crevice on the seafloor that shows evidence of growing larger. It seems that a volcano may soon erupt. At risk are several Mediterranean coastal cities. Experts disagree as to whether these cities should be evacuated.

SITUATION 9: Treasure hunters locate a pirate ship filled with loot. Because the discovery was made in international waters, the discoverers want to claim the treasure privately—but because of the nature of the treasure (booty), an effort is made to determine the owners.

SITUATION 10: A deadly sea organism is spreading, and biologists look for ways to prevent it from infiltrating coastal waters, especially where populations are dense (the coasts of the United States, Japan, India, and South America). But existing measures of control are having no effect.

CATEGORY 10: WILDERNESS EXPLORATION OR EXPLOITATION

As the global population rises and natural resources become increasingly scarce, wilderness areas diminish. Conflict between preservation and exploitation is ongoing, resulting in environment-themed stories that need to be told.

SITUATION 1: Ecologists deem a pristine segment of Amazon old-growth rain forest endangered; but in 2050, lumber is desperately needed due to climate change and resultant widespread forest fires. Both preservationists and developers strive to resolve the crisis—but mutual animosity interferes.

SITUATION 2: Several nature lovers venture deep into a Cambodian wilderness. A couple of them become so enraptured by the place that they refuse to leave. When a doctor examines the couple, she discovers mysterious bites.

SITUATION 3: Biologists protecting endangered species in a rain forest encounter squatters in the process of slashing and burning an area. The squatters, evicted elsewhere, need the land, but if the species in question is not protected, it will go extinct.

SITUATION 4: A naturalist hiking in Yosemite comes face-to-face with the ghost of John Muir, who shares some of the park's little-known wonders. When the hiker prepares to leave, Muir's ghost asks to meld with the naturalist in order to persuade state officials once again to demolish the Hetch Hetchy dam and restore the valley and river to its original condition.

SITUATION 5: Astronauts exploring the wilderness of an earthlike planet discover plants whose sap reverses the aging process—they sell it to people the world over. But the sap causes some unexpected side effects, one of which is a loss of desire to explore. Now scientists must search for an antidote, though the very idea of searching has become distasteful.

SITUATION 6: A search party penetrates difficult terrain in a mountainous wilderness where several teenagers disappeared. After nearly giving up hope, the party finds the teens but they have been inexplicably transformed—it's as if the wilderness itself has control of them.

SITUATION 7: Radical environmentalists guard a wilderness area from a developer after they get word that the developer intends to turn the area into a golf course. A confrontation leads to violence and sabotage.

SITUATION 8: Radiation-deformed people, driven out of the cities in this postapocalyptic earth, seek sanctuary in one of the few remaining areas of wilderness. There some of them want to use their strange powers—an unexpected by-product of the radiation—to wreak revenge on the "normal" people who drove them out.

SITUATION 9: In the future, Walden Pond is no longer a nature lover's mecca but a venue for boaters. One day, a boater encounters an apparition on the lake that looks to him like the ghost of Henry David Thoreau—and the ghost is furious.

SITUATION 10: Militant poachers ambush any preservationists who try to protect wildlife in this African mountain rain forest, but that doesn't stop the protagonist. She launches a counterattack that she hopes will eradicate the poachers before the species go extinct.

CHAPTER 11

THE GROWTH OF X

CATEGORY 1: THE GROWTH OF AN ARTISTIC MOVEMENT

Beauty may be in the eye of the beholder, but new modes of artistic expression (if sufficiently intriguing) tend to break down old assumptions about the nature of art and the human condition that new art depicts. Generally this happens only after initial shock and protest. Stories that capture the growth of artistic taste make for fascinating reading.

SITUATION 1: A teenager creates a new style of painting that her art teacher ridicules but others find enchanting. She attracts the attention of a TV station and becomes a media star. However, the teacher, with the help of those who find her paintings offensive, launches a counterattack.

SITUATION 2: "My kid could do that!" exclaims many a parent in response to some works of modern art. With this thought in mind, an art teacher has trained a group of child prodigies to create innovative paintings—and the results cause a sensation.

SITUATION 3: Artistically inclined sentient computers start an art revolution. The paintings the computers produce reach far beyond anything humans have created. Two critics—one for and one against computer art—argue whether art produced by machines should qualify as art at all.

SITUATION 4: Taking advantage of the growth of installation art, an artist creates a walk-in installation consisting of objects that viewers walk or crawl through. Unbeknownst to the viewers, hidden elements of the installation put them in a trance.

SITUATION 5: Artistic homeless people create sculptures out of trash. Defying those who call their work mere junk (i.e., city officials who want the homeless off the streets) these artists launch an art fair and use the proceeds from their sales to help homeless people find jobs.

SITUATION 6: An inner-city dance teacher works with a musically inclined street gang that has invented a new dance. Despite the dangers of working with street-hardened teens, she snags the attention of a professional dance company.

SITUATION 7: Neighborhood kids create a new kind of sidewalk art using multicolored chalk and want to take it to the next level, but they must battle police, parents, city officials, and other kids before their project gains momentum. Finally, an official interested in supporting inner-city youth lends a helping hand.

SITUATION 8: A creator of environmental art—outdoor sculptures, assemblages, etc., that are intended to interact with their surroundings—has become popular, but a group of dissenters wanting to put an end to his movement begins to vandalize the art.

SITUATION 9: Several artists who are also aviators begin creating sky paintings so mesmerizing that they enthrall entire communities who become unwilling to do anything else except behold the aviators' artistic creations. When one of the community leaders tries to stop the sky artists, the people protest violently, but he may have a point about the damaging economic effects of the art.

SITUATION 10: Chimpanzees are taught to express themselves with clay. These "ape sculptures" start out as curiosity pieces and then become a fad. Everyone wants to own an ape sculpture, and prices skyrocket. The narrator battles those getting rich at the chimps' expense.

CATEGORY 2: THE GROWTH OF DANGEROUS ENTERTAINMENT

People enjoy watching entertainers flirt with danger, within limits. But sometimes those limits are stretched to include the life-threatening, especially when the entertainers are highly skilled. The line between what is fun and what is deadly can become blurry indeed—or eliminated altogether.

160

SITUATION 1: A new game encourages young people to become ruthless despots in virtual-reality environments. Insisting that their games teach leadership skills in a ruthlessly competitive world, the game-makers continue to issue ever more troublesome games.

SITUATION 2: In the future, a casino features unusual games, such as a roulette wheel that has a space on it that "wins" the player a flogging ... or worse. Other numbers result in lavish prizes, but in order to be eligible for those prizes, one must risk the whiplash.

SITUATION 3: In this fictional world, virtual reality has allowed us to simulate any dangerous feat without harm. But the downside is that people then risk serious mishaps in real life without considering the consequences. Is the public too addicted to the virtual-reality aspect of their lives to tell the difference anymore?

SITUATION 4: Daredevil games abound in this society, where the more daring you are, the higher you climb on the social ladder. When the death-defying narrator vows to walk across Niagara Falls wearing a blindfold, a rival aerialist schemes to sabotage the narrator's performance.

SITUATION 5: A deranged billionaire will give ten million dollars to anyone who plays Russian roulette with him. If the gun aimed at his volunteer's head does not fire after three tries, he wins. But one woman who takes the gamble wants an even higher-stakes wager.

SITUATION 6: A music craze has been altering teens' brain chemistry—and only when the music becomes widespread do psychologists warn that the brain changes may be irreversible. But the fans threaten violence if anyone tries to prohibit the new music.

SITUATION 7: Fraternity initiation rites rise (or fall depending on one's values) to a new level when a frat house devises a wrestling match whereby a pledge must face one wrestler out of five—knowing that one of the five is hiding a syringe containing a substance that causes the initiate's body to break out in hives if they are pinned and injected. Little does the frat know that the injections lead to unexpected side effects later in the week.

SITUATION 8: Imagine an ice-skating competition on thin ice: The skaters must not only perform well but ignore the possibility of breaking through the ice. Rescue teams are on hand, but the risk of drowning or hypothermia still exists.

SITUATION 9: Wizards face off in a harrowing competition whereby they must summon—and then subdue—a demon. The danger lies in the possibility that the demon will subdue the wizard and carry him or her off to the infernal regions.

SITUATION 10: The focal character is a magician who, like her mentor, Houdini, entertains by performing death-defying escapist stunts; unlike Houdini, she relies on magic for her escapes. But one evening, her magic fails her in the middle of one of her most spectacular tricks.

CATEGORY 3: THE GROWTH OF ALTERNATIVE FAMILY RELATIONSHIPS

Over the years, the modern family has undergone noticeable changes. Although the traditional family structure endures (man as head of the household, wife as homemaker, etc.), alternative models are becoming widespread. As with all societal changes, the changes in family dynamics often generate conflict, especially between generations. Good stories can help us determine what best contributes to healthy family relationships.

SITUATION 1: Distressed over the growing strife in his family, a successful business executive who is used to being in a position of authority confronts his wife, insisting she has not done enough to maintain harmony. She in turn implores him to take a hard look at his attitude and assumptions as well. Meanwhile, their son and daughter suggest opposing ways of restoring harmony, one of which might actually destroy the family dynamic, which might be for the best.

SITUATION 2: A gay man decides to illuminate his parents (whom he always thought to be open-minded) on the virtues of same-sex marriage—but his effort goes horribly wrong. Now he is torn between losing his family forever if he marries his partner and losing his partner forever if he sides with his parents' view that same-sex marriage is an abomination.

SITUATION 3: Menage à trois, anyone? Two best friends in love with the same woman decide they want to live together as a threesome. At first, their seemingly perverse setup seems to work for them—but then, little by little, things start to fall apart.

SITUATION 4: A marriage counselor uses unusual methods to save his clients' marriages. Some methods seem premature (e.g., getting them to renew their vows) and others seem fringe (e.g., having the couples act out the parts of lovers), but he is confident that such methods are becoming widely accepted. Ironically, when the counselor uses these techniques to improve his own marriage, he makes matters worse.

SITUATION 5: In the near future, traditional marriage has been largely replaced by all sorts of alternative cohabitation, and to the narrator, a spiritual leader, this portends the decay of civilization. Using her widespread influence, she strives to bring back traditional marriage before (as she sees it) it's too late.

SITUATION 6: In a fourteenth-century feudal community, the overlord plans to exercise his right to sleep with every bride on her wedding night. But one of the grooms is determined to stop him. His efforts fuel the growing intolerance toward this tradition.

SITUATION 7: A social reformer in India of the Brahmin caste is determined to marry an "outcast" woman, in gross violation of tradition. His efforts endanger not only his life and his would-be bride's but also their families'. His ultimate goal: Destroy the caste system forever. He is encouraged to pursue this dangerous goal by ever-growing numbers of those who despise the caste system.

SITUATION 8: A rapidly growing trend among teens, called "sudden hookups," is based on the notion that first impressions are the best determiner for romance, and it eliminates the need for awkward getting-to-know-you rituals. But when the narrator and his "sudden" girlfriend hook up, mayhem ensues.

SITUATION 9: The rapidly growing popularity of automated matchmaking results in comical (and not-so-comical) matches despite the high-compatibility protocols the computers follow. Mayhem erupts at a reception for the matched couples. Case in point, the protagonist and her match (both psychology junkies) end up having it out with each other.

SITUATION 10: Now that communal parenting has become the norm in this utopian society, the likelihood of dysfunctional parenting has diminished—or so it seems. But when two siblings, disenchanted with the system, look for a way out, they are met with hostility.

CATEGORY 4: THE GROWTH OF AN OUTCAST INDIVIDUAL OR GROUP

Individual destinies are often predetermined by class or circumstance, but one of the crowning attributes of the human condition is the ability to triumph over these barriers. Here are ten situations to motivate you to dramatize this powerful aspect of human nature.

SITUATION 1: Born into a family of outcasts, the protagonist struggles to break free of her pre-established societal bondage and to destroy the caste system that has done so much harm to untold millions of people.

SITUATION 2: Exiled for being born out of royal wedlock, a child journeys across a desert and finds her way to a village where her supernatural powers are recognized. She also proves to be a natural leader and is groomed to assume a position of leadership under the queen.

SITUATION 3: A homeless man, who once had a career but threw it away thanks to a drinking problem, wants to make a comeback but needs a patron to give him a financial head start. He eventually finds someone, but she makes a difficult demand.

SITUATION 4: A young girl raised in poverty in her third-world country surmounts great obstacles to become a physician. She then devotes her practice to helping the sick in her native country, despite the political turmoil.

SITUATION 5: The protagonist is a charismatic teacher who is exiled because her views on religion are considered blasphemous. But instead of seeking out a more hospitable community, she returns home to raise the consciousness of those who spurned her.

SITUATION 6: Atheists are barred from this utopia because they are considered at best amoral. Closet atheists remain, pretending to be believers, but they plan to expose the hypocrisy in society of the closet atheists and of society generally.

SITUATION 7: When self-proclaimed social reformers become popular after successfully lobbying for tax cuts, they advance their anti-immigration agenda. The protagonist, cast out by the group for supporting diversity, travels the country to expose the reformers' true agenda: a freeze on immigration.

SITUATION 8: Dangerous levels of ultraviolet radiation have led to people wearing artificial skin of varying colors—lavender and green among the most popular. Those who spurn artificial skin and instead wear extreme sunscreen become outcasts.

SITUATION 9: Persons deemed to be overweight are outcasts in this society, where weight is a factor of height and gender. Thus women who are 5'7" must weigh no more than 150, or they are required to enter "weight-rehab." The narrator, who is considered "overweight," aims to rid society of this weight obsession.

SITUATION 10: The military draft has returned. All persons between eighteen and twenty-two must serve or be arrested, jailed, and become outcasts. The narrator is an army defector who aims to end this trend by exposing corruption in the military. His life is in danger as a result.

CATEGORY 5: THE GROWTH OF A POLITICAL MOVEMENT

Some political movements fizzle out quickly; others trigger a revolution. They often exhibit the best—and the worst of mob consciousness. In an era of social change such as ours, political movements often convey the needs and desires of the people, however imperfectly. The possibilities for suspenseful tales abound.

SITUATION 1: In this future society, anarchists become a political force to reckon with. They hold conventions and attract celebrities to their cause. But, true to their name, anarchists have a difficult time organizing themselves, and chaos ensues as some of them run for political office.

SITUATION 2: This story takes place at a time when global warming is flooding coastal cities, and researchers have discovered a way to rid deadly diseases with stem cells. Scientists try to persuade the people to take climate change seriously, but an ultraconservative movement led by a charismatic, popular politician is on the rise and urges people to trust God to keep the planet healthy.

SITUATION 3: Driven by the desire to improve public education, a new political movement arises during extreme budget cutbacks in education. The protagonist, refusing to identify herself with any ideology, argues for better instruction in history, science, communication, and art. Her opposition is fierce.

SITUATION 4: A political group supporting space exploration argues that international collaboration in human expeditions to Mars and beyond would contribute significantly to world peace. Opponents ridicule the movement and want to use the space program for military purposes only.

SITUATION 5: When a new political party devoted to scrapping the Environmental Protection Agency becomes popular, environmentalists stage demonstrations in an effort to discredit that party. Things get out of hand when members of the anti-EPA party are harassed and threatened.

SITUATION 6: An Orwellian fable: Conservative chimpanzees, liberal gorillas, libertarian orangutans, and anarchist baboons battle for control of a federation of apes. The narrator is an apolitical outsider who reports on the scheming and blunders of each group.

SITUATION 7: The Mob, riding a wave of popularity, forms a political party. They spend hundreds of millions of dollars on campaign ads for their candidates. The protagonist is determined to stop them—but his life has been threatened.

SITUATION 8: Vegetarians form a political party and use campaign contributions to discredit the meat industry. In retaliation, the meat industry launches a massive attack against the vegetarians.

SITUATION 9: Cannabis lovers form their own political party, and before long a revolution is at hand. Not only do they want pot legalized; they also want it promoted as a staple—and society's greatest hope for peace.

SITUATION 10: Native Americans in this future scenario have consolidated their influence and populations, and an American-Indian political party is formed. The protagonist is a charismatic Sioux congresswoman with an eye on the White House.

CATEGORY 6: THE GROWTH OF A RELIGIOUS OR SPIRITUAL MOVEMENT

We tend to associate religion with permanence, but most religions, no matter how "traditional" change over the ages. Doctrines are reinterpreted; new doctrines are adopted. And sometimes entirely new religions or religious cults are created. Many stories can be told from the perspective of a new religious movement.

SITUATION 1: Ostracized for their strange religious practices, several mystics establish a colony where they conjure up formidable spirits and set them loose on the society that shunned them.

SITUATION 2: In a future world, the ambassador of the human race returns from an interstellar voyage, during which she made contact with an advanced species. The contact has so transformed her that she has taken on the demeanor of a priestess ... and has founded a religious movement.

SITUATION 3: Inspired by the American transcendentalists, a reformer attempts to promulgate a reawakening based on the ideals of Emerson, Thoreau, and Whitman. His biggest obstacle is colleagues who think he has lost his mind. To advance his cause, he sets up a commune (inspired by the Brook Farm utopian experiment in 1840s Massachusetts)—but dissenters of the plan plot to sabotage the project.

SITUATION 4: The narrator leads a movement to create a new religion based on the mystical visions of Hildegard of Bingen and amplified by the spiritual insights of modern-day women from all walks of life. But male clergy, and even many women, impede her efforts.

SITUATION 5: Native Hawaiians, fearing the demise of their culture, plan a revival of their ancient pagan religious practices. It catches on with the younger generation, who spread the beliefs to the mainland. But Fundamentalists prove to be a powerful counterforce.

SITUATION 6: Vegans establish a church and create imaginative and aggressive propaganda to win converts. They associate vegan dietary strictures with God and eternal bliss and meat-eating with damnation. One of the vegan priestesses goes too far and infuriates Fundamentalists, many of whom are meat lovers.

SITUATION 7: Reincarnation cults are on the rise in this society. Adding to their popularity is the claim from pseudoscientists that hard evidence exists that proves reincarnation. Adding to the absurdity are those who insist that one can choose when and into what kind of body one may be reincarnated.

SITUATION 8: Spiritual vampires are the focus here: One of the fallen angels presents herself as the patron demon of vampires. Worshipping her will bring power and extraordinary opportunity to the vampires who follow her. Of course, being a demon-angel, she requires compensation.

167

SITUATION 9: An atheist teacher gets into trouble when she characterizes a sense of wonder (with regard to natural phenomena) as the healthiest kind of spirituality. Traditionally religious people in the community demand her resignation, but she finds a way to make them reconsider.

SITUATION 10: In this dystopian society, adolescents are conditioned to religious conformity through electronic devices. Several teens escape conditioning and establish a new religion, one based on the natural world. But they must evade capture by the authorities.

CATEGORY 7: THE GROWTH OF A ROMANCE

A love story may very well be the quintessential story. Of the many kinds of love stories that exist, perhaps the most intriguing are the ones in which we witness the growth of a romance despite daunting obstacles. Love stories often invoke the full spectrum of human emotions: jealousy, hate, and despair—but also inspiration, ecstasy, and hope.

SITUATION 1: Burned by too many ill-fated romances, the narrator vows never to fall in love again. But then he meets a woman whose talents as a mystic and otherworldly temperament enchant him. Still, he holds back ... until the woman casts a spell on him that breaks down his last line of resistance.

SITUATION 2: A career-focused ballerina feels uninspired and is determined to find the ideal mate to bring romance and passion back into her life. But her ideas about what "ideal" really is are challenged when she becomes injured and is unable to perform, which leads her to become jealousy of the successful dancer she was falling for before the injury.

SITUATION 3: A chemist has produced a powerful love potion, which an assistant steals from her lab and spreads everywhere. The result is romantic mayhem: People start falling in love indiscriminately. The chemist is ordered to find an antidote—but someone has stolen her lab book containing the formula.

SITUATION 4: The protagonist is in the middle of a divorce from a vengeful woman and his lover is plagued by psychotic breakdowns, yet their love inspires each of them to accomplish amazing things. Will these accomplishments keep them together, or will circumstances outside their control force them apart?

SITUATION 5: Two deaf people fall in love, wooing each other with letters and paintings. But the romance becomes complicated after the man undergoes an operation that restores his hearing: He now wants to explore a relationship with a woman who can hear.

SITUATION 6: A prosecuting attorney and a defense attorney fall in love during a trial that pits them against each other. But when the defense attorney wins, the prosecutor tries to break off the relationship.

SITUATION 7: Two patients in a mental hospital fall in love and are determined to triumph over their disabilities—but the severity of their respective illnesses undermine their intentions. A sympathetic psychiatrist, however, may hold the key to their success.

SITUATION 8: When a high-school student becomes infatuated with a teacher, the teacher does all she can to neutralize the attraction, but the harder she tries, the more smitten he becomes. She reports the problem, but the principal's extreme reaction has an ironic effect.

SITUATION 9: Two persons with diametrically opposed political views participate in a debate that ends in hurtful mudslinging. Afterwards, the narrator (among the mudslingers) tries to apologize to the person she offended, but she is rebuffed. A second effort at reconciliation leads to a romantic bond.

SITUATION 10: Two teenagers, escapees from a repressive society, fall in love while hiding in the forest. One is captured but refuses to cooperate in locating the other. In the meantime, the teen still on the lam plans a rescue attempt.

CATEGORY 8: THE GROWTH OF A SOCIAL CUSTOM OR MOVEMENT

Societal customs change continuously. Occasionally they become part of the culture. Other times, they fade quickly. Some customs are quirky, generated by entertainment media; others are downright bizarre and have the potential to become the basis of good stories.

SITUATION 1: Charismatic teachers influence young people to study the liberal arts rather than business-related subjects. A pragmatic educator upsets the status quo by insisting that the purpose of schooling is to train for careers in business and technology.

SITUATION 2: When a progressive elementary school favors an accelerated learning program in music, language arts, and science literacy, the parents are incensed and accuse the teachers of robbing their kids of their childhood. The teachers insist that learning enhances childhood. In retaliation the parents sue the school.

SITUATION 3: The narrator leads coaches in a crusade to mandate sports in the elementary grades. Children, they argue, should be exposed to the healthy competition and intense exercise that sports provide. Several parents try to stop these "jock fanatics" from disrupting classroom learning.

SITUATION 4: A city planner wants to transform a slum into a nature center, complete with a museum, a park, and eco-friendly businesses. But officials favors investors who want the area turned into rental property.

SITUATION 5: Holography is a basic mode of learning and entertainment in this future society. Some holo-architects, however, design and display frightening scenarios that can cause psychological problems. A holo-vice squad tries to maintain the society's normalcy.

SITUATION 6: Robotic Santa Clauses are the rage in the near future. They can do so much more than people who dressed up as Santa can. They can mimic comic-book heroes (and villains) and generate virtual-reality playrooms where the children can sample the toys they want. But lately, some of the robo-Santas are up to no good ...

SITUATION 7: Sculptors are transforming their city into a giant art gallery and not everyone is pleased: Vandalism of the sculptures is widespread, but law-enforcement officers are reluctant to stop it because they themselves dislike the movement and regard the sculptors as lawbreakers.

SITUATION 8: A town votes to initiate weekly "e-blackout" days on which no one uses the Internet or any other electronic devices (except for emergencies) in an effort to promote more social interaction. At first people resist, but gradually the movement takes hold and becomes a popular.

SITUATION 9: In this future society, street healing is widespread. Faith healers promise to rid people of a wide range of afflictions, at varying prices. One resident wants to stop what he thinks is a fraud—but one particular street healer gives him pause.

SITUATION 10: Tightrope walking has become a social custom in this society that lionizes those who risk their lives in public. High-wire acts are commonplace and have become an initiation rite for club memberships, job advancements, etc.

CATEGORY 9: THE GROWTH OF A SPECIAL INDIVIDUAL

Everyone is special in some way, but most people do not cultivate a one-in-a-million distinctiveness over the course of their lives. When they do, their activities often shape the lives of others, even shape history. Their lives sometimes appear in memorable stories and novels (known in German literature as the bildungsroman).

SITUATION 1: A reverse rags-to-riches story of a protagonist who scorns having been born into an affluent, privileged family. She forsakes it all, works menial jobs, and lives in deliberate poverty—all the while chronicling the decadence of the rich.

SITUATION 2: With a childhood marred by misfortune and delinquency, a nonetheless sharp-witted teen vows to turn his life around after being nearly fatally shot. It's a difficult battle because few people trust him. But he concocts a plan to improve his life that will either make him famous or homeless.

SITUATION 3: A dancer loses a leg in an accident and struggles through hopelessness as she painfully adapts to her prosthetic leg. Though ballet dancing seems out of the question, she finds a way to surmount her obstacles to become one of the finest ballet dancers ever.

SITUATION 4: This is the story of a drifter who dropped out of school and escaped his tyrannical parents to live a come-what-may life on the streets. After falling in with addicts and criminals, he meets a mysterious individual who sees in him a rare talent.

SITUATION 5: Thought to have been killed in battle, a soldier turns up years later in his hometown. The townspeople are jubilant, but then the soldier starts to behave strangely. Actually he has reassessed his life and his views on war, and he is determined to make radical changes in the world.

SITUATION 6: A teacher struggles to dispel his students' ethnic and gender stereotypes. Ironically he is the target of such stereotypes due to his ethnicity and sexual orientation. But one of his students, also a victim of stereotyping, works with him to advance his cause.

SITUATION 7: The hero of this story is determined to redo his life from scratch and become the honorable person he has dreamt of becoming. First, he gives up his bad habits—laziness, smoking, drinking—next, he attempts to win the good graces of those he has wronged. But some refuse to forgive him.

SITUATION 8: Regretting her decision to abandon philosophy to pursue a lucrative career, a shop owner liquidates her business and reenters academe. Disappointed with the pragmatic leanings of students and faculty, however, she strives to return the academy to its Platonic origins.

SITUATION 9: A woman finally shakes off her codependency to an abusive husband and pursues her lifelong dream of becoming a pianist. But she worries that she will be unable to master the instrument at her age. Others reinforce that pessimism, but one admirer is convinced she has the talent to succeed.

SITUATION 10: Growing up in a traveling circus, a clown experiments with ways to delight children and make them laugh. Over the years, he acquires a reputation as the world's funniest clown. Ironically, the more successful he becomes, the more his private life falls apart.

CATEGORY 10: THE GROWTH OF UNUSUAL TECHNOLOGIES AND INDUSTRIES

As science advances, new technologies and industries evolve. Some of these at first seem fringe, but then, as they become integrated into our culture, their strangeness fades—which in itself might be cause for alarm. Writers can find fascinating story material by paying attention to the ways in which new technologies and industries have infiltrated our daily lives.

SITUATION 1: When a huge oil shale deposit is discovered, a petroleum producer uses highly persuasive tactics to convince politicians to back his advanced methods of fracking but one dissenter is determined to stop them in their tracks.

SITUATION 2: Although surgery has become completely automated in this future society, some patients (like the narrator) demand a human surgeon. He is ridiculed, despite several stories of serious malfunctions, but a sympathetic nurse dares to help him with his wish.

SITUATION 3: It is the 2060s and self-driving cars are the rage, but plenty of old-style car lovers despise the trend and do all they can to discredit robotic cars— even to the point of deliberately causing accidents.

SITUATION 4: New-generation slot machines are sweeping casinos everywhere. They involve the gamblers in scenarios that are much more addictive than they first appear. The protagonist, a psychologist, sounds a warning, but the machines have become so popular that he is met with fierce opposition ... until several gamblers go insane.

SITUATION 5: A pair of inventors create a levitation machine that enables users to soar for hundreds of feet and descend safely; almost overnight, the levitation industry is born and people are soaring everywhere. But then problems arise: Some levitators develop faulty circuits and zigzag wildly through the air. People are hurt, and the inventors suddenly become villains rather than heroes.

SITUATION 6: Longevity has become a major industry. For a price, people can sign up to have their lives extended for as long as they want (up to a point). However, the more years they request, the riskier the chances that health problems will arise (exotic forms of dementia, for example).

SITUATION 7: In this near-future scenario, prosthetics technology has advanced, but some amputees continue to grapple with psychological disabilities. One amputee's goal: triumph over depression and despair. He founds an organization dedicated to helping amputees adapt to the new reality of their lives, but his new busy life leaves him feeling even more alone.

SITUATION 8: Virtual-reality technology has advanced to the point of competing with actual reality. Fearing that civilization itself could be severely compromised if technology advances any further, the protagonist sets out to bring people back to their senses—but faces a violent backlash as a result.

SITUATION 9: It is the mid-twenty-first century, and "retro-tech" has grown in popularity: Everywhere people are clamoring for passenger trains over jets, bicycles and streetcars over automobiles, print over pixels, handwritten letters over e-mails. But in a satirical twist on the present time, the older generation is desperate to restore their e-gadget culture to prominence.

SITUATION 10: Amusement-park technology has evolved dramatically in this future scenario. A ride at one amusement park is scary in ways never before imagined: The visitors experience being hanged, guillotined, drawn and quartered, etc. (all in good fun), but at least one visitor panics and runs amuck

CHAPTER 12

THE INVASION OF X

CATEGORY 1: ALIEN INVASION

True "alien invasion" conjures up space operas and science fiction flicks from the 1950s, but don't let the clichés discourage you from tapping into a venerable science-fiction motif. The possibilities for original and entertaining stories are inexhaustible. Here are ten of them to put your imagination into high gear.

SITUATION 1: Aliens invade Earth not by zapping cities with lasers but by bringing flowers—billions of flowers, far more exotic than those grown on Earth—and filling the cities with such loveliness and fragrance that people forget they're being invaded. But the flowers hide a dark secret of their own ... one even the invaders don't know about.

SITUATION 2: Shape-shifting aliens infiltrate the human population by assuming the forms of pets—cats, dogs, birds, etc.—and then reverting to their original forms after being adopted.

SITUATION 3: Aliens in the shape of balloons drift down to Earth. They are colorful and can move in strange ways. Humans are told the balloons must not be popped. Of course, despite warnings, children pop them ... just as the invaders expected.

SITUATION 4: Birdlike creatures that proliferate rapidly invade Earth. At first, they seem content to live on Antarctic mountaintops (akin to the climate of their home world)—but they want to manipulate Earth's weather to make the rest of the planet a tundra.

SITUATION 5: Long-hibernating wormlike creatures, which arrived on Earth via a meteor ages ago, begin to proliferate and grow much larger. They possess a protective outer layer that makes them nearly indestructible. They are also chameleon-like, which makes them difficult to spot until it's too late.

SITUATION 6: An alien invasion is underway through the process of taking over people's bodies, but no one knows who the aliens are or what they look like. People begin behaving strangely. For instance, some are able to do amazing things, like levitate.

SITUATION 7: Aliens invade the bodies of large mammals such as cows, horses, elephants, and tigers as a first step toward invading humans. Once they take over the bodies of chimpanzees, they communicate their intentions to the humans through sign language.

SITUATION 8: Humans from the future are invading Earth. Their goal is to prevent a nation from launching chemical weapons against their enemies and rendering sterile millions of people globally. But how can these future humans be trusted? What if they're the ones who want to sterilize the human race?

SITUATION 9: The Earth's surface is so contaminated in this future scenario that colonies have been built under the sea—and they are thriving. But the desperate surviving humans on land launch an invasion on these undersea colonies.

SITUATION 10: The aliens assure the people of Earth that they do not wish to invade but to cooperate. They want fair trade: their needs for ours. At first, the deal seems respectable, but then it becomes clear that their needs involve genetic manipulation.

CATEGORY 2: BACTERIAL OR VIRAL INVASION

Bacteria can become superbugs and they can trigger deadly epidemics. Scientists also speculate that viruses from outer space could do the same (think of Michael Crichton's *The Andromeda Strain*). Well-crafted stories about such invaders can raise consciousness about these possibilities.

SITUATION 1: An influenza virus mutates so that it feeds on antiviral agents. As the virus spreads, researchers rush to create an entirely new drug to combat the virus. They succeed but with a drug that has unforeseen side effects.

SITUATION 2: Several alien computer viruses attack communication satellites and power grids and wreak havoc on computer systems across the Earth. A team of ace hackers, led by the narrator, must produce an antivirus program before it's too late.

SITUATION 3: Lethal microbes, long dormant beneath Arctic ice, return to life due to the melting ice cap. A global health emergency is declared as scientists search for an antidote. The biggest problem is that initial symptoms mimic the common cold.

SITUATION 4: Children contract a disease that physicians can't diagnose. Symptoms include uncontrolled speech and changes in appearance. The narrator is an immunologist who decides to use her own son as a guinea pig for testing possible antidotes.

SITUATION 5: Astronauts return from deep-space exploration infected with a bacterial infection that escaped detection when the astronauts were in quarantine. Humans begin to mutate in bizarre ways.

SITUATION 6: A virus discovered in mice makes them resistant to infection and allows them to live past their normal life spans. A geneticist considers exposing humans to the virus, but her supervisor warns her not to pursue such an experiment.

SITUATION 7: After a plague sweeps a village, a botanist experiments with medicinal plants in the hope of concocting a serum. His inspiration is a physician from the future who instructs him. But as he attempts to administer the remedy, superstitious villagers try to stop him.

SITUATION 8: Researchers create a super virus intended to attack other viruses—but the supervirus escapes confinement and wreaks havoc on the environment, including valuable ecosystems and natural plants and fungi used for medicinal purposes. No one knows how to neutralize it ... until the narrator, a long-scorned microbiologist ignored by many scientific communities for his outrageous ideas, is recruited.

SITUATION 9: The protagonist discovers a meteorite that contains complex organic substances. After further analysis in her lab, she announces that she has discovered the first alien life form.

SITUATION 10: Scientists revive an unknown species of bacteria from a strange Egyptian-like tomb in Antarctica. Despite precautions, the bacteria escape confinement and cause a pandemic.

CATEGORY 3: BARBARIAN INVASION

It could be said that invaders are barbarians by definition, but some invaders are more barbaric than others. While some invaders sow the seeds of chaos and injustice, others sow the seeds of culture. The following scenarios lean more toward the former—although in some cases, it may not be easy to tell one type of invader from the other.

SITUATION 1: Barbarians attack a utopian city that has rid itself of crime, poverty, and ignorance, but its openness to outsiders has made it vulnerable to invasion. The barbarians exploit this weakness, but they fail to anticipate the utopians' ability to protect themselves.

SITUATION 2: In this strange parallel world, a remote territory explored by Nazis is home to a savage army of barbarians who are intent on banishing the Nazis from their land. But the barbarians' savagery is not enough to ward off the efficiently murderous Nazis.

SITUATION 3: When a group of religious extremists is no longer able to tolerate scientific teachings that contradict their interpretation of Scripture, it forms a movement that descends upon a town in order to make it their own and seal it off from the secular world. A teacher in the town tries to dissuade local officials from caving in to the group's demands.

SITUATION 4: Church leaders decry the presence of barbarians beyond the boundaries of their settlement. When the settlement leaders attempt to settle the differences with the barbarians, they discover the barbarians have abducted church leaders and demand their congregations adopt their own barbaric doctrines and behaviors. They insist this is the only way to avoid all-out war.

SITUATION 5: Cyborgs invade the last human outposts in this post-apocalyptic Earth. The humans are driven into the wilderness, but the cyborgs don't follow. Instead, they erect barriers to keep them in the wilderness assuming they will die out. The humans resort to barbaric tactics to survive. The narrator argues that such barbaric activities are what initiated the cyborg wars in the first place, and he is cast out of the human refugee camp.

SITUATION 6: Excluded from participating in the city's cultural life, the outcasts (as the city has branded them because of radiation-induced mutations) form their own colony and devote much of their energies to planning an invasion of the city.

SITUATION 7: A once-peaceful ethnic community is now experiencing oppressive treatment from city officials. When traditional legal channels fail to work, some members of the community decide to take matters into their own hands and commit acts of vandalism against their oppressors.

SITUATION 8: Invaders overtake a metropolitan area where most of the dwellers perished from a dirty bomb. Survivors ironically want to use a similar bomb against the invaders. Their rationale: They can survive in underground shelters until the nerve gas dissipates.

SITUATION 9: In this clash between invading barbarians and the pagan status quo, the latter promises the people social stability and a civil government—but their ruthless imprisonment and execution of "misfits" seems to tell another story.

SITUATION 10: On an alternate Earth, barbarians wielding magic powers invade their neighbors. Upon learning that the barbarians have targeted their village next, the narrator and his brother infiltrate the barbarian encampment to discover their source of magic ... but in doing so, they leave their own families unprotected.

CATEGORY 4: INSECT OR ARACHNID INVASION

Most insects and arachnids (spiders, scorpions) are frightening or at least unsettling. They creep, crawl, bite, have too many legs, and are as unlike us as it is possible for life-forms to be. Along with reptiles, they are the creatures most likely to be considered monstrous.

SITUATION 1: Locusts ravage a village with the devastation reminiscent of biblical times—but this is the twenty-first century, and these locusts are immune to existing pesticides—or rather, mostly immune. Scientists struggle to come up with a new way to eradicate the locusts.

SITUATION 2: A new strain of killer bees invades communities in the Southern United States, causing panic, as the stings cause severe illness and sometimes death. Initial efforts to counteract the stings only make the situation worse. One scientist, though, pursues an unconventional means of eradicating the threat.

SITUATION 3: Mutant spiders proliferate—perhaps as a result of genetic experiments gone awry. Their venom is not lethal, but it changes the victims in strange ways. Also, their enormous size causes widespread panic.

SITUATION 4: An invasion of aggressive centipedes is panicking a community. Scientists suspect radiation is to blame but from where? While the scientists search for a cause, the centipedes invade homes and cause bizarre illnesses.

SITUATION 5: At first the newly discovered species of ants seemed harmless, but then they began building weird mounds. When the narrator probes one of the mounds, she discovers intricate tunnels and chambers ... and makes a startling discovery inside one of them.

SITUATION 6: Wasps invade an upscale Hollywood neighborhood, and exterminators are brought in, but their efforts are futile. The wasps invade the studios as well and interrupt numerous TV and film shoots.

SITUATION 7: Larvae from an unknown species of insect discovered in a cave hatch and escape confinement. Despite efforts to eradicate them, they proliferate wildly. They also have an affinity for human blood.

SITUATION 8: Ordinary bedbugs are bad enough, but genetically modified bedbugs are a nightmare. Instead of being vulnerable to a new kind of pesticide, they thrive on it and become more aggressive than ever.

SITUATION 9: People are contracting tapeworms inexplicably, and health experts are working around the clock to locate the source(s). Meanwhile people are grossly overeating and losing weight drastically.

SITUATION 10: Scorpions infest a suburban neighborhood. Unlike the stings of typical scorpions, these stings cause people to change in grotesque ways. Attempted antidotes to the venom only worsen the problem.

CATEGORY 5: MILITARY OR PARAMILITARY INVASION

In any state or country, dissenters will arise; if they are powerful and charismatic enough, they may form a militia. The larger their numbers, the likelier the victory—assuming their forces are more powerful and resourceful. Fierce confrontations and inevitable bloodshed typify such invasion stories.

SITUATION 1: A militia of white supremacists invades a city—not to kill minorities but to take civic leaders hostage and order the city to exile minorities. Two officials infiltrate the militia in an effort to sabotage them from within.

SITUATION 2: Refusing to surrender to an invading army, inventive resistance fighters use new kinds of weapons to attack the enemy encamped outside the city walls. But the army captures the lead fighter and learns the secret of their new weapons.

SITUATION 3: At the height of the Gallic Wars, vigilante fighters attack one of Caesar's garrisons. They then engage Caesar himself in battle. Impressed, Caesar promises to spare their lives if they switch loyalties. The fighters agree but secretly plan to attack the Romans from within.

SITUATION 4: Even though the Civil War has come to an end at Appomattox, several Rebel soldiers against the surrender plan an invasion of a Union encampment. But a local farmer discovers the plot while he is out hunting, and must choose between warning the Union or confronting the Rebels.

SITUATION 5: Neo-Nazis invade a Midwestern city and redeploy Hitler's World War II strategies—this time with WMDs. It is up to the narrator, a military historian, to stop them.

SITUATION 6: Political extremists form a militia that recruits foreign demolition experts and snipers to launch an attack on the White House. But one of the militia members, a spy, leaks information to a Pentagon official.

SITUATION 7: A unit of the National Guard falls under some demonic influence; instead of protecting citizens, they attack them. Before other Guard units are called in, leaders must make certain they have not been infected as well.

SITUATION 8: Robots created specifically for warfare rewrite their programming and attack civilians—including the robotics engineers who designed them. Human military forces are deployed to stop them—but the robots have anticipated their arrival.

SITUATION 9: Native Americans form a militia and set out to reclaim South Dakota as their sovereign nation. Although they have little chance of winning, their grievances are heard and reparations are considered. But will they accept anything less than victory when their movement appears to gain momentum?

SITUATION 10: Outraged by the closing of clinics for women, numerous women with military training form a militia and invade the state-capitol building while in session, demanding the clinics reopen and all reproductive rights be returned to them.

CATEGORY 6: MUTANT INVASION

During the 1950s, fears concerning nuclear bombs led to many mutated creature flicks. Today fears of radiation poisoning via malfunctioning nuclear power plants, the genetic manipulation of plants and animals, and possible nuclear attacks provide the fodder for apocalyptic stories.

SITUATION 1: Residents of a town near a nuclear power plant begin to suffer mutations due to a radiation leak. But even after the leak is repaired, the mutations continue. Some are horrific, and they proliferate before quarantine is established. Scientists struggle to deal with the crisis.

SITUATION 2: In a postapocalyptic world, mutant humans invade a peaceful colony and turn it into a terrorist base from which they plan to attack nonmutant human enclaves. One of the colonists disguises herself as a mutant and infiltrates the invaders, hoping to sabotage their plans.

SITUATION 3: Cats contract a disease that causes them to mutate into dangerous creatures. Because the mutations are not always visible, cat owners panic. The protagonist leads a research team to find an antidote.

SITUATION 4: Someone casts a spell that causes the women of the village to mutate into witches and the men into warlocks. The children, unaffected by the spell, must find a way to neutralize it.

SITUATION 5: Following a rash of UFO sightings that most reporters dismiss as hoaxes, eyewitnesses experience changes in their bodies. After a while other people are similarly affected. After scientists regard the sightings as genuine, they launch a quarantine campaign.

SITUATION 6: Fish from a contaminated river mutate. The mutated fish proliferate and spread to other waterways and ultimately are ingested by people and wildlife alike. The result is a massive invasion of mutated life.

SITUATION 7: Geese invade a waste dump and mutate into ferocious beasts—but the mutation is strictly behavioral: Their outward appearance remains the same, deceiving those who attempt to re-domesticate the geese.

182

SITUATION 8: Radiation has caused the chicken on a farm to mutate into grotesque beasts that subsequently escape confinement and invade surrounding farms. When scientists try to contain the radiation, they too begin to mutate.

SITUATION 9: Some unknown virus is causing animals in a metropolitan zoo to mutate, escape confinement, and invade adjoining neighborhoods. Anyone who touches the escaped animals will mutate as well.

SITUATION 10: Dolls of all kinds come to life, morph into grotesque caricatures of people, and invade the bedrooms of children and adults alike. The protagonist traces the cause of the mutation to a little girl with magical powers.

CATEGORY 7: MOB INVASION

Mobs are often associated with rioting, criminal activity, and boorish behavior. "Mob consciousness" overrides or represses individual intentions. For that reason, mobs are powerful forces that are difficult to control or diffuse. Of course, "mob" has another meaning—as in the Mafia, also a great source of story ideas.

SITUATION 1: Militant conservatives seize control of a community known for its free-thinking ways. on grounds that the proper upbringing of young people has been discarded. Ironically, the militants are the ones who commit one crime after another in an effort to rid the town of atheists and secular free-spirits.

SITUATION 2: In this future scenario, the arts are on the verge of extinction now that the government has terminated support. Only privatized support exists, and these organizations only fund commercially driven projects. Avant-garde artists are silenced by mobs that fear these artistic dissidents.

SITUATION 3: It is Prohibition, and the Mob has taken over the liquor business in a small town. One of the mobsters, attracted to the peacefulness of the town and its rural surroundings, wants to quit the Mob—but doing so would put his life at risk.

SITUATION 4: When mass-media propaganda demonizes a particular ethnic group, mob consciousness overtakes individual judgment and mobs of frightened people attack members of the ethnic group. The protagonist must find a way to undo the brainwashing before it's too late.

SITUATION 5: Fans of a champion team go berserk when their team loses after a long winning streak. They vandalize the city of the winning team and assault individual players. The city's mayor decides to use them to set an example that squelches the folly of sports fanaticism once and for all.

SITUATION 6: A mob of cannabis advocates invades a community where the weed is outlawed and, in a circus atmosphere, offers free joints to any who want them. This transitions to a more sedate and open dialogue between the advocates and the public. When the police attempt to arrest key leaders of the movement, the public strongly objects.

SITUATION 7: When the legislature of a border town strikes down an immigration reform bill, a group of undocumented workers protest at city hall. Although the town's mayor vows to reconsider the bill, she guts it. This time, the protestors become an angry mob.

SITUATION 8: Fans of a champion race-car driver become distraught when he announces his retirement. A small group kidnap him and demand that he teach them his secrets and help them build a car of their own. When the news does break that the driver is being held somewhere in town, a mob of fans from all over the state gather to find him, and some threaten death to the kidnappers.

SITUATION 9: A mob of senior citizens storms Congress to protest a bill that, if passed, would drastically reduce medical benefits to the elderly. Energized by the intensity of the protest, the narrator urges her fellow seniors to stage similar protests for other causes.

SITUATION 10: Leprechaun mobs invade Irish towns in reaction to the clearcutting of woodland that is already scarce. They warn people that unless the trend is reversed—that new trees are planted and new woodlands preserved—all magic will vanish from Ireland.

CATEGORY 8: INVASION OR UPRISING OF THE MARGINALIZED

The marginalized or outcast in society are often underestimated. They may be largely uneducated and resigned to their lives of servitude, but too much deprivation leads to ever-growing anger and frustration—until they reach a flashpoint and revolt.

SITUATION 1: A group of gypsies revolt against those who have bought into stereotypes about gypsies and have mistreated them and denied them their rights. The focal character is a gypsy who disguises her ethnicity and infiltrates mainstream society to become an attorney. Now she will use her knowledge of the law (and her license to practice law) to change the public's attitude.

SITUATION 2: Overweight people organize a series of protest marches to argue that thinness is not a requirement for attractiveness. Ironically, after weeks of marching, they begin losing weight. Now they must eat more to regain their weight and maintain their credibility.

SITUATION 3: In this cyborg-dominant world, people without mechanical or electronic parts are targets of injustice and prejudice, but an underground movement of noncybernetic humans has begun. The narrator leads a movement for an all-out revolt, though the cards are greatly stacked against them.

SITUATION 4: Outcast and considered insane, poets in this future dystopia invade the city that exiled them and stage a mock trial of the officials. Alas, the poets acquire the insensitive attitudes they once accused their captors of harboring.

SITUATION 5: By 2050 everyone is linked to a social network ... except for those rare few who do not care to be "social" in the electronic sense. Ironically, the networked communities attempt to brand and ghettoize the "separatists"—but the separatists fight back.

SITUATION 6: In this future society, eye color determines status; the darker one's pigmentation, the higher one's status. Those with light pigmentation (blue, green, gray, hazel) are at the bottom, and are marginalized. False-color contact lenses are illegal and highly valued.

SITUATION 7: Marginalized for being precocious, several high school students stage an uprising at their school, demanding that learning standards be set higher. But the teachers insist that everything must be done to help the disadvantaged and that the high achievers can take care of themselves.

SITUATION 8: Colonists returning to Earth after living on Mars for several years are first quarantined. When tests detect unexpected changes in body chemistry, they are sequestered and treated like outcasts. In desperation, the colonists decide to break out of quarantine.

SITUATION 9: Men in this future society must take testosterone enhancers at puberty to ensure a proper level of aggressiveness. Passive males are marginalized and persecuted. Women, likewise, must conform to standards of femininity;

they take estrogen enhancers at puberty. The narrator heads an underground effort to end this madness.

SITUATION 10: Outdated androids are relegated to labor camps where they are divided into groups based on competency. The least competent androids are forced to do the most dangerous or foulest labor (mining, waste-dump reclamation, etc.). A sympathetic human encourages these androids to revolt.

CATEGORY 9: PARANORMAL INVASION

Even in our scientific age, bizarre phenomena occur that seem to defy any scientific explanation. For the horror writer's sake, this is a good thing. Society seems to have an insatiable appetite for weird occult tales. Stories of invasions by creatures from the dark side of reality are especially spine-chilling.

SITUATION 1: They materialize only in the dead of night—organisms from deep underground that wriggle to the surface and take over the brains of sleeping hosts. Once infected, the hosts begin building a fortress of truly alien design and purpose.

SITUATION 2: A man's dwelling is invaded by the ghosts of his dead family members stretching back for generations who all want him to complete certain tasks before they can rest in peace, but he refuses ... at first.

SITUATION 3: A demon takes refuge in a church to keep from being apprehended by other demons. Finding sanctuary in a church would be impossible, if not for the intervention of a sympathetic priest. But the priest worries that the demon wants to make a fool out of him.

SITUATION 4: Renegade angels disguise themselves as gang members and infiltrate a slum. Existing gangs try to scare them off, and quickly regret their actions when the angels afflict them with muscle spasms, facial blotches, etc. When the gangs realize that the new gang members are angels, they suggest a crime partnership.

SITUATION 5: Realizing they can exert more influence on people by working together, rogue ghosts work in teams, not just to haunt houses per se, but to force occupants to retaliate against certain individuals.

SITUATION 6: Poltergeists invade businesses in a small town. The narrator, a paranormal investigator, searches for a cause. After fruitless searching, he encounters a poltergeist who explains what the vandalizing spirits want.

SITUATION 7: A ghoul army invades a kingdom in search of treasure that the humans stole. Learning of the coming invasion, a human guardian encases the treasure in a force field. The ghouls warn that unless the treasure is released to them, they will decimate the kingdom.

SITUATION 8: Diabolical angels invade a community of worshippers by disguising themselves as benevolent angels. But one of the worshippers discovers the scam and retaliates by deceiving the demon angels.

SITUATION 9: The spirits of African Americans and other minorities who had been lynched in the South and elsewhere during pre-civil-rights days have come together to haunt those institutions in which racial discrimination is still practiced.

SITUATION 10: Known for its horrific conditions, a centuries-old European prison is haunted by souls who have been unjustly imprisoned and tortured. They collude with existing prisoners to force the warden to accept an ultimatum: Make reparations to the descendents of the ghosts, or terrible things will happen.

CATEGORY 10: VERMIN INVASION

Destructive pests like rats, roaches, or certain kinds of worms (*vermis* in Latin, origin of the word *vermin*) are aggressive survivors. Rats are especially troublesome because of the diseases they carry. Because vermin proliferate just about everywhere, their influence on civilization has been significant.

SITUATION 1: Superintelligent rodents invade a city by gnawing wires of all kinds, thereby sabotaging communication systems. Humans fight back with robots programmed to attack the rats and mice. But the rodents figure out a way to dismantle the robots.

SITUATION 2: In this postapocalyptic scenario, irradiated roaches grow to ten times normal size and invade homes. To combat them, a scientist who has studied roaches creates a robotic roach programmed to destroy the real ones. But until he figures out a way to get his robotic roaches to reproduce, the experiment will be useless.

SITUATION 3: Vermin have infested this formerly sanitary, upscale urban community, and no one can explain why ... until the narrator uncovers clues left by organisms smuggled from a region that had been quarantined after a top secret experiment failed.

SITUATION 4: After termites overwhelm an African village, scientists realize that the species of termite in question had been genetically transformed by an unknown organism. Having become carnivorous, the termites target animals ... and people. The narrator must find a way to undo the mutation.

SITUATION 5: Centipedes inexplicably proliferate in a wilderness area. Existing pesticides backfire, and the centipedes spread everywhere. The worst danger is in their bite, which transforms a human into a monstrous human-centipede hybrid.

SITUATION 6: Mice genetically enhanced for medical research purposes escape confinement, proliferate, and invade homes. The greater the attempt to eradicate them, the more they retaliate.

SITUATION 7: Someone trains rats to destroy electronic systems. The mysterious trainer posts a ransom demand of fifty million dollars or the invasion of rats will continue. The narrator and her team look for ways to neutralize the rats.

SITUATION 8: Engineers try to determine why their city's sewer system is infested with rats. Officials worry that the infestation may carry over to food storage facilities. Exterminating techniques are not working. Clues suggest that someone is deliberately breeding the rats.

SITUATION 9: People are being attacked at night by genetically engineered cockroaches, which invade even the most sanitary residences. The narrator, an exterminator, believes that the cockroaches are an act of terrorism.

SITUATION 10: A breeder of nightcrawlers for fishing enthusiasts is mystified by the changing behaviors of his worms: He finds evidence that they are burrowing into his house and worries that they may be invading the entire community.

CHAPTER 13
JOURNEY OR PILGRIMAGE TO X

CATEGORY 1: JOURNEY TO AN ANCESTRAL HOME

Many people feel the need to not only trace their lineage but to visit their ancestral homes. Often the discoveries are fascinating. Sometimes, though, they are disturbing. Whatever the outcome, rich story material can be mined from such a quest. The following ten scenarios should stir your storyteller's imagination.

SITUATION 1: Ostracized from his family for certain taboo indiscretions, a writer visits his European ancestral village. There he encounters a ghost who teaches him about his true ancestral history, which is very different from what he was told by his parents. Then he meets a living relative who also has been ostracized and is seeking redemption.

SITUATION 2: While overseas, the protagonist inexplicably feels compelled to remain in a town she never visited before. Strangers there regard her as a lost relative. Curious, she discovers her surname in the village's records; one document that is at least 400 years old includes not just her family name but her own full name.

SITUATION 3: A young professional traces his ancestry to an isolated town, which he visits. But by digging into his past, he learns that he is descended not from heroes, as recent family members have insisted, but from villains.

189

SITUATION 4: Under hypnosis, the narrator recalls a village where she lived in a previous lifetime. Using her hypnotists' notes, she identifies the village and visits it. There she discovers the descendents of persons who knew her in her previous life.

SITUATION 5: Adopted as an infant, a journalist visits the city of his birth parents and discovers disturbing facts about them. When those who knew his parents learn that he is visiting, they hold him accountable for his parents' transgressions.

SITUATION 6: An octogenarian visits her ancestral home and learns about the restorative folk medicine her great-grandparents used. She realizes that they stayed healthy into their nineties. Finally, she tries the herbal concoctions herself.

SITUATION 7: Although she has been living and working in a large Midwestern city, a Native American feels the tug of her ancestral home in New Mexico. During her visit, she tracks down several of her distant relatives now living in poverty.

SITUATION 8: When a man returns to his ancestral village, the residents avoid him. An ancient document revealed that his ancestors had been associated with witchcraft, and at least one resident fears that he may still possess some of that evil power.

SITUATION 9: A Haitian American returns to her ancestral country, hoping to write about her roots. In Haiti, she explores religious and folk medicine practices and even the drug smuggling in which one ancestor was involved. The research leads her to dangerous people.

SITUATION 10: In researching his family tree, a historian learns that one of his ancestors was a Puritan judge in a witchcraft trial. Intrigued, he visits his ancestral home only to discover that the descendents of the wrongly tried and executed women want to punish him for his ancestor's alleged misdeeds.

CATEGORY 2: JOURNEY TO ANOTHER WORLD

There may be tens of billions of planets in our galaxy alone. Despite their enormous distances from Earth, we love to conjure up journeys to some of these worlds, especially if they are at least marginally Earth-like. What strange and exciting experiences would we encounter?

SITUATION 1: Humans have colonized the moon, Mars, and elsewhere to escape an environmentally ravaged Earth. A social reformer, however, wishes to stay behind to launch a vast reclamation project—but she needs thousands of volunteers to make the project work.

SITUATION 2: A spiritualist trains people to migrate to other worlds through mental discipline alone. When a young woman undergoes the training, she winds up in a nightmare world and is unable to return. Her only hope is to find someone in this nightmare world that can help her.

SITUATION 3: Astronauts journey to a newly discovered dwarf planet at the outer edge of the solar system. It is a top-priority mission because a robot probe has shown that the world is artificial. When they arrive, they discover that the planet is heavily guarded.

SITUATION 4: A multigeneration starship has gone into orbit around an Earth-like world. Although no intelligent life has been detected, one crew member wonders if they're using the right criteria for detecting it.

SITUATION 5: An expedition heads to Venus after a probe detects signs of life on this hellish planet. It doesn't seem possible: The atmosphere is toxic, and the surface is hot enough to melt lead. But life signs lead them deep underground.

SITUATION 6: Survivors from a damaged spaceship land on a world where they encounter bizarre life forms that seem intelligent ... and also carnivorous. They struggle to find a way to communicate with the creatures before they get eaten.

SITUATION 7: Astronauts travel through a wormhole to a mirror Earth. There they encounter mirror cities with mirror inhabitants (including themselves), but this Earth's history is radically different. The astronauts will not escape easily.

SITUATION 8: The world upon which the first sign of intelligent life beyond the Earth is discovered consisting entirely of artificial life. But who created these intelligent artificial beings? The astronauts who arrive there look for clues.

SITUATION 9: Explorers journey into an artificially designed cyberworld and get lost. The designer of the cyberworld, along with several of her associates, enters that world to search for the lost explorers.

SITUATION 10: An extraterrestrial-intelligence investigator intercepts an invitation from beings to visit their world orbiting the nearest star, Alpha Centauri. But subsequent messages seem less like invitations and more like warnings to stay away.

CATEGORY 3: JOURNEY INTO A WASTELAND

Wastelands can be literal symbolic, or both. A land that has become infertile can be the basis of a story about desperate farmers and at the same time a story about sterility on the human level. Journeys into such lands can embody the struggle of life over death, a strong premise for many potential stories.

SITUATION 1: The crops of a once-successful farmer die prematurely. Despite sufficient rainfall and protection from pests, the region is becoming a wasteland of ruined crops, and that fact is driving people away. An agronomist suspects an unknown organism. But further inspections reveal a more serious threat to those who have stayed behind.

SITUATION 2: Explorers defy a warning based on an old legend, and enter a canyon that's considered cursed because no one who ventures there ever returns. The explorers expect to find treacherous crevasses or geologic instability, but the landscape they encounter defies all expectations.

SITUATION 3: Geologists head toward an island that straddles a notoriously active earthquake fault; they regard the site as an ideal laboratory for seismic research despite locals long ago abandoning the area. When they investigate the island's fault zone, the scientists discover something much more ominous.

SITUATION 4: A giant chamber materializes near a desert town, and after the townspeople spread the word, hundreds flock to the site to witness what seems to be a divine manifestation. One of the residents is skeptical and finds a way to enter the chamber, just to prove that it's some weird kind of mirage. What happens to him defies comprehension.

SITUATION 5: To visit a fabled city, pilgrims must cross a wasteland filled with obstacles, both natural and supernatural. Only three people have ever returned and each are in various states of delirium The narrator and a companion decide to take the trip anyway.

SITUATION 6: Using an improved method of earthquake prediction, a seismologist fears that a megaquake will occur within the next seventy-two hours in an area that has not had a quake in decades. Unfortunately she must travel across many miles of desert wasteland to reach those who would be affected, most of whom are without phones (by choice).

SITUATION 7: Oceanographers detect a giant fissure in the sea floor and decide to investigate it. What they discover is frightening: An enormous magma chamber seems about to erupt with the force of a supervolcano.

SITUATION 8: A virus transmitted by a tick turns people into zombies. The ticks have infested a forest, turning it into a wasteland, but exterminators dare to infiltrate the infected area to keep the ticks from spreading.

SITUATION 9: After a war transforms a city into a wasteland, an international team journeys to the site to determine ways of resurrecting it. But the ruined city still harbors deadly obstacles—and one precious prize.

SITUATION 10: Pilgrims trek across an expanse of Judaean desert where a young nomad experienced a vision of Christ. But as they approach the alleged site, they experience a vision that seems more diabolical than heavenly.

CATEGORY 4: JOURNEY TO A FORGOTTEN OR NEGLECTED PLACE

> Many journeys are therapeutic: to relive an experience, to exorcise a demon, to rekindle a lost love. Such stories are often suspenseful because obstacles both expected and unexpected must be overcome. It's tough for your characters, enjoyable for your readers!

SITUATION 1: Neglected for decades after a chemical-plant accident, this city lies dormant. An engineer, whose roots stem from this city, places his entire personal fortune on the line to save it. But first he must risk his life by going there to assess the damage and design a restoration plan.

SITUATION 2: When a middle-aged woman is reminded of a particular place from childhood, she becomes dizzy or disoriented or has a panic attack. With the help of a therapist, she finally manages to come face-to-face with the traumatic event that occurred there.

SITUATION 3: A legendary city long ago fell into neglect and the narrator wants to learn why. She and her team venture through a jungle to reach the city. When they arrive, they find that the main road has recently been barricaded. Obstacles become more complicated after they pass the barricade.

SITUATION 4: Explorers visit the remnants of a villa that has been submerged in the Aegean for millennia. The underwater investigation is treacherous because of unstable slabs of stone. But the risk is worth taking because clues suggest that a profound secret lurks within.

SITUATION 5: Scientists journey to the middle of a desert where, according to satellite infrared-detection methods, a long-lost city is buried. But as the scientists excavate, they encounter several warnings that the city must not be disturbed under any circumstances.

SITUATION 6: Some horrific disease has affected the inhabitants of a desert outpost, yet the residents will not allow anyone to come to their aid. A physician figures out a way to penetrate their defenses and find out what happened.

SITUATION 7: Decades after lunar colonists cut themselves off from Earth, envoys journey to the moon to investigate. They discover that the colonists have radically changed, both physically and psychologically.

SITUATION 8: Missionaries journey to a leper colony years after it had been deemed a forbidden zone by the king. Instead of finding lepers, however, the missionaries find a strangely altered race of beings, and they are hostile to outsiders.

SITUATION 9: Explorers undertake a treacherous journey through the Andes in search of a city that is mentioned only in legends. But the team leader is convinced the city exists because she uncovered telling artifacts nearby. In the meantime, local residents refuse to welcome her investigations.

SITUATION 10: In the not-so-distant future rising sea levels resulting in widespread flooding have forced residents to abandon several coastal cities. The protagonist ventures into what is left (on dry land) of San Diego to find a way to save a secret research facility from disaster.

CATEGORY 5: JOURNEY TO A MAGICAL PLACE

Magic can be a trick or illusion—in which case it isn't really magic; and if it is really magic, it can't be reality, since reality and magic are opposites. A journey to a magical place, then, would be a journey outside the real world. However, magic sometimes infiltrates reality, leading to a type of fiction called magical realism.

SITUATION 1: After finding a magical city in a dream, the narrator is unable to shake off the sense that the magic city really exists. Using clues from things the guide in her dream had said to her, she locates him—an old man in a rest home. He gives her the information she needs to journey to the city in waking life.

SITUATION 2: The White Rabbit (from *Alice's Adventures in Wonderland*) materializes in a boy's bedroom and invites him to accompany him on a journey to a little-known place in Wonderland—a place where things move backwards, including time itself.

SITUATION 3: A social outcast journeys to a fabled kingdom where, according to legend, a remote ancestor of his had been in service to the throne. There, in the ruined castle, the ghost of his ancestor appears and whisks him back in time to save the kingdom from invaders.

SITUATION 4: Passersby report strange goings-on in an abandoned hotel. Detectives decide to check out the place, wondering if the hotel is being used as a hideout. They discover instead an entrance to a magical world, which they decide to investigate.

SITUATION 5: Teenagers escape from a juvenile correctional facility to visit a circus—but it's a bizarre circus indeed, full of dark magic. The teens get involved with the dark magic and become adept at wielding it, which they try to use against their enemies back home.

SITUATION 6: A young woman embarks on a pilgrimage to a land where, according to testimony passed down from her ancestors, magic exists, but when she arrives at the alleged site, it is no longer the magic place.

SITUATION 7: A brother and sister enter an amusement park attraction that had been shut down. They get inside a rail car that whisks them to a haunted palace. When they try to leave, they discover to their horror that all the doors are locked.

SITUATION 8: While an eight-year-old boy is playing with his toy soldiers, one of them comes to life and leads him to a magical kingdom in which the childless king has been desperately searching for an heir. When he meets the boy, the king proclaims him to be his successor.

SITUATION 9: The March Hare and the Mad Hatter have been kicked out of Wonderland. The two of them journey across the dreary (to them) real world in search of another magical realm. About to abandon hope, they encounter a magician who can help them get where they want to go.

SITUATION 10: Two siblings find a map that gives directions to a hidden tunnel leading to (the map claims) a magical place. After finding the tunnel, they decide to see for themselves where it goes. After a long journey, they find the magical place, but the magic there is not what they expected.

CATEGORY 6: JOURNEY IN SEARCH OF ONE'S DESTINY

Although we often long for a glimpse of what the future holds, we also dread looking ahead. We regard our destiny as unknowable one moment, and then we make a strong effort to shape it the next. The following story situations draw from both impulses.

SITUATION 1: After a brother and sister escape from the orphanage where they've been living unhappily, they stumble upon information regarding their parents, who were supposedly dead—but not according to one of the documents.

SITUATION 2: An adopted child wonders why her birth parents had given her up for adoption. The deeper she probes, the greater the mystery becomes—there's some indication that one or both of her birth parents were criminals. The closer she gets to solving the mystery, the more resistance she encounters.

SITUATION 3: A pauper stumbles upon clues that her father was of royal blood and had been exiled. After gathering sufficient evidence to demand restitution from the crown, she is threatened with her life.

SITUATION 4: When an amusement park fortune-teller tells the protagonist to travel to a city she's never visited before, she searches for clues about how the city may be related to her past but she cannot find any. Finally, she visits the city and discovers a dark secret about her family.

SITUATION 5: According to family lore, the narrator's grandfather died in a tractor accident, but when she visits her ancestral farm (still owned by an uncle), something feels off. She decides to dig deeper (since she has training in forensic investigation), and the death begins to look like foul play.

SITUATION 6: Desiring to know if his preparations for success will bear fruit, an inventor uses his latest machine to journey ten years into the future. Disappointed by what he sees, he returns to undo everything—but is restrained by one who had ventured into the future for the same reason.

SITUATION 7: Attempting to escape what many consider to be his inescapable destiny as the inheritor of his father's business, a young man dissatisfied with his life visits sacred sites around the world in search of his soul.

SITUATION 8: Before tying the knot, the overcautious groom-to-be journeys five years into the future to see if it will be a happy marriage. But when he discovers

196

that certain things he wanted to happen did not occur, he returns to the present to confront his fiancée about certain demands—hers as well as his.

SITUATION 9: While she is asleep, an inventor is transported by an angel into the future and shown the social impact her invention of a habit-forming virtual reality program will trigger. When she awakens, she decides to destroy her invention—but someone has stolen it.

SITUATION 10: Refusing to believe that biology is destiny, the daughter of schizophrenic parents journeys far and wide to meet with psychologists and geneticists, and anyone else who can prevent her from falling into the prison of severe mental illness.

CATEGORY 7: JOURNEY TO A THIRD-WORLD COUNTRY

Many nations have large populations that exist below the poverty line. And while there are organizations that work hard to alleviate poverty, there never seem to be enough of them. Volunteers are always needed. Stories about such widespread human suffering can do a lot to raise awareness and encourage volunteerism.

SITUATION 1: In this alternate universe, the United States is a third-world country and Mexico is a prosperous nation that has set up extreme border-security measures to prevent illegal Americans from sneaking into Mexico. But many still attempt to cross.

SITUATION 2: A small overlooked nation slips into poverty when the product of their principal export runs out. A loyal citizen seeks a way to resuscitate their economy and save what is left of an idyllic society.

SITUATION 3: In an effort to put an end to an African nation's famine, the leader of a food drive persuades farmers around the world to donate grain shipments. In order for the grain to get through, however, a passage that avoids militants (who want to eradicate the starving people) must be found.

SITUATION 4: An artisan creates objects both beautiful and functional in an effort to persuade the occupiers of her people's land to accept them instead of grain and livestock. After the occupiers refuse and force her into slavery, her brother risks his life by journeying to the capital to rescue her and finds an underground movement enthralled by her works already planning a rescue.

SITUATION 5: Human-rights workers journey to a war-torn country to rescue its inhabitants from militants. But the inhabitants, despite their lack of freedom, side with the militants and resist the workers.

SITUATION 6: When two students learn about children starving in Sudan, they travel there to volunteer with rescue efforts—but instead get entangled in the political instability that has led to the impoverishment.

SITUATION 7: A reclusive tribe of Amazonian natives needs rescuing in spite of themselves; several of them are suffering from a deadly virus. A missionary worker and her team venture into this forbidden segment of the Amazonian rain forest with medications—but the healthy natives warn them to stay away.

SITUATION 8: When a tyrannical regime takes over an already impoverished country, the ethnic and political minorities there are cut off from government aid and protection. It is feared that the minorities will next be ghettoized and systematically executed or used for menial labor until they die. A charismatic fighter for human rights gathers a group to help free these people, but mob mentality has already taken a strong foothold.

SITUATION 9: The narrator's girlfriend breaks off their relationship and returns to her home country, preferring her impoverished land and its people over America and Americans. The narrator follows her, determined to bring her back, but when he gets there, he undergoes a transformative experience.

SITUATION 10: Several teachers journey into a third-world country to strengthen its schools—specifically to implement a "fast-track-to-self-sufficiency" core curriculum that will help the young people find jobs. But the country's officials are resistant and accuse the teachers of subversion.

CATEGORY 8: JOURNEY INTO THE PAST OR FUTURE

> Journeying into the past to change terrible events slated to happen or into the future to escape terrible events is a popular plotline in fiction. Whether or not it's actually possible does not deter writers from brewing up exciting stories like these.

SITUATION 1: A sociologist travels fifty years into the future to get some idea of where humanity is heading. Trends she hoped would evolve have not and vice versa. She must return to the present to prevent ominous trends from flourishing.

198

SITUATION 2: The protagonist is a medical researcher who feels she is on the verge of finding a cure for one of the deadliest diseases. She finds a way to travel fifty years into the future to learn the procedure. But when she returns to her own time to apply the procedure, it backfires.

SITUATION 3: A theologian journeys to Galileo's trial for heresy (1633, Rome) to convince the Inquisition that their arguments are fallacious, but they wind up trying him for heresy too.

SITUATION 4: Bent on wreaking havoc with U.S. history, a criminal mastermind hauls an arsenal of high-tech weapons back to the Revolutionary War, intending to instruct the British how to use them. A time detective goes after him.

SITUATION 5: A hitherto undisclosed talent of the goddess Aphrodite is that she can travel through human history and wield her power (and charms) in any age. Prometheus steals that secret ability from her and offers it to a mortal ... for a price. The mortal pretends to consider the offer and then schemes to steal the secret from Prometheus.

SITUATION 6: In this world, suspended animation is a reality, and the narrator opts to sleep for fifty years—until a time when her doctors are confident that a cure for her terminal illness will have been discovered. But because of some mix-up, she is not revived for five hundred years, by which time society has an unfavorable view of longevity.

SITUATION 7: Time travelers journey into a distant future where time travel is forbidden, but when they try to escape, they are seized by a group of outlaws who want to use the time machine for ignoble purposes.

SITUATION 8: Severely lacking in self-confidence, the focal character repeatedly takes short journeys through time (now that such technology is possible) to check on the consequences of his actions. Ironically, his confidence only deteriorates with each successive journey.

SITUATION 9: The inventor of the first time-travel machine, sensing that journeys to witness major historical events will become a lucrative business, takes people into the past or the future ... for a heavy price. But things go terribly wrong when criminals hijack her machine.

SITUATION 10: Dissatisfied with her family's loss of good fortune (financially and otherwise), the eldest daughter travels back a century to prevent her ancestors from making bad investments. As a result of her intervention, her family becomes involved with organized crime.

CATEGORY 9: PILGRIMAGE TO A SACRED OR PAGAN SITE

A sacred place can range from the conventionally religious to anything that lifts the spirit, including pagan sites (modern day as well as ancient). Ever the wellspring of horror tales, paganism continues to enthrall readers. Perhaps one or more of the following situations will spark your creative imagination.

SITUATION 1: Young followers of a Druid cult go on a pilgrimage to Stonehenge. While on the Salisbury Plain, two of the followers come under the spell of Druid spirits and start speaking in a strange language. One of the others translates some of their utterances, something about ghouls rising from the earth.

SITUATION 2: Not the least concerned about voodoo practices, adventurous (and mischievous) youths visit a site in Louisiana that's notorious for voodoo rituals. Alas, after getting into an altercation with a voodoo priestess, the youths discover that they are cursed.

SITUATION 3: An atheist visiting a European cathedral experiences a spiritual epiphany. She chalks it up to the church's architectural splendor, but then she has a vision as she stands before the altar. Still unable to accept supernatural events, she consults a therapist—but the spiritual experiences continue.

SITUATION 4: Entranced by Aphrodite, goddess of love, a young pagan woman embarks on a pilgrimage to her shrines in Greece. One shrine in particular has a transformative effect, convincing the young pagan that the love goddess is not only real but living on one of the Greek islands in the Mediterranean.

SITUATION 5: Despite her skepticism, the protagonist journeys to Lourdes (the holy site where the Virgin Mary once appeared to St. Benedict) to pray for her cancer to go into remission. But while there, she encounters many whose suffering is greater than her own and prays for them instead.

SITUATION 6: A pilgrim journeys to the shrine of Athena to ask for the goddess's protection when he returns to the kingdom from which he'd been exiled. But before Athena agrees, he must perform a series of difficult tasks for her.

SITUATION 7: Feeling that she is losing her faith, a woman who's suffered a string of misfortunes goes on a pilgrimage to the Holy Land. There, on the Via Dolorosa (the path Jesus took on the way to his crucifixion), she experiences a vision that rekindles her faith; she also learns that there is a task she must fulfill.

SITUATION 8: Archaeologists uncover a shrine dedicated to a lost pagan deity. Engraved on some of the artifacts are symbols that suggest a connection to a sinister force. As the archaeologists explore further, they fear that somehow they may have unleashed the sinister force.

SITUATION 9: After discovering a map to what could be an ancient citadel, the protagonist and her team journey to the site, where they discover artifacts of great and controversial religious significance. They also discover that they're not alone in this quest.

SITUATION 10: When Homer enthusiasts follow Odysseus's journey through the Greek Isles, they are visited by a goddess who was never mentioned in *The Odyssey*. This goddess demands that her temple, buried on one of the islands, be excavated and refurbished ... or else.

CATEGORY 10: PILGRIMAGE TO A WAR-RELATED SITE

> Whether it is Pearl Harbor or Gettysburg, or a far-older battleground, the memories of bloody battles often become memorialized. Still, others have been virtually forgotten. In any event, stories abound in these special places.

SITUATION 1: A veteran visits Omaha Beach, not just for a D-Day anniversary memorial but for a much more personal reason—to reconcile himself to a combat error he'd made on that fateful day. While there, he encounters the ghosts from that bloody battle.

SITUATION 2: Enthralled by Homer's *Odyssey*, a classical scholar journeys to region in Turkey reputed to be the site of the Trojan War. As she examines the artifacts associated with that legendary battle, she is transported back to the seventh century BCE, into the midst of battle.

SITUATION 3: While visiting the Pearl Harbor Memorial, the protagonist establishes a psychic link with her grandfather, who was killed on the day the Japanese attacked. He wants to share a terrible secret with her, hoping that doing so will give him the eternal peace he craves.

SITUATION 4: The widow of a soldier killed in Afghanistan visits the place where her husband had struck a land mine. While in the region, she assembles a team of demolition experts to develop sophisticated land-mine detectors. Meanwhile the enemy plants land mines that evade detection.

SITUATION 5: The descendent of a Civil-War soldier visits the battleground where his ancestor had fallen. Intent on writing a biography of the soldier, she stumbles upon an undisclosed fact about the battle and her ancestor's role in it.

SITUATION 6: A Vietnam veteran thinks he can alleviate his combat-related nightmares by revisiting combat sites there. But while there, he encounters villagers who remind him of the reason for his nightmares.

SITUATION 7: For his memoir, a writer needs to remember a suppressed traumatic moment experienced during his combat mission in the Middle East. He returns to the site in the hope of remembering an event too terrible to contemplate. Instead he is swept up in a new military operation there.

SITUATION 8: While researching the causes of recent Arab-Israeli conflicts, a reporter becomes involved in underground efforts to establish a lasting peace. At the same time, she runs into a group planning to sabotage any future peace programs.

SITUATION 9: A war correspondent returns to a war zone where she had risked her life reporting combat as it occurred. Her goal is to purge traumatic moments that have given her nightmares for years. But what she learns on this pilgrimage traumatizes her further.

SITUATION 10: While visiting the 1890 Wounded Knee (South Dakota) massacre, a young Sioux has a vision of his warrior ancestors. They want him to continue the fight for Indian rights in a very specific way.

CHAPTER 14

LOVE BETWEEN
X AND Y

CATEGORY 1: FORBIDDEN LOVE

Forbidden is an enticing word when it comes to romantic fiction. It implies the kind of conflict that is generated when romantic impulses confront long standing social customs or family values. Stories of forbidden love often probe these traditions for both their strengths and their flaws.

SITUATION 1: The hero is a sorcerer in love with a princess, but her father, the King, exiles him because of his illegal practice of dark sorcery. No matter how the sorcerer pleads for a second chance, the King will not change his mind. But then the sorcerer has a dangerous idea that could make the King reconsider.

SITUATION 2: Despite the growing public acceptance of homosexuals, a gay college freshman is convinced that his father will no longer finance his education if he comes out. But he comes out anyway, which causes a rift between father and mother, as well as father and son.

SITUATION 3: A dance instructor falls in love with one of her students, despite her promise to herself never to let that happen. The student's infatuation with her complicates the problem. She worries that breaking off the relationship would not just undermine his dance skills but also cause him to harm himself.

SITUATION 4: When a social worker finds herself attracted to a parolee, she asks to be taken off the case, but the parolee continues to pursue her, insisting that she is his only motive for staying out of trouble.

SITUATION 5: Finding herself attracted to her best friend's fiancé, a career woman cuts off her friendship with both of them rather than risk the consequences. But the friend demands to know the reason for the rift. Moreover, the friend's fiancé suspects the reason.

SITUATION 6: Everything seems harmonious about this superstitious woman's love affair, but she insists that before the relationship can continue, an astrologer must sanction it with a detailed horoscope. Her boyfriend refuses, insisting that horoscopes are bunk.

SITUATION 7: A long-standing prophecy forbids a prince or anyone else in the kingdom from marrying someone from the rival kingdom on the other side of the mountains. But when the prince encounters a woman exiled from that other kingdom, he falls in love with her.

SITUATION 8: Though her parents forbid her to marry outside her social class (threatening to deny her an inheritance), the protagonist chooses to forfeit financial security to marry a charming, handsome laborer. She believes that she can inspire him to fulfill his dream of owning his own business, but when his dream fails, she has second thoughts about their marriage.

SITUATION 9: The heroine's Asian parents do not want their daughter marrying her Anglo fiancé. The daughter insists that if her parents get to know her fiancé better, they will change their minds about him, but they refuse.

SITUATION 10: In this distant-future scenario, a law is passed to prohibit humans from continuing to interbreed with humanoid aliens—a method of preventing Homo sapiens from going extinct. The law has triggered an outcry of species racism. The counter-argument is that interbreeding with the aliens is the only way to ensure survival.

CATEGORY 2: LOVE BETWEEN MORTALS AND IMMORTALS

Mythology and fairy tales are filled with stories of ordinary mortals falling in love with supernatural beings and vice versa. Such tales might be regarded as metaphors for the enchantment that can infuse any love relationship. The following scenarios should help you compose a modern-day romantic fantasy.

SITUATION 1: A guardian angel falls in love with the mortal he was assigned to protect. Warned by an archangel to end the romance at once or lose his immortality and angelic powers, he opts for the former—but soon realizes he can no longer perform his angelic duties without his love.

SITUATION 2: When a centaur falls in love with a mortal woman, he asks Zeus to change him into a human. Zeus agrees to grant him the wish, provided he allows the woman he loves to become Zeus's paramour.

SITUATION 3: Horrific and deadly as Medusa is, she still has the capacity to fall in love, but everyone she falls in love with turns to stone. When she begs Minerva (who punished her) to exempt her new potential lover from the same fate, Minerva refuses ... but then changes her mind when she sees Medusa's new object of affection.

SITUATION 4: Dido, Queen of Carthage, falls in love with Aeneas, the Trojan War hero compelled by Zeus to fulfill his destiny as the founder of Rome. Virgil never recorded this, but Aeneas is willing to forsake his destiny for Dido. Zeus, however, intends to sabotage this affair.

SITUATION 5: An Argonaut is mesmerized by a Siren's singing and jumps overboard, but instead of drowning, the singing Siren rescues him, takes him to her island home, and falls in love with him. His fellow Argonauts try to rescue him, but he refuses to leave his new home.

SITUATION 6: A wood nymph is punished for falling in love with a sea god, whom nymphs generally fear. But this sea god is gentle (even though he possesses great power). He will have to prove his civility to her people, or he will never be allowed to see the wood nymph again.

SITUATION 7: Imagine that Sisyphus (who, for his wanton ways, was condemned by Zeus to roll a rock up a hill in the Underworld throughout eternity) becomes a goddess's object of affection. Despite her efforts to persuade Zeus to release Sisyphus from such cruel punishment, Zeus refuses. But then the goddess makes Zeus a tempting offer.

SITUATION 8: In the ancient story of Echo and Narcissus, Narcissus is cursed to fall in love with the first person he sees—himself, reflected in a pool. For this retelling, Narcissus is a playboy who expects women to fall all over him, and they do. But he meets a reporter disguised as a socialite, and she aims to give narcissists a taste of their own medicine. Alas, she falls for him, too.

SITUATION 9: A modern-day pagan expresses her love for Eros (Cupid) who, like most of the Olympian deities, gets involved in human affairs. Apollo and the protagonist carry out their love affair, which infuriates Eros's mother, Aphrodite (Venus).

SITUATION 10: A goddess falls in love with a prince, but immortals are forbidden to make love to mortals. However, when the prince discovers the goddess watching him, he pursues her, and soon finds himself pleading with Zeus to let them consummate their love.

CATEGORY 3: LOVE BETWEEN PERFORMER AND DIRECTOR (OR ANOTHER PERFORMER)

Romantic attraction can be powerful, even among the most disciplined people who highly value professional and ethical standards. Stage and film professionals may be more challenged, considering the role-playing they engage in. Plenty of opportunities for intriguing love stories are found here.

SITUATION 1: During a production of *Romeo and Juliet*, in which the Montagues are played by African Americans and the Capulets are played by Anglos, the eponymous heroes not only fall in love in character but offstage as well. The situation causes animosity between their parents—thereby paralleling the play.

SITUATION 2: The director of the play uses her manipulative powers to make the protagonist, an actor in her play, leave his love interest and fall in love with her. The harder he tries to break free of the director's grip, the more helpless he becomes.

SITUATION 3: During orchestral tryouts, a violinist enchants the conductor to such a degree that the latter becomes hypnotized by her playing and falls in love with her. The only problem is that the violinist is married.

SITUATION 4: While rehearsing together, a harpist and a bassoonist fall in love. They develop a way to communicate their intimate thoughts through their instruments. Unfortunately a jealous rival performer finds a way to sabotage their musical communications.

SITUATION 5: A diva and her onstage lover begin an offstage romance that at first parallels the progress of the romance in the opera—but then takes a very different turn. When it does, it affects their performance onstage. The director must figure out a way to get them back on track.

SITUATION 6: A circus aerialist falls in love with a fellow aerialist, but then their relationship sours. Now they are faced with the task of repressing their animosities during death-defying acrobatic acts.

SITUATION 7: When a conductor discovers that her first and second violinists are falling in love, she gives them an ultimatum: End or suspend the romance or leave the orchestra. But without the relationship, neither performer can play as well.

SITUATION 8: So fully into portraying a witch in a horror film, an actress discovers she cannot break out of character—a problem that undermines her budding romance with the film's director. To preserve their romance, the director implores the scriptwriter to revise the witch's part, but the writer is also in love with the actress.

SITUATION 9: Two stand-up comedians, bitter rivals, begin to admire each other's routines, and this leads to romantic feelings. But the stronger those feelings become, the less edgy their routines become.

SITUATION 10: Forced to perform silly tricks, two circus dogs fall in love and plot to escape from their trainer. Before the trainer knows what is happening, the dogs have instigated a circus-wide revolt.

CATEGORY 4: LOVE ACROSS CLASSES, CULTURES, ETHNICITIES, RELIGIONS

Love animates the world, including the world of story. Love elements are important to stories even when they're not "love stories" per se. In the following situations, love is both the generator and the resolver (although not always happily) of conflict.

SITUATION 1: When he becomes attracted to a Muslim woman in Morocco, a Mormon missionary tries to convert her to his faith, and she attempts the same with him. Their debates over religion become as heated as their growing romance, despite their mutual effort to keep romance at bay until the religious issues are resolved.

SITUATION 2: An atheist falls in love with a man of faith, who will not marry her unless she converts—mainly for his parents' sake. At first she agrees, hoping the issue will fade into the background once they're married, but then he insists they must teach their children to be believers as well and she begins to doubt her desire to marry him.

SITUATION 3: When a Western news correspondent asks the parents of his Afghan sweetheart for her hand in marriage, they say they will consent only if he converts and adheres to the strictures.

SITUATION 4: A Peace-Corps worker in Africa falls in love with a woman he had been trying to nurse back to health. Together they face animosity from the woman's family, especially from her father.

SITUATION 5: While visiting an Indian reservation, a social worker meets a Native-American activist filled with bitterness toward Anglos. But the social worker gradually wins the activist's trust—and, ultimately, his heart—as they collaborate on improving conditions.

SITUATION 6: To win his girlfriend's parents' approval, the protagonist must submit to a series of culturally specific "tests," such as eating (and enjoying) certain foods and rituals. He does his best to "pass" the tests—but ultimately fails one of them.

SITUATION 7: During the Civil War, a Union soldier falls in love with the daughter of a plantation owner. She secretly harbors abolitionist views but vowed always to uphold her family traditions. Nonetheless, when her father learns of the romance, he is determined to end it.

SITUATION 8: Although he received a huge inheritance, the once-poor protagonist continues to give the impression that he is poor because he does not want his girlfriend to commit to him for the wrong reason. But she learns the truth from a friend and accuses him of deception.

SITUATION 9: Steeped in ancient Egyptian rituals, a modern-day pagan falls in love with a man who convinces her that he is the avatar of Osiris, and she—the modern pagan—the avatar of Isis. However, she begins to suspect that the man is a con artist.

SITUATION 10: A veteran suffering from post-traumatic-stress disorder (PTSD) falls in love with the therapist who cares for him. At the same time, the therapist reminds him of a civilian woman who protected him after an injury behind enemy lines.

CATEGORY 5: LOVE BETWEEN DOCTORS, OTHER HEALTH-CARE PROVIDERS, AND PATIENTS

It's called the Florence Nightingale effect, whereby a physician or nurse (or any other health-care worker) develops romantic feelings for a patient. Such situations can develop into thorny predicaments in which the need to maintain professional distance is pitted against the power of love. In other words, great story possibilities!

SITUATION 1: Like most physicians, the protagonist strives to maintain a professional distance between his patients and himself—and he has been successful for many years. But the woman now in his care has an overwhelming effect on him, and he is not quite sure how to deal with it.

SITUATION 2: A schizophrenic patient falls in love with his psychiatrist, but she skillfully discourages the affection from developing ... until, inexplicably, she finds herself falling for him—or more precisely, for one side of her patient's personality.

SITUATION 3: Two patients in a state mental hospital fall in love, even though their respective emotional disorders prevent their relationship from evolving. One of the nurses in the facility seeks to end the relationship entirely, while another nurse tries to preserve it.

SITUATION 4: A woman who was severely disfigured in an accident falls in love with her plastic surgeon, but when he fails to reconstruct her face to his satisfaction, he does all he can to nix the romance.

SITUATION 5: When a celebrity patient is admitted, three nurses vie for his affection, but the celebrity is more interested in winning the heart of a candy-striper volunteer, who is at least twenty years younger than he is.

SITUATION 6: An army medic suppresses her attraction for one of the soldiers wounded in her platoon, assuming romance is incompatible with combat. Ironically, the harder she tries to suppress her feelings, the more they interfere with her duties.

SITUATION 7: When a comatose patient comes under her care, a neurologist searches for new ways to bring him out, as established ways have failed. Her efforts lead her to fall in love with him.

SITUATION 8: Fearing that he is going blind, an artist puts himself under the care of an ophthalmologist, who suspects that the artist's vision problems are partly psychological. Her unconventional treatments lead to a romance that threatens her objectivity.

SITUATION 9: A nurse in an assisted-living community discovers that she has rejuvenating powers. Her ministrations actually make the elderly patients younger. One octogenarian in particular not only grows younger under the nurse's care; he falls in love with her as well.

SITUATION 10: Once abused by men, a massage therapist struggles with negative emotions when giving massages to male customers—especially when she finds herself attracted to one of them, against her will.

CATEGORY 6: LOVE BETWEEN FRIENDS, RIVALS, AND ENEMIES

> Friendship between the sexes can sometimes be as much of a barrier to romance as rivalry or enmity, but human relationships are complex and what may seem to be mutually exclusive states can prove to be more compatible than anyone realizes. Each of the following scenarios should help you shape a love-rivalry story of your own.

SITUATION 1: Trained to be a spy, a princess successfully infiltrates an enemy kingdom. Everything goes as planned, but then she encounters the enemy prince and, while spying on his activities, falls in love with him.

SITUATION 2: The narrator falls in love with a woman whose father had once mistreated the narrator's mother. When his mother learns of her son's romance, she demands that he break it off at once, but he cannot bring himself to do that. She then resorts to drastic measures.

SITUATION 3: A journalist from an enemy nation is attracted to the daughter of a politician known for his hawkish views. When he discovers the relationship, the politician schemes to have the journalist arrested on a fabricated charge.

SITUATION 4: Love or money? After thinking she has found the ideal man, the focal character learns that her ex-boyfriend has sold his startup company for a staggering amount of money and he wants her back.

SITUATION 5: No male can resist her charms—which is why the daughter of the emperor's physician is ordered to woo an enemy prince ... and in so doing steal a precious secret that he has been guarding.

SITUATION 6: Although they are fierce rivals on the tennis courts, the up-and-coming narrator finds herself powerfully attracted to a champion she wants to defeat at all costs. The rival, knowing this, uses her charms to undermine her game.

SITUATION 7: Love on the slopes: Competing skiers struggle to keep their rivalry from giving way to a romantic attraction. As they find themselves competing for the top prize, they overcompensate and suffer serious mishaps.

SITUATION 8: An assistant professor of anthropology studying the remains of Native Americans in an ancient burial site falls in love with a Native-American woman. She believes that removing the bones for scientific study is sacrilege, but unless the assistant professor completes his proposed study of the bones, he could be denied tenure.

SITUATION 9: Despite his precautions, a detective falls in love with the loyal daughter of a Mafia boss. Even though he's convinced she is pretending to love him in order to manipulate him, he cannot bring himself to break off the affair.

SITUATION 10: A hunter and firearms enthusiast confronts a supporter of gun-law reform. No matter how heated their debates, they become romantically involved, and as their relationship evolves, so do their views regarding their respective positions on gun control.

CATEGORY 7: LOVE MIX-UPS, FOUL-UPS, AND MISSED OPPORTUNITIES

> Literature is filled with cases of mistaken identity in romantic contexts. Such tales can be serious or lighthearted, realistic or whimsical; regardless, they quite often mirror romantic situations most of us have experienced at one time or another.

SITUATION 1: During a costume party, the narrator flirts with a strange woman dressed in a costume that makes him believe she is his fiancée. When she unmasks, he apologizes profusely. But it's too late: The love arrow has been shot.

SITUATION 2: The protagonist is convinced that the man sitting across from her in a restaurant was her junior high school crush, someone she had dated several years earlier, even though the resemblance is slight. When she introduces herself, he insists she is mistaken and quickly leaves. But she feels certain he's covering up—although she can't figure out why—and follows him.

SITUATION 3: Too shy to establish a relationship with a fellow student whom he fantasizes to be the woman of his dreams (because of their apparent similar academic interests), the narrator laments her relationship with a mutual friend. Finally, he decides to act, but it might be too late.

SITUATION 4: A street magician notices that one of her regular admirers is a young man whose admiration seems to extend beyond her magic. She keeps hoping that he will speak to her, but he never does. Finally, she decides to make the first move, using some of her magic.

SITUATION 5: While deciding whether to begin a romance with another passenger on the cruise ship, the narrator watches his roommate beat him to the punch. He tries to woo her away from his roommate by accusing the roommate of being a dangerous man, but this only angers the woman. It also makes her wonder if he might be telling the truth.

SITUATION 6: The narrator intercepts a love note intended for his twin brother, with whom he recently had a falling-out. When the other brother finds out, he plans revenge.

SITUATION 7: Rather than going next door to meet the neighbor he'd been admiring for months, the reclusive narrator sends her flowers anonymously, but she assumes that the flowers came from the narrator's archrival down the street.

SITUATION 8: The woman with whom the narrator is in love is unhappy with her face. Despite the narrator's insistence that she is beautiful, she undergoes plastic surgery without letting him know. His reaction suggests she made a terrible mistake.

SITUATION 9: Overhearing a young man's lamentations over his failure to kindle a romance with a co-worker, a guardian angel grants the young man a new opportunity to do so—but this time, he will face much greater obstacles.

SITUATION 10: Two traveling carnival workers, male and female, become romantically involved, but a jealous clown, a former lover of one worker, aims to break up the relationship by blackmailing them.

CATEGORY 8: LOVE IN STRANGE OR EXOTIC PLACES

Love stories acquire added flare when played out in an intriguing part of the world, for such settings enhance the romance. Think of the love stories in James Michener's *Tales of the South Pacific*, set in Hawaii, or Emily Brontë's *Wuthering Heights*, set in the haunting Yorkshire Moors.

SITUATION 1: While conducting research in the Arctic, a marine biologist meets an Inuit woman who sees the world through religious eyes only, but as their relationship grows, each takes to the other's way of perceiving the world.

SITUATION 2: The narrator and another rival mountain climber team up with others to scale a dangerous and difficult peak. During the excursion, their rivalry reaches a heated pitch. But then one of them has an accident.

SITUATION 3: On a lush tropical island, a surfer becomes involved with a native woman whose allure is undercut by her uncontrollable desire to bring men to their destruction. Another native islander attempts to intervene.

SITUATION 4: A member of an elite demolition team falls in love with one of his colleagues while searching for undetonated bombs in a combat zone. One argues that his love is true, while the other believes that their dangerous work is what makes their relationship exciting, which means it won't hold up in the real world. After a tense and dangerous incident dealing with an unexploded bunker bomb, they are both sent on leave to recoup, and they attempt a real relationship.

SITUATION 5: Two scuba divers share coral-reef explorations together. During a dive, one of them has an accident, and the other is wrongly blamed for it. Could a malicious rival have been the cause?

SITUATION 6: When a reclusive rare-manuscripts archivist realizes that a scholar is after her heart, she requests and receives a transfer to another part of the library. The scholar manages to learn of her whereabouts—but knows that showing up at her new location would backfire. Instead he plans to secretly help her with her research.

SITUATION 7: Two skydivers become more attracted to each other with each dive. But then, one of them has an accident that leaves her injured, and the other suggests they both quit skydiving for good. The suggestion sours the relationship. She aims to continue skydiving, but only he sees the peril in her decision.

SITUATION 8: Spelunkers wander off the beaten path of a newly discovered cave and get lost. As they try to find their way back, two of them—originally mere acquaintances—become enchanted with each other among the stalactites.

SITUATION 9: Meeting in a temporary shelter during a hurricane evacuation, a middle-aged man and woman explore their shared interests and discover they have only one. But this one thing draws them together romantically.

SITUATION 10: During a cat-show competition, two of the contestants become romantically involved and must find a way to balance their growing affection with their rivalry. But when one of them is disqualified, the other tries to reinstate her, at the risk of disqualifying himself.

CATEGORY 9: LOVE IN THE WORKPLACE

> The professional workplace is often a stage for romance, albeit one that is accompanied by challenges such as maintaining optimal work performance, maintaining a professional demeanor, and/or sidestepping policy that discourages or forbids office romances. In any case, such situations make for compelling stories.

SITUATION 1: Despite the fact that a manager imposed strict regulations against office romances, she herself falls for one of her employees, but instead of admitting it, she tries to cover it up.

SITUATION 2: Worried that resisting her boss's amorous advances would jeopardize her job, an employee pretends to be flattered. But doing so only encourages the boss to become more amorous. Torn between warning him to stop and playing along, she lets co-workers assume she is gay.

SITUATION 3: Junior members competing for a managerial position in the firm, the protagonist and her competitor become romantically involved. Both are equally qualified, but the protagonist has a fiercer competitive spirit, which (her competitor fears) may sabotage both the romance and the possible promotion.

SITUATION 4: Ignoring his lab's anti-harassment policy, a senior researcher becomes infatuated with one of the post-doctorate students he is supervising. When she, in turn, flirts back, things start to get out of hand. She senses that unless she allows the infatuation to advance to the next stage, her research project will be in jeopardy.

SITUATION 5: A corporate executive finds herself attracted to the night janitor because he reminds her of a childhood sweetheart. The more they interact, the likelier it seems that he really is her childhood sweetheart. However, the janitor seems to suddenly develop a deep grudge against her and she isn't sure why.

SITUATION 6: Accused once of sexual harassment, a manager has lost the trust of his employees, especially now that he has fallen for one of them. Assuming it to be another example of harassment, the woman is debating whether to file charges.

SITUATION 7: A police detective becomes infatuated with one of the rookie officers. Worried that their relationship may compromise their job performance, the chief keeps them from working together. When the rookie pursues a robbery suspect and vanishes, the detective drops everything to find her.

SITUATION 8: Two aspiring chefs competing for a master-chef award become romantically involved and channel their affections for each other into the dishes they must prepare. Their romance is challenged, however, when the final competition comes down to just the two of them.

SITUATION 9: Even though he was prudent in conveying his affection for an office co-worker, the co-worker accuses him of harassing her. As a result, he avoids her, and she eventually realizes that she had been unfair.

SITUATION 10: When a closeted gay employee makes advances toward a co-worker, the manager tries to blackmail him: "Unless you do such-and-such, I will expose you." But the employee counter-blackmails when he finds out that the boss's mistress is the CEO's daughter.

CATEGORY 10: YOUNG LOVE

Love can affect even the very young, and when it does, the emotions can go just as haywire as adult love. Sometimes young love can be dismissed as mere infatuation or puppy love, but sometimes it can be quite mature.

SITUATION 1: Convinced they are in love and not merely infatuated with each other, two fifteen-year olds engage in extraordinary acts of maturity to impress their doubtful parents. But one of the parents will not allow the relationship to continue because of its apparent seriousness.

SITUATION 2: A couple below the legal age for marriage heads for Nevada with fake IDs. While waiting their turn at one of the wedding chapels, they become dismayed by the kitsch and the fakery and decide to delay their nuptials so they can think things over.

SITUATION 3: Despite his vowing to marry her when she tells him she's pregnant, the narrator's boyfriend panics and disappears. When the baby is due, he resurfaces—but she has become engaged to someone else. Distraught, he searches for a way to win back her love and trust.

SITUATION 4: A high-school senior falls in love with one of his teachers twice his age. At the same time, the teacher is recovering from a disastrous marriage and is vulnerable to the teen's kindness and maturity. But the teen's parents scheme to sabotage the relationship.

SITUATION 5: Jealous that one of his favored teenage mortals has fallen in love with another young mortal, Zeus turns them both into snakes—but their love continues. Moreover, they win the favor of Hades, who gives them the power to return to human form for one month out of the year. Hades urges them to exact vengeance on Zeus during that time, but they have other ideas.

SITUATION 5: Two teens from an underprivileged neighborhood fall in love, despite the hardships they endure. They work together to overcome those hardships and the meddling of neighbors and friends who want to sabotage their relationship.

SITUATION 6: Shocked by the realization that they are both gay and attracted to each other, the narrator and her college roommate decide not to share their feelings with friends. One of the friends finds out anyway and instigates trouble for the pair.

SITUATION 7: When a teen is arrested for shoplifting, his girlfriend is urged to break off the relationship, but she wants to give him another chance. After his second arrest, she breaks off the relationship, but then he does something extraordinary to win her back.

SITUATION 8: A shy adolescent becomes infatuated with a librarian who's engaged to an abusive man. After he encounters the two of them quarreling in a restaurant, he lifts her spirit by thanking her for recommending a book. He mistakes her delighted response for romantic affection.

SITUATION 9: Two high-school students fall for the same girl, for very different reasons. One does so because of her love of science, the other only because she seems like an easy "conquest." Despite her high intelligence, the girl finds herself attracted to the latter because of his self-confidence.

SITUATION 10: Despite his efforts to discourage a teenager's infatuation with him, the narrator, who is in his thirties, is accused of instigating the infatuation. Nothing he can say or do persuades the girl's parents otherwise.

CHAPTER 15

THE MYSTERY OF X

CATEGORY 1: MYSTERIOUS BOOKS, PACKAGES, AND DOCUMENTS

Many a gripping mystery centers on a book or document in which clues are hidden, sometimes very cleverly, and require a combination of creative and analytical thinking to decode them. The following story situations will give you a sense of the possibilities for mystery-making via handwritten or published materials.

SITUATION 1: After her father disappears, the protagonist opens his safe, hoping to find clues relating to his disappearance, but all she finds is a single sheet of paper, on which is written a number that is clearly the combination to another safe.

SITUATION 2: A CIA employee receives a letter written in code. Unable to decipher it, he seeks the expertise of cryptographers one of whom thinks she can break the code. After partially decoding the letter, she realizes that it conveys information about a military coup being planned.

SITUATION 3: An unaddressed package appears outside the narrator's front door. Against her better judgment, she opens it and finds nothing but wadded newspaper inside. Her boyfriend (an amateur sleuth) suggests that some of the words on the wadded newspaper, those underlined in pencil, contain a hidden message.

SITUATION 4: While searching through old books at an estate sale, a history teacher finds what appears to be a codex (a medieval manuscript book) of a lost play by Sophocles. But when she sets it aside while continuing to browse the items for sale, someone runs off with the codex. The teacher catches only a fleeting glance of the thief.

SITUATION 5: A down-and-out veteran receives a conciliatory letter from his fiancée ten years after she broke off the engagement because of his mental disorder. But during those intervening years, the veteran has endured a series of misfortunes and has become an alcoholic. He contacts her to tell her this and to assure her that he has been successfully treated by a psychiatrist—which is not entirely true.

SITUATION 6: When a book collector discovers a cryptic message scrawled in the margin of a holy book, she takes it to a cryptographer, who thinks the message is part of a set of instructions for locating a mythical weapons arsenal.

SITUATION 7: A historian discovers a letter written by a political leader during World War II that may change the way a particular battle has been interpreted. Despite efforts to safeguard the letter, someone manages to leak its contents, triggering a political backlash and halting the announcement for a new joint memorial planned between two nations often at odds with one another.

SITUATION 8: Despite her father's plea not to publish her exposé about his CIA experiences, an ambitious writer proceeds with her publication plans. Now the father threatens to even the score by divulging a secret his daughter would not want revealed—unless she withdraws her book from publication.

SITUATION 9: A special book, one in which prophecies appear only to readers voicing the proper incantation, vanishes from its magical universe. Clues uncovered by the book's guardian lead to our universe—more specifically, to a university where the book may have been hidden.

SITUATION 10: The viewpoint character receives a land deed from her cousin, with the accompanying explanation that his father (the narrator's uncle) willed it to her. But she is suspicious of the deed because she and her uncle had never gotten along.

CATEGORY 2: MYSTERIOUS BURIED OR HIDDEN OBJECTS

The very idea of buried objects conjures up adventure quests from childhood like the search for treasure chests and lost tombs. The adventure intensifies when the object uncovered mystifies or frightens. The following situations can open up numerous story possibilities for you.

SITUATION 1: While planting flowers in his backyard, an ex-con uncovers a tin box filled with gold coins. When he has them appraised, the appraiser, who recognizes the infamous former convict, rushes into the back of his shop to call the police—but the ex-con anticipates this move.

SITUATION 2: A map bequeathed to him by a recently deceased relative directs the protagonist to a series of dead ends: boxes filled with electronic equipment, a pile of auto parts, stashes of old magazines. Was he duped? A friend thinks the junk may hold clues to the real treasure.

SITUATION 3: Inheriting a mystery box from a deceased relative, a woman discovers that it is filled with rare books. She struggles between the need to sell them (she needs the money badly) and the desire to retain them as heirlooms. She begins to sell some and then discovers the books hide a deeper secret.

SITUATION 4: While remodeling her home, the focal character finds a stash of documents written in code that had been hidden under the floorboards. No one can explain their significance until she shows them to a retired military official.

SITUATION 5: Prospectors digging in an abandoned mine discover the vein of an ore they cannot identify. An expert thinks the ore is rich in rare-earth elements—vital for electronics—and demands a share of the take for his assistance. But the expert has no intention of sharing anything with the prospectors.

SITUATION 6: A fifty-year-old time capsule is unearthed and contains clues that could solve several mysteries that have baffled the town, including murders that resemble a current unsolved murder.

SITUATION 7: The purchaser of an antique desk inspects the desk more closely and discovers a hidden compartment containing a document written in an unknown language. An expert thinks the document may hold clues to a long unsolved local mystery involving a missing fortune.

SITUATION 8: Someone has been spying on a chemistry professor who serves as a consultant to the FBI. His home, car, and office have been bugged. Suspecting that the spies are actually thieves who want to steal the strange substance he is researching in connection with a highly secretive investigation, he hires a private detective to find the spies and protect him. But is the detective who he really says he is?

SITUATION 9: This genie, hiding inside an ancient lamp, does not grant wishes. Instead, he can peer into the near future and reveal what he sees, but he can only do this three times before he moves on to a new owner. However, his current owner finds a way to keep the genie's services against his will.

SITUATION 10: Middle-school students digging in a field unearth an alien artifact. Rather than inform their parents or any other adults, they try to determine the object's function on their own—and are overwhelmed by what they discover.

CATEGORY 3: MYSTERIOUS ILLNESSES

> Today's illness-combating and prophylactic drugs are miraculous, especially when compared to their forerunners a couple of generations earlier. Yet medical research is continually challenged by newly discovered and antibiotic-resistant pathogens. Such challenges, while frustrating, serve as solid foundations for stories.

SITUATION 1: During a Mediterranean cruise, passengers begin falling ill—first with headaches, then with fever and disorientation. The ship's physician suspects contaminated food, but he can't find any evidence of it. And then some of the passengers start behaving very strangely.

SITUATION 2: Vacationers staying at a tropical island resort begin to exhibit strange symptoms like hot flashes and hallucinations. One of the vacationers is a physician who looks into the resort's operations and makes a startling discovery.

SITUATION 3: Residents in a neighborhood suddenly break out in bizarre skin discolorations. As medical researchers rush to find a cause, the afflicted experience changes in behavior as well. When one of the researchers acquires the symptoms despite taking precautions, panic sets in.

SITUATION 4: In this suburban community, people inexplicably start sleepwalking. A neurologist conducts tests on some of the sleepwalkers and traces the cause to a chemical in the water supply. Meanwhile some of the sleepwalkers undergo a radical personality transformation.

SITUATION 5: Despite NASA precautions, an alien virus carried by a robotic probe that has just returned from giant asteroid (where it collected subterranean materials) escapes quarantine and infects lab personnel. They in turn infect family and friends, triggering an epidemic.

SITUATION 6: A new deadly sexually-transmitted disease spreads rapidly among straight and gay couples alike, causing widespread panic. The Centers for Disease Control rushes to isolate the bacterium or virus involved. Meanwhile the CDC insists upon a ban on sexual activity until further notice.

SITUATION 7: People in a small town awaken with their perceptions greatly enhanced ... but with their capacity for self-control greatly diminished. A medical researcher suspects airborne alien bacteria.

SITUATION 8: Hallucinations are running amok in this town. Health officials trace the likely cause to a previously unknown species of plant that grows in a large ring surrounding the town. In the meantime, no one knows how to stop the hallucinations, which are affecting behavior in bizarre ways.

SITUATION 9: Neighborhood children have been experiencing strange growths on their hands and feet. Doctors suspect contaminants from a nearby waste-disposal site; but the symptoms are unlike anything ever before seen.

SITUATION 10: After thousands of people (mainly adolescents) suddenly experience problems with their vision, scientists trace the likely cause to a new kind of video game. When the decision is made to confiscate the games, riots break out.

CATEGORY 4: MYSTERIOUS MESSAGES

> A message, especially a cryptic one, whether it originates from an enemy nation or outer space or from some sinister family member, makes for a great story premise. What is the motive of the message writer? What are the hidden implications? The following ten story situations will set your imagination spinning.

SITUATION 1: Detectives searching for a missing woman are baffled by a letter she wrote in code and left for her husband. Nobody can decode it until one of the detectives shows it to an expert in extinct languages.

SITUATION 2: The protagonist awakens from a nightmare in which she receives a frightening message from a strange person. She can only recall part of the message; but under hypnosis, she is able to recall the whole thing, as well as the identity of the person.

SITUATION 3: Astronomers intercept a message from deep space. At first they think it's from aliens in another solar system—but the language seems strangely familiar. One of the astronomers wonders if they intercepted a message from humans in the distant future.

SITUATION 4: On a subway train, a woman presses a slip of paper into a young man's hand: HELP ME. At the next stop, the woman gets off, and against his better judgment, the young man follows her into a dangerous neighborhood.

SITUATION 5: After receiving a second message from a stranger who claims to be her brother, the narrator decides to find out if the claim is valid. In doing so, she discovers disturbing information about her family's history.

SITUATION 6: Every night for the past several days, a ghost has appeared before an elderly man, bringing one mysterious message after another. At first the messages seemed cryptic, then they start to make sense, and finally they become terrifying.

SITUATION 7: The narrator keeps receiving phone and e-mail messages from someone who claims to be from the future, and who pleads with her to follow his instructions to avoid terrible consequences. She dismisses him as a fraud, but then he tells her things that prove his claim.

SITUATION 8: An Alzheimer's researcher discovers that if she hypnotizes some of the patients, they can remember things more effectively when hypnotized than when they're awake. But frequent hypnosis has negative side effects she must find a way to avoid.

SITUATION 9: After breaking up with her abusive partner (and getting a restraining order against him), a woman receives bizarre messages from him in places he is not permitted to enter—like her office or the apartment she just moved into.

SITUATION 10: Terrorists have been leaving mysterious messages near the sites they have bombed or invaded. The messages seem to be part of a mega-message that could allude to a vast-scale terrorist attack.

CATEGORY 5: MISSING-PERSONS MYSTERIES

The premise of many a mystery is that someone has gone missing. Perhaps the person willfully disappeared; perhaps he or she was abducted ... or worse. A good missing-persons mystery will keep the reader guessing and turning the pages rapidly.

SITUATION 1: When a retired weapons designer invited to be the guest of honor at a company reunion fails to show, foul play is suspected because of the nature of his research. The detective assigned to the case soon finds herself embroiled in an international conspiracy.

SITUATION 2: A journalist disguised as a homeless man (to investigate poverty in his city) discovers that a street peddler he recently spoke to has disappeared. An eyewitness thinks he was abducted by the Mob for speaking to the journalist. Together the witness and the journalist set out to find the peddler.

SITUATION 3: Police are wondering why circus performers are being abducted. One enterprising detective has an idea after interviewing several members of a traveling circus whose performers have disappeared.

SITUATION 4: When a group of anthropologists journey into the depths of a rain forest to study an obscure tribe, one of the group's members disappears. When they reach the village, they find clues that he was there but none of the villagers claims to have seen him. Soon a village leader also disappears, causing a panic.

SITUATION 5: Agents from an enemy government have kidnapped an autistic child. They demand government secrets as ransom. Why this particular child has been abducted is a mystery—but the child's therapist has an idea.

SITUATION 6: When a popular street vendor disappears, few people give it much thought. The detective assigned to the case discovers that the vendor had been involved in a biotech corporation's secret beta tests.

SITUATION 7: Time travel has become possible, but time travelers cannot remain outside their original time frame more than twenty-four hours. After that, they are automatically catapulted back to their original respective times. But when a time traveler returns to a moment in the past to repair an anomaly, she takes more than twenty-four hours to complete the job and vanishes. Her colleague sets out to find her, but it's like a wild-goose chase through the ages.

SITUATION 8: Santa Claus has vanished from his North-Pole home, and Mrs. Claus is worried. Meanwhile she has taken over Santa's duties, much to the disdain of traditionalists ("Mother Christmas? No way!"). But who could have kidnapped Santa?

SITUATION 9: Someone has kidnapped the Pope. Vatican police suspect a member of the Pope's inner circle or maybe even members of the Swiss Guard. Before long, a list of demands is discovered inside the Sistine Chapel.

SITUATION 10: When the president of an enemy nation disappears, the United States is blamed, but evidence points to a faction within the enemy nation itself. They seem to have recruited an American defector to assist with the abduction.

CATEGORY 6: MYSTERIOUS PHENOMENA

Even in our scientific age, we occasionally encounter inexplicable phenomena. Usually an explanation arrives (those strange lights in the sky were experimental aircraft, not alien flying saucers). Even so, plenty of phenomena defy explanation and that is good news for storytellers. Here are ten scenarios to get you going.

SITUATION 1: Something is ticking behind the safe of a controversial public figure, but when he opens it, he finds nothing. The ticking resumes somewhere else in his house. Is someone trying to drive him insane?

SITUATION 2: Bizarre lightning storms develop over various parts of the country. Whenever they occur, animals begin acting strangely. One scientist fears that the phenomena may have something to do with two realities colliding.

SITUATION 3: Scientists are at a loss to explain the sudden eruption of steam vents in a region where such geologic activity should not exist. A geologist sees a similarity between these vents and those in Yellowstone and fears that a lava chamber deep underground may be awakening after thousands of years.

SITUATION 4: A nearby unstable star has a 30 percent chance of going nova, thereby jettisoning lethal radiation toward earth. Do the odds warrant spending countless billions of dollars on protective measures which may or may not work? Heated debates take place, but one fact is beyond dispute: Once the star explodes, it will be too late to take precautions. The plot thickens when a mysterious message is received from one of the unstable star's planets.

SITUATION 5: Strange mushroom-like plants have been cropping up everywhere. Some think they're not from earth. Daredevils eat them and claim they're not only delicious but rejuvenating. Reassured, everyone starts eating them—with bizarre consequences.

SITUATION 6: Communication satellites begin malfunctioning. The Internet and mobile phones are crashing; global chaos ensues. Some suspect a radiation bursts from deep space; others suspect technologically advanced terrorists.

SITUATION 7: Geneticists create an organic substance that could be the link to instant organ replacements, but they discover that it mutates on its own in unpredictable ways. Before the geneticists are able to terminate the experiment, the substance breaks confinement and disappears.

SITUATION 8: Mysterious metallic artifacts are discovered in a newly found cave. They could not possibly be of prehistoric origin ... unless the cave dwellers had contact with extraterrestrials. And then one of the artifacts comes to life.

SITUATION 9: Using DNA from different species, including humans, a precocious but unscrupulous graduate student has developed a substance that stimulates brain growth. Convinced it will increase intelligence dramatically, he injects the substance into himself.

SITUATION 10: The River Jordan has turned blood-red overnight. The faithful call it a miracle. Scientists fear that the red color is caused by contaminants. When the river begins to glow, everyone suspects that something unearthly is to blame.

CATEGORY 7: MYSTERIOUS PLACES

We love to travel, mainly because unfamiliar places are mysterious (in varying degrees), a characteristic that adds to the enchantment of the place. Sometimes, though, the mysteriousness becomes uncanny or unnerving—ideal breeding ground for stories. Here are ten possibilities.

SITUATION 1: After oversleeping on a commuter train, a salesperson disembarks on the next stop, but the town is utterly unfamiliar to her. Because it is after midnight, the station is deserted, so she treks through the town in search of a room—but there are there no hotels; the entire town seems deserted.

SITUATION 2: An archaeologist may have stumbled upon her dream of a lifetime: Finding a lost city that's mentioned only in legends. Although the site bears all the signs of being this lost city, some of the artifacts excavated tell a much darker tale than anything on record.

SITUATION 3: While working amid the ruins of the five-thousand-year-old city of Tarxien, on the Mediterranean island of Malta, a historian examines remnants of structures that might have been a secret temple and makes a remarkable discovery that could rewrite history.

SITUATION 4: Residents in a small desert town explore a long-sealed-off mine. What they find inside the mine terrifies them. To make matters worse, the mine entrance collapses while they are inside.

SITUATION 5: Archaeologists find remnants of what appears to be a lost city beneath the ruins of another city. No record of the underlying city exists, fueling skepticism about its authenticity. But then the protagonist discovers a cache of documents ...

SITUATION 6: Following directions he found hidden in a secret compartment of a bookcase he purchased at a flea market, a prospector finds a ghost town partially buried in rubble from an earthquake. Items he discovers there suggest that the town had been guarding a terrible secret.

SITUATION 7: Scientists discover the site of a city that flourished at the dawn of civilization. The more they uncover, however, the more baffled they become: Nothing about this lost city resembles other cities of its time. Some of the structures and artifacts look more like those from modern times.

SITUATION 8: Within the Aztec capital city of Tenochtitlan (site of present-day Mexico City), the serpent god Quetzalcoatl, the mother goddess Ciuacoatl, and the sky god Tezcatlipoca warn the city's guardians through esoteric messages of the coming alien invasion from across the sea, but the guardians do not know how to interpret the warnings.

SITUATION 9: Nothing seemed at all unusual about the inner-city playground where the narrator's son played with other neighborhood children, but one day, the children begin to act strangely the moment they enter the playground. The narrator decides to investigate.

SITUATION 10: This parallel Earth has an extra continent about the same size as Australia, but it's a land where nature has run amuck, spawning bizarre life-forms. Those venturing into the continent's interior never emerge.

CATEGORY 8: MYSTERIOUS SOCIETIES

Most people enjoy being part of a larger group of people who share common interests. Sometimes though, the organization in question may be involved in unsavory practices or views and not all of the members are aware of these practices. Such situations make for interesting stories.

SITUATION 1: A former teacher receives an invitation to join a society of retired teachers from a small university, but he cannot find any other information about the society. He decides against joining, but in increasingly threatening ways, members of the group tell him he must join now that he knows of their existence.

SITUATION 2: After she is recruited into a sorority, a student becomes suspicious of the sorority's activities. The others rebuke her for "being paranoid," but when she decides to leave the sorority, she is ordered to stay or face unpleasant consequences.

SITUATION 3: What once seemed like an honorary club for accomplished business professionals now seems like a cult. When the narrator, a new member, shares his suspicions with his sponsor, a family member disappears. The narrator is then informed that he must earn the family member back through subversive activities or lose another.

SITUATION 4: When the president of a highly esteemed society for professional women invites the narrator to become a member, she accepts. But after doing some research, she discovers that the society wants to undermine several feminist objectives. When the narrator tries to bow out, the president tries to prevent her from doing so using threats and blackmail.

SITUATION 5: An organization working to improve opportunities for Native Americans is also working clandestinely to reclaim land the government confiscated long ago. As the woman heading the effort begins to make progress, a government agency sets out to stop her.

SITUATION 6: A cabal of magicians has its eye on a reclusive magician who performs only on rare occasions—and when she does, the magic is unlike anything ever seen. When a recruiter for the cabal asks her to join, she refuses, but the recruiter doesn't take no for an answer.

SITUATION 7: His friends call him charismatic, so it isn't surprising when the precocious teenager with strong leadership tendencies organizes a club ostensibly to curb the "loose" ways of his fellow youth. However, he has a more ominous agenda than he lets on.

SITUATION 8: In this future world, enigmatic spiritual societies rival traditional religious sects. One of these societies is based on fringe science, bordering on the occult—like training the mind to manipulate others' thoughts. The protagonist aims to put this group out of commission.

SITUATION 9: All of the senior citizens in a small town have been meeting in secret to plot ... what? That is what one of the younger citizens intends to find out, but first she must disguise herself as an old person.

SITUATION 10: An investigator has uncovered a secret society of people with paranormal powers. Led by a woman capable of controlling minds, the members seem to be plotting an insidious takeover of the community and beyond.

CATEGORY 9: THE MYSTERY OF MISSING OR STOLEN PROPERTY

Most people are quite good at losing things—after all, there are so many things to keep track of, from the small (keys, phones, documents, eyeglasses) to the large (tools, appliances). Most of the time, we chalk it up to the carelessness of misplacing things, but occasionally we suspect foul play which is bad for us but a good springboard for a mystery story.

SITUATION 1: For several weeks a wealthy widow's possessions have been disappearing. At first, only relatively insignificant things vanish: gloves, scarves, knickknacks, and such. But when precious jewels and heirlooms start to disappear, she contacts the police—a problem because some of the cops are members of a jewel-thief cabal.

SITUATION 2: When the narrator finds a stash of goods in her son's room, she fears that he is involved with pushing stolen goods, but when she confronts him, he swears that he has no idea where the stuff came from. Adding to the mystery, some of the goods begin to grow and change shape.

SITUATION 3: An engineer's lab notebooks have vanished—a cause for alarm because they were filled with notes for constructing top-secret robotics systems. The engineer fears that the thief could be an enemy spy—something his employers now accuse him of being.

SITUATION 4: A prized parrot has been stolen. The police think the thief wishes to cash in on the bird's well-publicized amazing gift of language; but unbeknownst to the detective investigating the case, the parrot's owner was using the bird to transmit secret information.

SITUATION 5: The narrator has spent a year doing research about a corrupt enterprise; now her notebooks have vanished. She does not inform police due to the sensitivity of the information. Finally, she entrusts a friend to help find the thief and recover her notebooks.

SITUATION 6: It must have happened on the subway train to work: A pickpocket managed to take from her purse the envelope containing top-secret encoded information. But how could the thief have known it was there?

SITUATION 7: Someone has stolen a young woman's identity: Her purse has been snatched and her computer hacked (including password files). She fears that the identity thief might access information no one must ever see.

SITUATION 8: The only copy of a map leading to a kingdom's most carefully hidden treasure has disappeared. The map's guardian, a loyal servant to the king, is nonetheless suspect. Swearing innocence, the king orders him to find the map—and the thief—or lose his head.

SITUATION 9: A woman's ruby necklace has somehow been replaced by a fake. Clues suggest that her husband is the thief, but that theory proves wrong. The detective on the case has another hunch, but it will require some creative sleuthing to substantiate it.

SITUATION 10: Why would anyone steal a homeless person's lucky rock? Apparently only a hunk of iron ore, it surely has no intrinsic value, but ever since he found it, the homeless person has grown increasingly more optimistic about his life. A private detective suspects the rock might be more than a lucky stone ... possibly a rare meteorite with strange powers.

CATEGORY 10: MYSTERIOUS STRANGERS

Strangers—the very word implies mysteriousness, and although it is true that the more we get to know someone, the less mysterious that person becomes, a residue of mystery often remains. That's because human beings are inherently complex and unpredictable. That's a good thing for writers of fiction!

SITUATION 1: Several children mysteriously show up in a small town. Although they keep to themselves, rumors spread about them, raising suspicions and fears. When the paranoia reaches a fever pitch, the children explain their intentions ...

SITUATION 2: A reclusive retiree purchases a long-abandoned home on the outskirts of town. Because she never interacts with the townspeople, rumors start brewing about her. Then one of the residents disappears, and she is blamed for it.

SITUATION 3: When the butler of an aristocratic family exhibits anomalous behavior, members of the household suspect that he may be suffering from a psychological disorder. But one of the family members suggests something more ominous: The butler is an imposter, perhaps even a spy.

SITUATION 4: After a strange old woman follows a single mother as she shops in a grocery store, the mother finally confronts her. The old woman begs her to end the relationship with her boyfriend because if she doesn't, terrible things will happen.

SITUATION 5: Realizing she is being followed, a woman manages to confront the pursuer, who it turns out, is her ex-husband's reclusive brother. He claims she has something valuable of his. The woman has no idea what it could be and attempts to avoid him and his cryptic messages and visits.

SITUATION 6: A stranger claims to be the son of a famous business executive and that his mother was a prostitute with whom the executive slept years ago. When the executive refuses to believe it, the stranger provides evidence: a keepsake the executive had given his mother. The executive suspects that his newfound son wants to blackmail him, but the stranger seeks something unexpected.

SITUATION 7: One stormy night, a stranger passing through a small town begs a resident to give him shelter, despite his disheveled appearance. The resident agrees, against her better judgment. It turns out that the stranger is a very special person indeed.

SITUATION 8: An industrial workplace supervisor wonders if she's being paranoid when she suspects that her employees have been replaced by imposters, but others detect subtle differences, too. Eventually she becomes convinced. But what are the imposters' motives? And what have they done with the employees they're impersonating?

SITUATION 9: Strangers arrive in town and claim to be resurrected men and women who had been executed for crimes they never committed. They have returned to demand reparations. The sheriff agrees to compensate them if (a) they can prove their innocence and (b) they can prove that they are who they say they are.

SITUATION 10: Soapbox preachers come and go in this community, but one of them is able to enthrall all who listen to her. She has the makings of a true prophetess. However, someone in the community is telling everyone that she is dangerous.

CHAPTER 16

THE RESCUE OF X

CATEGORY 1: ANIMAL RESCUE

Our fascination with animals—in stories as well as in real life—stems from childhood. We care about their welfare, and we are outraged when they are abused or neglected. Good animal-rescue stories go a long way toward raising our collective consciousness about what needs to be done to ensure that animals continue to be loved and protected.

SITUATION 1: When the management of an underfunded and overcrowded animal shelter threatens to euthanize all their dogs and cats, one of the employees launches a campaign to save the animals. But not enough people will contribute enough money. The protagonist comes up with a startling idea to motivate donors.

SITUATION 2: Hunters (who are either ranchers and farmers or are funded by them) have been exterminating wolves and foxes in great numbers. When an animal rights activist and his team investigate, their lives are threatened.

SITUATION 3: Animal-rights activists break into a cosmetics laboratory to rescue guinea pigs and other animals used for testing various products. The activists are arrested for burglary and theft, but their attorney wants to expose the lab for animal cruelty.

SITUATION 4: Thieves run off with a chicken that can predict the future (by pecking out cryptic messages). They demand a million dollars or else. The chicken's owner, however, thinks she can swipe the chicken from under the thieves' noses.

SITUATION 5: A dog that has the potential to win a major prize in a show where animals are mistreated has run away. While a search is underway, someone who despises such shows finds the dog. He sends a letter to show managers and the owner stating: Improve the conditions and he will release the dog. If you don't alter the show, he will sell the dog to a good home far away.

SITUATION 6: A homeless man rescues an injured duck. When no animal shelter accepts it (they would only euthanize it), he decides to care for it himself. When he brings the duck to his temporary shelter, he and the duck are ridiculed and one of the managers threatens to turn the duck into a meal. But his friendship with the duck eventually leads to some surprising opportunities.

SITUATION 7: With the rise of animal abuse cases in a specific area of the city, animal-rights activists enter the neighborhoods involved in order to rescue the animals—but the neighborhoods also have reported high incidents of shootings and assaults.

SITUATION 8: Someone is poisoning dogs in a neighborhood. The narrator, a vet, struggles to find an antidote to the poison—but even when he does, the person committing the crime continues to get away with these criminal acts.

SITUATION 9: Animal-rescue workers look for a way to rescue dozens of cats hoarded by a homeowner who will not allow the cats to be removed even though she is no longer capable of caring for them. When one rescuer commits an illegal act to force the issue, the rest of the team must come up with a new rescue plan.

SITUATION 10: Malnourished horses are the targets of a rescue operation—but the ranchers owning the horses refuse to allow anyone on their land. The protagonist, an aggressive animal-rights activist, will not let that stop him.

CATEGORY 2: RESCUE OF CULTURAL ARTIFACTS

When wars break out, our shared global cultural heritage becomes vulnerable to plunderers. Over the centuries, precious artifacts from books to works of art have been lost ... as well as rescued. The following ten scenarios should help you fashion stories that both raise consciousness and entertain readers.

SITUATION 1: Museum thieves make off with only one statuette, one from ancient Egypt. Detectives are baffled: Why didn't they steal other treasures? But an Egyptologist thinks she knows the answer and will use that knowledge as the basis for rescuing the object.

SITUATION 2: A newly discovered quarto of a Shakespeare play is stolen. Because the quarto will surely offer new insight into the play's composition, it is considered a major find. But the thief vows to destroy it unless he receives his outrageous demand.

SITUATION 3: When a civil war breaks out, the country's cultural minister rushes to protect the national museum that raiders are about to plunder. The museum's curator is prepared to risk her life protecting the treasures.

SITUATION 4: Outraged by paintings that, to them, blaspheme their religion, several radicals break into a museum with the intention of destroying the paintings. One of the guards, though he sympathizes with the vandals, is determined to stop them in their tracks.

SITUATION 5: A treasure trove of ancient religious artifacts is uncovered at an excavation site in a city under siege by terrorists. An archaeologist and volunteers risk their lives to penetrate the museum's entrance and rescue some of the treasures.

SITUATION 6: Rare manuscripts are stolen from a museum before they have been fully studied. Some fear the thief will sell them to private collectors. Because the manuscripts are frail, the curator arranges for a specialist to rescue them.

SITUATION 7: Having been lost for hundreds of years, several documents revealing an important historical event are recovered, but someone inexplicably tries to destroy them by planting a bomb where the documents are kept. The archivist must find a way to rescue them.

SITUATION 8: A curator for a museum's mummy collection discovers precious jewels sealed inside one of the mummies. She tries to extract them, though doing so could destroy the mummy. When a colleague discovers what she is up to, he proceeds to rescue the mummy.

SITUATION 9: An ancient monument is threatened by rising sea levels and must be moved to higher ground if it is to survive. Archeologists beg for help, but neither the government nor any private company seems willing to fund the massive engineering project, perhaps because the monument celebrates a religious cult now considered blasphemous by modern religious groups. A businessman steps forward to help, but he is a mysterious figure with an eerie past.

SITUATION 10: Archaeologists in a strange, distant future are puzzled by fragments of electronic devices—laptops, e-readers, tablets, etc. They try to ascertain the kind of culture these artifacts represented—and whether they are worth preserving.

CATEGORY 3: RESCUE OF ENDANGERED SPECIES

We have learned to save species on the brink of extinction: The bison, bald eagle, and condor are three famous examples. Other species, such as the passenger pigeon, we were not so lucky. Thanks to animal-protection measures and well-written stories about endangered species, even greater protection measures may be taken. Stories about such endeavors need to be told.

SITUATION 1: A plan is launched to rescue endangered gorillas from their natural habitat in Rwanda as poachers, more militant than ever, penetrate their sanctuary. But the rescue plan is somehow leaked to the poachers, who design their own brutal attack.

SITUATION 2: Elephants are nearing extinction as poachers continue to kill them for their ivory tusks. An activist dares to infiltrate a major poacher operation, but the chances of bringing them down are slim.

SITUATION 3: Conservationists are ridiculed when they lobby for protection of an endangered mouse species. Despite a conservationist's explanation of the mouse's importance to the environment, opponents launch a counteroffensive full of falsehoods to protect the value of their aggressive development plans in the region.

SITUATION 4: Zoo officials clash with animal-rights activists over the preservation of an endangered species. The activists want the creatures released into the wild; the zoo officials believe that doing so would hasten their extinction.

SITUATION 5: It is the 1880s and thousands of hunters are shooting countless passenger pigeons out of the sky and selling them for a penny apiece. The protagonist strives to rescue this bird from extinction by making people understand the magnitude of such folly.

SITUATION 6: Anthropologists go back in time three million years to study members of a hominid ancestor with unusual skills, only to find that the hominids are being killed off by ruthless competing hominids. Defying their prime directive not to interfere with the course of evolution, the anthropologists try to rescue the endangered hominids.

SITUATION 7: Komodo dragons are being killed off en masse in Indonesia (mostly for food), and ecologists launch a plan to rescue the giant lizards before the species goes extinct. The hunters, however, argue that they feed the local population. In any case, they will not tolerate interference from environmentalists.

SITUATION 8: A species of tarantula is rapidly being exterminated, and an environmentalist fights to save the species—but she must first convince non-environmentalists that saving what many consider to be a dangerous spider (which it is not) is worth the bother. In doing so, she discovers a unique method of combating society's general fear of spiders.

SITUATION 9: To the disdain of many biologists, genetic engineers resurrect certain species that had become extinct during the last few centuries, arguing that resurrecting them would help the environment. But one such species seems to be having the opposite effect.

SITUATION 10: A mysterious virus causes dogs to revert to their lupine origins. Geneticists try to manufacture a retrovirus to reverse the plague, but it only causes even more frightful mutations. In the meantime, the infected dog-wolves are attacking humans mercilessly.

CATEGORY 4: RESCUE OF HOSTAGES

Hostage-taking situations make for white-knuckle suspense. We know from frequent headlines that hostages have roughly a fifty-fifty chance of surviving the ordeal. It takes clever planning to rescue hostages without casualties—either to the hostages or to the rescuers. Such stories make for exciting reading.

SITUATION 1: Terrorists seize control of a skyscraper and hold everyone inside, booby-trapping the perimeter. They demand that U.S. troops evacuate from designated regions in seventy-two hours or the entire building will be demolished.

SITUATION 2: The hostage being rescued in this scenario is actually an enemy of the rescuers, who, ironically, are not aware of this. The rescuers believe the hostage possesses valuable information, which they intend to extract from him.

SITUATION 3: When a young slave rescues a Roman senator from a gang of insurrectionists, the senator offers the slave his freedom, which he refuses, requesting instead that his parents be given their freedom. But the young slave's parents, who in the past have spoken out against the Senate, have been deemed a threat to the state.

SITUATION 4: After seizing an embassy and holding everyone inside hostage, terrorists demand that the ambassador recall her country's nuclear-inspection team. The ambassador agrees, to buy time, but then carries out an ingenious plan to rescue the embassy workers.

SITUATION 5: Militants hold Santa Claus and children hostage in a shopping mall. The terrorists, brandishing automatic weapons, threaten to kill the hostages the moment a SWAT team appears or if their demands aren't met. Meanwhile, Santa, alongside his most trusted elves, has a plan.

SITUATION 6: Disguised as security personnel, terrorists seize hostages inside an airport terminal and announce that they have planted bombs inside suitcases placed on random flights and will detonate them if their demands are not met. The airport's security manager, however, has reason to believe that the terrorists' explosives are fakes.

SITUATION 7: Inhabitants of a small island are held hostage by a legion of pirates who managed to booby-trap the island's seaport and heliport. As negotiations proceed (they demand a billion dollars), the protagonist, a seaplane pilot, plans an ingenious rescue operation.

SITUATION 8: During a government shutdown, extremists plant explosives around several unattended national monuments and threaten to destroy the monuments unless their demands are met. The narrator captures and interrogates one of the terrorists in an effort to defuse the explosives.

SITUATION 9: Terrorists seize control of Liberty Island and hold the Statue's visitors hostage. They will destroy the Statue and everyone inside it unless a certain member of the president's cabinet is turned over to them. The cabinet member wants to go, but the president refuses.

SITUATION 10: Bank robbers lock several hostages inside the vault that they've just cleaned out; then they booby-trap the vault—any attempt to rescue the hostages or nab the robbers will result in detonation of a bomb. Only after they escape will they defuse the bomb via remote control. But one of the thieves has a change of heart during the robbery.

CATEGORY 5: RESCUE FROM NATURAL OR ENGINEERING DISASTERS

Volcanoes erupt, and dams burst; tsunamis ravage coastal cities and oil rigs explode: It seems that engineering disasters keep pace with natural ones. The two dovetail when it comes to natural disasters caused by humans—carbon emissions contribute to melting Arctic ice, for example. Plenty of stories in this vein are waiting to be told.

SITUATION 1: Nursing-home residents are stranded when a flash flood isolates the building from the rest of the area. The protagonist leads a team to rescue the residents. The crisis is aggravated by the fact that the building is in danger of collapsing.

SITUATION 2: People are trapped inside a building that all but collapsed in a gas-leak explosion. First responders enter the building, keenly aware that it could collapse at any moment; they, too, become trapped.

SITUATION 3: Fearing that a faultily constructed dam is likely to burst, engineers try to evacuate the village nearby—but some of the residents deny the danger and refuse to leave. One of the engineers tries to come up with a way to persuade the villagers to evacuate before it's too late.

SITUATION 4: A bridge is in danger of collapsing, following a powerful earthquake. Rescuers are faced with evacuating hundreds of people stranded on the bridge, unable to proceed in either direction because of buckled pavement.

SITUATION 5: Skiers are trapped in a cable car, and rescuers are getting ready to airlift them by helicopter—a dangerous maneuver under ideal conditions. The crisis worsens when one of the cables snaps and a snowstorm heads their way.

SITUATION 6: Several families are marooned in their homes after molten lava from a long-dormant volcano surrounds them. Rescuers use helicopters in the rescue operation, but the smoldering volcano makes the operation difficult.

SITUATION 7: Fighting against time to dig through a rockslide (triggered by an earthquake), rescuers work to extricate people trapped in their cars. Conditions are made worse by aftershocks, and disagreements among the rescuers over how to proceed also cause delays.

SITUATION 8: A levee bursts during a storm, homes are rapidly being flooded, and elderly residents are trapped. Teams set out to rescue them but are held back when the storm develops into a hurricane. One of the rescuers risks her life to bring a group of residents to safety.

SITUATION 9: Dozens of miners are trapped when an earthquake causes the mine to collapse. They are so deep underground that only a technological breakthrough would enable rescuers to reach them in time.

SITUATION 10: When a gas line explodes near a remote natural-gas plant, dozens of workers are trapped in the rubble. First responders enter the building and become trapped themselves when part of the building collapses, with no timetable for a second wave of rescuers.

CATEGORY 6: RESCUE OF POLITICAL PRISONERS OR PROTESTERS

Rescuing political prisoners makes ideal thriller scenarios of the *Mission Impossible* variety. Rescuers typically must concoct ingenious, life-threatening schemes to get the prisoners to safety. The more inventive the twists and turns become, the better the story.

SITUATION 1: Health-care workers are taken hostage by a country that sponsors terrorism. Their demand: Release the imprisoned terrorists, or the hostages will be executed. A diplomat with ties to one of the terrorists thinks she can negotiate with them even though government policy forbids such negotiating.

SITUATION 2: The child prodigy of a powerful political figure is taken prisoner when the enemy abductors discover that she has a photographic memory. Rescuers must navigate a labyrinth to get to the child—and once they do, they must rely on the child to lead them out, even though the kidnappers now know of their presence.

SITUATION 3: When a tourist is detained by the secret service of this politically unstable nation, the narrator, a CIA agent, initiates a plan to rescue him. The agent has discovered that the tourist, who is pretending to be a blue-collar American on vacation, is a nuclear physicist.

SITUATION 4: Hikers are arrested after they accidentally cross into an area where top secret nuclear research is being done. When the hikers' embassy fails to win their release, a plan is presented to rescue them—but the enemy country has threatened to execute the hikers if there's a rescue attempt.

SITUATION 5: Students protesting stringent policies established by the new tyrannical regime attempt to take control of a government building and clash with police, who use tear gas to subdue them. But when some of the students don gas masks, the police resort to battery and gunfire. A group of students make it inside and take control of the building, but now they are surrounded by chaos and some have a change of heart.

SITUATION 6: When police prevent protesters from occupying a government park, a riot breaks out and the protesters are hit with Tasers. The leader of the protest goes into cardiac arrest and must be rushed to an ER, where someone sympathetic sneaks him away from his police guards during his recovery.

SITUATION 7: A bloodthirsty emperor has just taken his latest prisoner—a sorceress who dared proclaim that her powers exceeded his own. Because the sorceress is revered, a plot is hatched to rescue her—but she must combine her powers with those of a rival sorceress.

SITUATION 8: Journalists are being rounded up and imprisoned by their country's censors, on grounds that they are inciting an antigovernment uprising. Ironically, the people demand that the censors be arrested, and they work up a plot to rescue the journalists.

SITUATION 9: Even though they were assured of the right to criticize their government, a theatrical troupe is imprisoned for ridiculing the dictator in a satiric play. When conventional negotiations for their release fail, a celebrated but controversial actor thinks she can stage a rescue.

SITUATION 10: In this medieval kingdom, the court jester is thrown into the dungeon after he crosses the line by poking too much fun at the royal family. But the princess and her secret lover plot a rescue for the jester.

CATEGORY 7: RESCUE OF REFUGEES

Wars and civil strife uproot many citizens, particularly those who are victims of ethnic cleansing. Suddenly homeless and vulnerable, they seek asylum in neighboring countries or find places to hide. Such personae non gratae can serve as tragic heroes of gripping stories.

SITUATION 1: Refugee rebels from their country's civil war are detained by a bordering nation that has just sided with the loyalists. One of the refugees, a journalist, tries to convince their detainers that the loyalists are corrupt and secretly intend to invade them.

SITUATION 2: Although war refugees were permitted to enter a neighboring country, that country's policy toward refugees was reversed when a new leader took office. Now the refugees are being persecuted. The protagonist works feverishly to get the new government to reverse its policies.

SITUATION 3: A refugee from a military coup, in possession of top-secret information, is the target of a rescue operation, but the refugee wants to deliver his information to someone in a country that is a haven for terrorists.

SITUATION 4: A ship carrying refugee children is denied asylum even though many are suffering from malnutrition. Because onboard supplies are rapidly running out, a third group attempts to rescue the children, even though their capabilities are limited.

SITUATION 5: Some of the refugees that have been given asylum in the United States are now suspected of being spies or terrorists. A Homeland-Security official must weed these people out before they infiltrate government agencies.

SITUATION 6: Refugees are accepted into a nation that's only pretending to be friendly. The nation's ulterior motive is to confiscate the refugees' valuables, including art collections, as payment for asylum. Corrupt officials think the art collections are worth far more than their refugee owners realize.

SITUATION 7: A Mexican refugee camp is brutally attacked for no apparent reason. No one claims responsibility. The protagonist works with a forensics expert to ascertain those responsible. Clues point to a group of anti-immigration extremists.

SITUATION 8: Guards open fire on a prisoner of war as he is being rescued, severely wounding him. Doctors must now fight to save his life—an urgent matter because the prisoner possesses top-secret information.

SITUATION 9: Thousands of refugees, victims of chemical warfare, are denied entrance by the bordering country, fearing that the refugees have been infiltrated by secret agents. The protagonist tries to organize a rescue operation for the refugees, who now face imprisonment.

SITUATION 10: A ship filled with refugees from a country engaged in ethnic cleansing is denied admission into the country that once promised them safe haven (when that country was under another regime). One government official hopes to find a loophole before the ship is sent back.

CATEGORY 8: RESCUE AT SEA

Large bodies of water are wildly unpredictable; treacherous conditions can arise almost instantly, and not being prepared can spell doom. Sea-rescue stories often combine high adventure with fascinating insight into navigation challenges.

SITUATION 1: Sailors navigating a reconstructed ancient ship encounter foul weather, and the ship is in danger of capsizing. Rescuers try to save both the crew and the ship—but it becomes apparent that attempting this will cause the loss of both.

SITUATION 2: Several prized dolphins in a marine research facility escape confinement and become stricken with an unknown pathogen. It is up to the narrator, a dolphin specialist, to rescue the dolphins (which possess rare abilities) before they succumb to the disease.

SITUATION 3: A cargo ship suspected of carrying contraband to a terrorist nation has capsized, and rescuers are faced with saving the lives of those aboard (and simultaneously arresting them) and confiscating the contraband.

SITUATION 4: Pirates have captured a cargo ship and threaten to blow it up if their demands are not met. Two counter-terrorism agents masquerade as pirates to get onboard the ship and attack the terrorists, but the pirates soon discover the deception.

SITUATION 5: A plane makes an emergency landing on one of the Great Lakes, and a flight attendant struggles to keep passengers from panicking so they can exit the plane before it sinks. The ordeal is aggravated by stormy weather and a disabled escape chute.

SITUATION 6: Marine biologists attempt to rescue a whale severely injured by a harpoon. They must deal with difficult maneuvers, unreliable equipment, and other whales in the vicinity.

SITUATION 7: During exploration of a sunken city, the archaeologists become trapped. A rescue team is deployed, but they too become trapped. No one is able to explain what is trapping the explorers, until one of them spots a bizarre lifeform inside one of the city's structures.

SITUATION 8: After an airliner crash-lands in deep water, rescue teams scramble to reach the survivors before the plane sinks. However, a storm is brewing nearby, threatening disaster to all.

SITUATION 9: A ship carrying African animals for a zoo capsizes; rescuers will give priority to the humans onboard, of course, but the narrator is willing to break safety protocols to rescue the animals as well.

SITUATION 10: An oil spill in an ecologically sensitive bay threatens a colony of endangered marine mammals and birds. The head of the rescue operation wants the oil company to finance the project, but they argue that they're only responsible for the oil cleanup. The rescue operation launches a campaign to convince the Environmental Protection Agency to side with them.

CATEGORY 9: RESCUE FROM (OR BY) ALIEN OR SUPERNATURAL BEINGS

One never knows when aliens, ghosts, or demons will materialize out of the sky or the ground and terrorize or transform us. How does one escape? Who has the power or the cunning to rescue mere mortals from such beings? See what imaginative stories you can conjure up using the following situations.

SITUATION 1: While exploring his grandmother's cellar, a brother and sister stumble upon a boarded-up doorway. They pull away the boards and are pulled in by a demonic force. The grandmother knows how to rescue the siblings but is too frail to attempt it, so she calls the person who originally rescued her all those years ago.

SITUATION 2: In this world, demons are a constant threat, and mortals must continually seek new and clever ways of avoiding them. The protagonist heads a team devoted to establishing a permanent barrier against the demons. Naturally she is the demons' number-one target.

SITUATION 3: Alien beings abduct several schoolchildren to their secret base in the mountains. When a search party stumbles upon the alien hideout, they too are abducted, and they soon discover the aliens' true mission, a plan that divides the group as they decide between escape and joining the aliens.

SITUATION 4: When a ghost hunter is trapped by vindictive ghosts inside a haunted hotel, a benevolent ghost sets out to rescue her. The ghost hunter is suspicious of the nice ghost, whose motives will be revealed only if the ghost hunter cooperates.

SITUATION 5: Evil aliens attack human explorers on this Earth-like world. Their benevolent counterparts attempt to rescue the humans but in the process trigger a war. The humans side with their rescuers but soon discover that each side has valid points in the war to keep their alien planet free of outsiders.

SITUATION 6: Demons possess residents in a quiet neighborhood but their human host bodies soon become afflicted with a wasting disease so they must choose new host bodies every few days or risk their own death. They do their best to disguise themselves as healthy individuals as they take over a small town. Would-be rescuers must figure out a way to distinguish the true living from host bodies, as well as find a way to banish the demons.

SITUATION 7: Rescuing people from these ghouls will not be easy since they take their victims deep underground, but one of the ghouls is captured above ground and persuaded to reveal the others' whereabouts.

SITUATION 8: Ghosts of Crusaders enter the bodies of the archaeologists excavating in a cemetery where they were buried. The ghosts say they will not release the archaeologists until the ghosts fulfill their sacred mission, but one of the archaeologists convinces the ghost inhabiting him to do things a different way.

SITUATION 9: Alien envoys offer to protect humanity from an impending invasion of malevolent aliens—provided humans will share the planet with the good aliens. Fearing that the good aliens and the bad ones are the same, the protagonist heads a plan to save humanity.

SITUATION 10: Two clans of vampires vie for dominion over a remote city, but one group of vampires, who seem much more trustworthy than the others, offers to deliver the humans to a safe haven ... for what they say is a modest price, but some feel the price is still too steep.

CATEGORY 10: RESCUE OF WAR WOUNDED

Combat often demands a precarious balance between assault against enemy forces and rescue of wounded fellow combatants and both operations occur simultaneously at times. Narratives depicting such moments make for gripping reading.

SITUATION 1: In the middle of a fierce clash, a Union soldier defies orders and rescues a Rebel soldier after the latter's leg is blown off by cannon fire. The Rebel soldier survives, and after an arduous journey back to Union lines, the rescued soldier divulges important information regarding future combat strategies.

SITUATION 2: A wounded soldier in the Afghanistan-Pakistan tribal region struggles to rescue a comrade more severely wounded than she, even though her chances of succeeding are slim. Her only hope is to find a temporary shelter where she can tend to her comrade's life-threatening wounds.

SITUATION 3: After her helicopter crash-lands, the copilot, despite her injuries, struggles to pull the pilot and another crew member from the wreckage. At the same time, she tries to save top-secret materials from going up in flames.

SITUATION 4: An Army nurse uses his combat training to stave off attackers so that he can rescue several wounded soldiers—but their injuries are too severe and the attackers too fierce to give him much chance of success.

SITUATION 5: In this future war, a robot that specializes in foxhole infiltration is severely damaged, and one of the human soldiers sets out to rescue it, despite the sergeant's order never to rescue robots.

SITUATION 6: Wounded during a sneak attack on a remote military outpost in the Afghanistan outback, a soldier is captured by the enemy. When his surviving comrades disobey orders to remain at the camp until reinforcements arrive and they can attempt a rescue, a fierce battle ensues. Hope of rescue is lost ... until a young enemy soldier decides to defect.

SITUATION 7: Three of the most elite members of an advanced recon unit have been incapacitated by a land mine. Two of the soldiers are the only ones in a position to find a way home—but one of the wounded cannot be moved, and the enemy is closing in.

SITUATION 8: A bomb-sniffing dog is wounded in the line of duty, and a soldier decides to disobey his commanding officer and attempt to rescue the dog, thereby risking a court-martial. The soldier's rationale: The dog has saved the lives of at least a dozen soldiers. But in taking on this rescue mission, the soldier is trapped on the wrong side of the lines during a sneak attack.

SITUATION 9: SWAT-team commandos infiltrate an enemy stronghold to rescue a diplomat captured while trying to gather top-secret information—information that could compromise the security of the United States.

SITUATION 10: Women and children, used as human shields by the enemy, are wounded and trapped inside a building in which a terrorist leader is hunkered down. Commandos devise a plan to rescue the children and take out the terrorist.

CHAPTER 17
THE SEARCH FOR X

CATEGORY 1: THE SEARCH FOR ALIEN OR EXOTIC LIFE

Organisms from sponges and jellyfish to alligators and orangutans fill us with wonder. And new creatures continue to be discovered in remote deserts, rain forests, and the fossil record. What will we discover tomorrow? The following scenarios should pique your storyteller's imagination.

SITUATION 1: Several dogs genetically enhanced for a secret military-combat operation have disappeared. Special agents must locate the animals and retrieve them before they fall into the wrong hands. Locating them is one challenge; retrieving them is quite another.

SITUATION 2: While visiting an African wildlife preserve, a photographer tries taking close-up photos of an unknown creature when it suddenly attacks her. She escapes and later returns to the site with natives who are familiar with the region to help track down the strange creature.

SITUATION 3: An elephant zoologist searches for a special young elephant with telepathic powers that escaped after realizing that there is a whole world outside of the zoo. When the zoologist reconnects with the elephant, now hiding in a dense forest outside the city, the elephant begs him leave him alone.

SITUATION 4: Investigators search for an escaped chimpanzee. The animal fled a research facility that specializes in DNA mutations, and doctors had just injected the animal with what investigators believed to be the DNA of a "missing-link" type of animal. The investigators cannot determine the results of the injection unless they recover the chimpanzee.

SITUATION 5: A botanist searching for new species of edible plants (in order to help alleviate famine in an African country), finds a strange moss-like substance that tastes delicious, but soon proves to cause bizarre side effects.

SITUATION 6: When a biologist disappears after studying dangerous pathogens in his lab, the biologist's former lover sets out to find him. When she does, she realizes that he is infected with one of the pathogens and may have infected someone else—someone he did not want her to know about.

SITUATION 7: Astronauts search for primitive life in Martian soil, but their search becomes complicated when they find an object that appears to be the petrified remains of some creature. They bring it into their compound for further study: a big mistake.

SITUATION 8: After a UFO crash-lands in the Sahara Desert, several search groups scramble to locate it. The group that gets there first is mystified by what they find and must work with the other groups to make sense of the discovery.

SITUATION 9: Undead beings that were once Jack the Ripper and Lizzie Borden terrorize the country. It is up to the narrator, who learned from a shaman how to stop such beings, to destroy them. But the shaman's techniques don't work, so he must figure out what to do on his own.

SITUATION 10: The insane Roman emperor, Caligula, has been catapulted into the present day by a sorcerer, and he proceeds to wreak havoc everywhere he goes. The world's best-known expert on Caligula's life searches for a way to stop him.

CATEGORY 2: THE SEARCH FOR ARTIFACTS, MANUSCRIPTS, OR RELICS

> The following scenarios will help you take your readers on a treasure-hunting adventure. If the object of the quest is not a magic ring like the one in J.R.R. Tolkien's Lord of the Rings trilogy, then maybe it's a lost manuscript or an object that someday could become a treasure.

SITUATION 1: Two archaeologists search in exotic locales for the manuscript of a lost biblical episode that would reinforce or invalidate extant texts dealing with those episodes (e.g., Noah's Ark, the Exodus into Egypt). Their efforts are undermined by one who is intent on destroying the manuscript for the same reason.

SITUATION 2: A child who witnessed a member of a satanic cult (her neighbor) worshipping a sacred artifact has been kidnapped by the cultists to prevent her from giving away their secret. Her parents suspect the neighbor and fear that the cultists will try to brainwash her into joining their sect.

SITUATION 3: Divers scouring a shipwreck find a vellum map sealed in a ceramic jar. It directs explorers to a cache of pre-Colonial artifacts—some of which could change history profoundly. Their biggest challenge is to deliver the artifacts to safety before thieves (who know about the find) try to get a hold of them.

SITUATION 4: A parent searches for the lost diary of their runaway teenager, hoping for clues that will help them find her. They eventually do find clues, but they reveal unexpected and disturbing reasons for why she ran away. And she included a warning: Do not search for her.

SITUATION 5: A newly excavated map etched in stone contains a clue to the whereabouts of a trove of unknown sacred scrolls. However, the scrolls (according to the map) are buried in enemy territory. Even so, the discoverer knows someone there who (he hopes) will assist him.

SITUATION 6: Archaeologists from the future search for ancient technological artifacts in a region once known as Silicon Valley. One of the archaeologists fears that some of the artifacts they discover there could cause their society to devolve into slaves controlled by supercomputers.

SITUATION 7: An anthropologist, following clues taken from a recently excavated Mayan burial site, searches for what may be a lost city on the Yucatan Peninsula. But superstitious villagers near the site do all they can to keep the scientists away and for good reason.

SITUATION 8: An artifact discovered inside an Egyptian sarcophagus releases a zombie pandemic that mystifies scientists. The scientists search desperately for the one Egyptologist who might know how to stop the plague.

SITUATION 9: A monastery in sixteenth-century England is destroyed, and the monastery's librarian searches the ruins for a magic book—one that contains a spell that could prevent the monastery's destruction.

SITUATION 10: A literary scholar teams up with an archaeologist in the search for a lost play of Sophocles that, according to clues recently unearthed, could lie beneath a church in Athens. The challenge will be obtaining permission to excavate inside the church or doing so without being detected.

CATEGORY 3: THE SEARCH FOR AN ELIXIR

We associate elixirs with magic—they are nectars or foods that will restore youth or youthful vigor, heighten perceptions, or bestow immortality—but elixirs are part of everyday reality too—vitamins, for example. Catholics restore their state of grace by ingesting an elixir of "the body and blood" of Christ through the Eucharist. Here are ten situations for taking readers on an elixir search.

SITUATION 1: A geneticist searches for a gene responsible for aging. After finding it, she manipulates it to extend a friend's life—but with unexpected negative results. She must now search for an antidote.

SITUATION 2: After someone steals an elixir capable of restoring one's youth, it is up to the protagonist to recover it. But the thief is reputed to have demonic powers, including the power to reverse the elixir's effects and accelerate age.

SITUATION 3: Biologists in a rain forest search for an elixir that enhances one's sexual drive. They find one, but others get a hold of it and misuse it.

SITUATION 4: People are searching for a self-proclaimed sorcerer who is said to have discovered an elixir with the power to rid people of terminal illnesses. When they finally find him, he is near death. They realize he is dying from an unknown disease that, ironically, is resistant to his elixir; it is up to the protagonist to find a way to prolong his life using everyday medicines.

SITUATION 5: Villagers have lost track of a snake whose venom, if injected in tiny quantities (by a shaman), imbues one with supernatural strength. A herpetologist (the narrator) is recruited to search for it—a daunting assignment because the rain forest is filled with a similar species of snake and the missing snake's bite is lethal.

SITUATION 6: An ancient document said to contain recipes for becoming invulnerable to deadly diseases has been discovered. However, the recipes include rare herbs, which a group of researchers set out to find in a remote rain forest.

One of the scientists worries that some recipes may have undesirable side effects, and they soon discover this to be true.

SITUATION 7: A recovering alcoholic searches his home desperately for the liquor-cabinet key that his wife hid. When his wife returns home and finds him trying to destroy the cabinet to get to the liquor, she takes the step she always dreaded taking to ensure that he stays on the wagon.

SITUATION 8: After years of searching for a way to enhance intelligence, a psychologist succeeds in ways he never anticipated—first with animals, then with humans. But when the public learns the details of his project, there is widespread outrage. But the human patients step up to support the doctor's unorthodox methods.

SITUATION 9: Medical researchers create a drug that dramatically improves memory, but there are painful psychological side effects because the drug prevents users from forgetting anything. A search is launched to neutralize the drug before users lose their sanity.

SITUATION 10: In the near future, after marijuana becomes fully legalized, botanists cultivate a superpotent version of the drug that offers great medical benefits but is also as addictive on the level of much harder drugs. Efforts to find a way to counteract the addiction are met with fierce resistance because of the extreme euphoria the drug produces.

CATEGORY 4: THE SEARCH FOR A FUGITIVE

Fugitive-hunting situations make for suspenseful plots, often with dead ends, false clues, and harrowing chases. Here are ten scenarios for creating gripping twist-and-turn stories—perhaps emulating Marlow in his search for Kurtz in Joseph Conrad's *Heart of Darkness.*

SITUATION 1: A police detective searches for a serial killer who has escaped from prison and is stalking victims in upper-class neighborhoods and nightclubs in a posh city. The problem is that the killer is female, well-mannered, attractive, and has a knack for altering her appearance.

SITUATION 2: A posse is organized to search for an arsonist who has been burning down Western towns. The leader of the posse (the protagonist) also tries to figure out the arsonist's motive and is shocked by what he discovers.

SITUATION 3: Police search for a charismatic cult leader who, like Charles Manson, is able to brainwash followers into committing acts of brutality and murder. When an undercover investigator finds him, he must risk becoming brainwashed himself.

SITUATION 4: The teenage daughter of a mob boss is kidnapped. No one knows who the kidnappers are, except for the narrator, who fears that sharing his hunch could threaten the daughter's safety and bring suspicion upon himself. He sets out to find her as a way to pay back the mob for a favor they rendered years ago.

SITUATION 5: CIA agents search for a former agent who has infiltrated an enemy organization by luring them with top-secret information. Is she a traitor, or is she merely using the classified documents as bait?

SITUATION 6: When an enemy-encrypted transmission is intercepted, the only cryptologist who can decipher it disappears. Because the message is time-sensitive, a search is undertaken to locate the cryptologist, who may have been an enemy agent all along.

SITUATION 7: Two children who possess the ability to read minds escape custody (or were they abducted?) before they are recruited (and given posthypnotic suggestions) to track down perceived enemies of the state. The recruiters find one of the children and send him on their manhunts.

SITUATION 8: A serial killer escapes from confinement and evades every effort to find him. As a last resort, the protagonist—an ace fugitive finder but a highly unstable personality with a criminal record of his own—is recruited to track him down through the most dangerous neighborhoods of the killer's hometown.

SITUATION 9: How does one find a fugitive who is a master of disguises? That is the challenge for the narrator, a detective who is tracking down an assassin who seems to be able to impersonate almost anyone, even the detective, which makes him a suspect in the case.

SITUATION 10: An art thief who has served her sentence for grand theft is hired to track down thieves responsible for stealing paintings from the local museum. Many, however, worry that she might collaborate with the fugitives to pull off an even more ambitious art heist.

CATEGORY 5: THE SEARCH FOR FREEDOM, SIMPLICITY, SELF-SUFFICIENCY

Those who live and work in urban areas know how easily one can become detached from the natural world and how rejuvenating it can be to reconnect to the Earth. Here are ten situations that dramatize the need to simplify one's life—following Thoreau's ideal— to restore one's sanity before it is too late.

SITUATION 1: A latter-day Thoreau quits his high-pressure job and searches for a way to follow the great naturalist's precepts. But no matter how cleverly he tries to sever his connections with the corporate world, his old habits keep coming back—until he tries one more strategy, one he learned from a Native -American tribal leader.

SITUATION 2: In a fast-paced urban world, the protagonist searches for ways to slow down. She seeks out sanctuaries of peace and quiet, including cloisters, houses of worship, and libraries. After frustrating outcomes, she finds her ideal sanctuary in an unlikely place.

SITUATION 3: Tired of urban life, a business executive takes his family on an extended vacation in the wilderness but with unanticipated complications— not so much from animals or from difficult terrain or weather but from other vacationers.

SITUATION 4: No matter how cleverly an aspiring career woman negotiates with her controlling but otherwise good-hearted husband, she cannot convince him to stop micromanaging her every move. Finally, she tries one last unusual ploy before seeking a divorce.

SITUATION 5: During a stressful period in his life, the narrator finds refuge from the real world in a fantasy world he creates based on childhood daydreams, but he decides that the real world offers plenty of opportunities for solace. However, when he tries to return to the real world, he cannot.

SITUATION 6: In a postapocalyptic world, surviving families struggle to regain self-sufficiency without resorting to savagery, but on certain occasions, many families decide that a few desperate measures have to be taken. One woman, however, looks for ways to keep her family from resorting to savagery.

SITUATION 7: An astronomer searching for remnants of the Big Bang stumbles upon what appears to be proof of a Divine Being. Despite his colleagues' taunting, he insists his findings are correct.

SITUATION 8: After living most of his life in big cities, the narrator seeks a simpler, quieter life by taking over her brother's farm. But before she can have a simpler and quieter life, she needs to learn a few lessons about farming.

SITUATION 9: No longer finding pleasure in what he sees as a sterile, mechanized world, an aspiring artist is determined to find fulfillment in painting. Ironically, his artistic impulses drive him back to the frenzied modern world—but with a transformed perspective.

SITUATION 10: After the Civil War, a freed slave who had learned to play his former owner's piano struggles to find work as a musician in a land still dominated by racial discrimination. Through his dazzling performances, he manages to cut through most but not all of the prejudice.

CATEGORY 6: THE SEARCH FOR IDENTITY OR ROOTS

> Who am I? The question lies at the heart of much literature, from Hamlet to Alex Haley's *Roots*. The easiest, if not the most reliable, means of discovering one's identity is by consulting family records—diaries, photographs, other memorabilia—another is through oral histories. The scenarios that follow will help you shape stories centered on the search for identity.

SITUATION 1: When a relative gives an unemployed drug addict a document showing that the addict's missing father is/was a military hero, he sets out to find the man, despite his own precarious health and drug dependency.

SITUATION 2: A teenager living with his adoptive father sets out to find his birth father after finding evidence that his birth father, a successful business executive, gave him up for adoption when he was an infant. He is concerned, however, that his birth father will think he is only tracking him down because of his wealth.

SITUATION 3: A ghost visits an abused child to tell him that he is an exiled king from a magical world and that his kingdom desperately needs him to return

255

and restore order. Alas, the portal to that magical world has been lost, and it is up to the child to find it. The spirit has only a few meager clues to offer, but it's enough for the child to get started.

SITUATION 4: After tracing his ancestry, an American citizen born in Britain uncovers a clue that suggests his father may be the illegitimate son of the royal family and therefore he deserves a share of his royal father's estate. But first, he must find harder evidence to validate the claim.

SITUATION 5: A sick and homeless Oglala Sioux man learns that he is the descendant of Sitting Bull. He vows to restore himself to health and lead the people on his reservation to a better life, but the odds are against him because of his advanced age.

SITUATION 6: After the narrator discovers records revealing that she is not who she thinks she is, she embarks on a quest to discover her true identity. However, someone unexpected is taking pains to ensure that she does not discover the truth about herself.

SITUATION 7: The child heir to a powerful kingdom is kidnapped by an enemy and becomes the adopted son of the enemy king. Years later, the grown son launches an attack against the other king, his birth father. A former childhood friend learns of the attacking prince's true heritage and attempts to fight through enemy lines to convince him of that truth.

SITUATION 8: An orphaned girl in ancient Rome becomes the servant of an aristocrat who secretly knows that the girl is the illegitimate daughter of the Emperor. The girl finds out and demands to know why her lineage has been kept a secret—but her master refuses to tell her.

SITUATION 9: When a white supremacist discovers that his paternal great-grandfather was an African-American slave, he vents his rage against his father for keeping the matter secret, but as he learns more about his great-grandfather's life, his sentiments change.

SITUATION 10: A retired German architect orphaned at age four has no idea of his lineage—genealogy searches always turn up blank. Finally, he conducts extensive research and arranges for a DNA analysis. He discovers to his horror that he is an illegitimate son of Adolf Hitler. Suddenly, his life is in danger.

CATEGORY 7: THE SEARCH FOR A MISSING PERSON

The scenarios that follow will help you set up stories about people who are missing against their will—those who are lost or kidnapped. Think of the 1962 film, *The Manchurian Candidate*, based on the novel by Richard Condon, in which a man is abducted and brainwashed to be an assassin.

SITUATION 1: A disgruntled CIA agent steals classified information and blackmails the organization, but just as the issue is resolved and he agrees to return the materials, he vanishes. It is up to the protagonist, a current CIA agent, to find him. It appears that an unknown third party has abducted him.

SITUATION 2: Twins capable of feats of magic go missing. Their parents, who had abandoned them when they were infants (fearing they were possessed by evil spirits) and are no wracked with guilt, search everywhere for them. In a last desperate measure, they ask a sorceress to help find the children.

SITUATION 3: Agents search for one of their own spies, one of the world's cleverest computer hackers, who has stolen secret information and disappeared. It is believed that the spy may have been kidnapped years prior and was brainwashed by a terrorist group to sabotage computer systems vital to national security.

SITUATION 4: The protagonist hears a rumor that a woman capable of performing health-related miracles has vanished, and she sets out to find her. But there are some who wants to make sure no one ever finds her.

SITUATION 5: In medieval France, an old woman is accused of being a witch and is hunted down. The protagonist risks his life to save her from being burned alive, convinced that the witch is actually a miracle worker. He hopes to prove her authenticity before they are both caught and executed.

SITUATION 6: A mentally unstable engineering genius vanishes into the wilderness just when her insights are most needed to solve a potentially disastrous communications network malfunction. The protagonist and a partner work around the clock to determine her whereabouts.

SITUATION 7: A pilgrim to the Holy Land follows clues in search of a seer whose extraordinary visions might hold the secret to peace in the Middle East. The only problem is that the seer is extremely reclusive and has hired guards to keep people away who determine his whereabouts.

SITUATION 8: Everyone assumes that the maternal grandmother of the protagonist is penniless, but after she disappears, rumors that she stashed away a vast fortune emerge. Some family members believe she ran away and set out to find her, while others believe she is being held captive.

SITUATION 9: The adopted daughter of a CIA agent is kidnapped by the daughter's biological father. The ransom is a certain top-secret document. Instead of giving in, the agent uses tenuous leads to search for his daughter.

SITUATION 10: A botanist vanishes in a Central American rain forest while searching for new species of medicinal plants. When his son, who goes searching for him, encounters militants in the process of deforesting the region, he begins to suspect foul play.

CATEGORY 8: THE SEARCH FOR RESOLUTION

> People in power sometimes mistreat those under their control. If the mistreatment goes unchecked, as is often the case with prisoners (think of the film *The Shawshank Redemption*, based on a Stephen King story), rioting can break out. The protection of basic human rights prevents such abuses of power from occurring.

SITUATION 1: When factory workers, led by a charismatic organizer, strike against their supervisors, the factory's CEO searches for a peaceful way to end the conflict without a strike—but the organizer will not relent. Finally, another worker comes up with a plan that just might satisfy both parties.

SITUATION 2: A prison warden tries to prevent an impending riot by negotiating secretly with one of the prisoners who is respected by most of his fellow inmates. The prisoner is torn between loyalty to his fellow prisoners and wanting his sentence reduced.

SITUATION 3: During the witch-hunting in late seventeenth-century New England, a woman accused of witchcraft must prove she is not a witch. But what seems to her compelling evidence is to Cotton Mather an excellent reason for condemning her.

SITUATION 4: In 1964, during the Civil Rights movement in the South, a white high-school teacher tries to change the racist thinking of his students after an

African-American student joins his class. However, he find that even his closest friends and loved ones cannot agree with his enlightened thinking.

SITUATION 5: After rioting breaks out in a community in reaction to the government's oppressive policies, a civic leader struggles to find common ground between the community's demands and the government's policies.

SITUATION 6: A tribal leader tries to defuse a growing Native-American rebellion, the aim of which is to regain land lost to them more than 150 years ago. At the same time, he is motivated to improve living conditions for his people through legal means.

SITUATION 7: In the future, two lunar colonies threaten to go to war to resolve disputes over natural resources. An emissary from Earth uses diplomacy to try to broker a truce, but all of his efforts fail ... except one that could backfire.

SITUATION 8: During a human-rights protest in a dictatorship (past or current), the protagonist attempts a peaceful protest march—but halfway through it, police try to disperse the protesters with tear gas and a riot breaks out.

SITUATION 9: In a village plagued by superstition and fear, unmarried women who are being persecuted as witches plan to revolt against the (all-male) clergy—many of whom, ironically, have been secretly engaging in sorcery. One of the men tries to prevent the revolt.

SITUATION 10: Because of escalating gang wars, a retired police officer is determined to search for creative ways to diffuse the hostilities, disarm the gangs, and even disband the gangs themselves—but the gang leaders offer formidable opposition to her plans.

CATEGORY 9: THE SEARCH FOR A SOLUTION TO A HEALTH CRISIS

Steven Soderburgh's 2011 film *Contagion* riveted moviegoers with its disturbingly real dramatization of the rapid-fire spread of a lethal pathogen. Novels like Michael Crichton's *The Andromeda Strain* have had a similar impact. Such stories remind us of our vulnerability to infection—but also of the need to maintain good health habits. The following situations involve health crises that could become the basis of riveting stories.

SITUATION 1: A recreational drug that drastically (and possibly permanently) alters the personalities of its users becomes widespread. The protagonist searches for an antidote (as well as a way to sabotage existing supplies of the drug) before it's too late.

SITUATION 2: Severe pollution in a large metropolitan area is causing widespread and unusual respiratory disorders—and there seems to be no solution to the problem until the protagonist discovers a promising fix. However, the fix requires a major sacrifice.

SITUATION 3: A deadly epidemic is sweeping the country. The protagonist, who thinks she can stop it, is kidnapped by members of a terrorist group responsible for spreading the virus.

SITUATION 4: When a love drug is made available, millions take it to experience or re-experience romance with their significant other. However, the drug has unforeseen side effects that are problematic enough to incite researchers to search for an antidote.

SITUATION 5: Medical researchers rush to create an antidote to a mutated syphilis bacterium resistant to existing antibiotics. The head researcher discovers a possible antidote, but it is highly controversial.

SITUATION 6: Someone has contaminated a community reservoir with a chemical that is causing people's faces to change. The narrator searches simultaneously for the culprit and an antidote to the contaminant's effects.

SITUATION 7: The suicide rate is becoming alarmingly high among business professionals. A clinical psychologist, with the help of his wife, a corporate executive, embarks on a search to discover the cause.

SITUATION 8: People everywhere are losing their memories, and psychologists search simultaneously for a cause and a cure. Things become even more confusing when people begin experiencing false memories.

SITUATION 9: An artificial antiviral agent, originally designed to give people lifelong immunity to all types of flu, mutates inexplicably, causing grotesque physiological changes in those who were immunized.

SITUATION 10: Mosquitoes carrying the dengue-fever virus proliferate inexplicably and migrate to northern latitudes. The narrator, an expert on this infectious disease, must find an antidote before hundreds of thousands of people perish.

CATEGORY 10: THE SEARCH FOR A WEAPON

Stories of war, criminal investigation, or espionage, often involve the search for a weapon and thereby generate the suspense readers crave. A good cinematic example is *The Hindenburg*, a 1975 film, which speculates that the cause of the destruction of the German zeppelin was a bomb planted by an anti-Nazi spy. Here are ten scenarios for you to develop into nail-biting suspense.

SITUATION 1: A group of domestic terrorists announce that they have planted a bomb somewhere in the protagonist's large city and will detonate it unless the government ceases all efforts to restrict the use of petrochemicals. The protagonist and her team use scant clues to search for the bomb.

SITUATION 2: After a scientist entrusted with top-secret information about a new military weapon vanishes, an agent is recruited to find her. However, the scientist has begun to send media contacts pieces of information about the program, and the military decides to not just find the scientist but dissolve the program and make everyone who had anything to do with it disappear, including the agent.

SITUATION 3: Demolition experts venture into enemy territory in search of a missing nuclear warhead that the enemy stole from a botched secret-ops mission. The narrator must resort to unusual infiltration methods to obtain information leading to the hiding place.

SITUATION 4: When a highway construction crew unearths a strange device, experts fear it may be a weapon—but no one is certain what kind or how lethal it might be. Archaeologists are brought in to determine the manufacturers.

SITUATION 5: Someone has contaminated a municipal water supply with a chemical that heightens aggression and makes people lose their ability to think rationally. An enterprising detective searches for the culprit as well as an antidote, but he must hurry: He drank from the water supply himself.

SITUATION 6: After a domestic terrorist hides a bomb in an office building and makes demands, he is killed in an unrelated incident. The protagonist must locate the bomb before it's too late.

SITUATION 7: Robots with advanced artificial intelligence plant a doomsday weapon designed to eliminate all human life on earth. It is up to a small group

261

of humans who have escaped from roving armies of robots and who learn about the weapon from a robot defector to find the weapon before it detonates.

SITUATION 8: A powerful bomb, presumably left over from a recent conflict, is found partially buried just outside a busy marketplace. The protagonist, a demolition expert, fears it may be remote-controlled and was deliberately buried.

SITUATION 9: An arsenal of nuclear warheads for missiles vanishes. A domestic militia is responsible for the theft. Eventually they announce that they are planning to launch an attack against a government institution unless their demands are met. It is up to the narrator, a CIA agent, to stop them.

SITUATION 10: Someone has placed a bomb in Jerusalem's Old City. An encrypted e-mail sent to the Israelis, the Palestinians, and the U.S. Embassy warns that the bomb, capable of destroying the Temple Mount, will be detonated unless a lasting peace between the Israelis and the Palestinians is established.

CHAPTER 18

THE SECRET OF X

CATEGORY 1: SECRETS OF ANIMALS

> No matter how thoroughly we study them, animals continue to mystify. We like to imagine their secrets, which they may never allow us to know, even if they can one day communicate them to us. Many species of animals have yet to be discovered; who knows what fascinating behaviors and abilities they might have?

SITUATION 1: Weird catlike creatures fill the forests of this magic land; the rebellious princess, tired of being cooped up in the castle, sneaks out with the help of a guard. She ventures into the forest and spies on one of the creatures, one that is intent on sharing its secrets with her.

SITUATION 2: Who would have guessed that frogs harbor strange secrets and that people can figure out what they are, if only they listen carefully enough to their croaking? That is exactly what a precocious girl is able to do. But the frogs warn her: You must not share these secrets with anyone else.

SITUATION 3: Lizard-like creatures that seem to possess humanoid traits have been stalking villages, managing to escape whenever the residents lay traps for them. But one villager discovers the cave from which they emerge and dares to venture inside.

SITUATION 4: An artificial sphere, a hundred meters in diameter, has been found partially buried in the desert; scientists discover that it contains creatures with characteristics that are both alien and familiar. They suspect that the sphere has been transported from the distant future—for reasons they hope to discover.

SITUATION 5: A curious young boy discovers a long-lost entrance to a world in which fearsome creatures have been exiled. All of the creatures harbor terrible secrets about the world they came from—secrets that the boy suspects have to do with wealth and magic. He must win their trust before they will divulge their secrets.

SITUATION 6: Giraffes are full of secrets, which a zoologist discovers. She has spent her professional life studying them but only recently found that giraffes share their secrets under special circumstances and in unusual ways. These secrets begin to affect her personal life in dramatic ways, some good and some bad.

SITUATION 7: While exploring a lake deep beneath the Arctic polar cap, scientists encounter a fishlike animal no one has seen before. While examining it in the lab, it begins to communicate with them with strange sounds.

SITUATION 8: When a sickly child sneaks out of the house one summer day, he is startled to discover that birds fly toward him and share their secrets in a bird language he can understand. Some of the secrets help him find ways to improve his condition, and some get him in trouble. Meanwhile a psychologist insists that he should be "cured" of this delusion.

SITUATION 9: A rare sea creature washes ashore, barely alive. When a child finds it, she is about to toss it back into the water when, in a faint voice, it speaks to her. It tells her an amazing secret about an enchanting undersea domain that must be rescued before it disappears forever.

SITUATION 10: Conscious her ability to establish mind links with animals, a teenager visits the zoo. There the animals share their secret thoughts with her. Many are unhappy. When one of the animals realizes her talent, it tries to persuade her to set it and its kind free.

CATEGORY 2: ANCESTRAL SECRETS

Those who research their family histories are often surprised— pleasantly or unpleasantly—by some of the long-forgotten activities of their ancestors, and the farther back they search, the more eye-opening the surprises, in many cases. Secrets, after all, are destined to be revealed eventually. Such intrigue spanning many generations makes for fine story material.

SITUATION 1: When a teacher uncovers a diary kept by her grandmother, she is shocked to discover that her mother's real father was a Nazi guard who had raped her. Moreover, the Nazi is still alive in a German prison.

SITUATION 2: While cleaning his attic, an elderly man stumbles upon a trunk that belonged to his great-grandfather. When he opens it, he is shocked to discover documents that tie his ancestors to a crime that has never been solved.

SITUATION 3: Following a string of career failures, the protagonist falls into deep depression, but then he discovers a journal kept by his deceased father who described a similar crisis in his life—which ended when he found a hidden talent, one his son has in abundance.

SITUATION 4: The head of a prosperous aristocratic family is being haunted by the ghosts of his ancestors. They claim the family prosperity was gained by the suffering of others—and it's time to pay the piper.

SITUATION 5: For the past decade, a once-prosperous family has been suffering one misfortune after another. The family's matriarch discovers the dark secret: Her father had swindled a business partner, a sorcerer who cursed the family. Now the matriarch is determined to do whatever it takes to break the curse.

SITUATION 6: Seeking to uncover the dark secrets her ancestors were alleged to have harbored, a writer returns to her ancestral Asian village and indeed uncovers more secrets than she bargained for. Some of them are too disturbing to write about.

SITUATION 7: A priest exploring his genealogy discovers that his grandfather worked for a family involved in organized crime and he committed a terrible misdeed for which he served a prison sentence. The secret had been hidden so that his family could maintain their sterling reputation. The priest wants to void that false reputation—but his family warns him not to.

SITUATION 8: While abroad, an art historian chances upon a portrait that resembles himself. He discovers to his amazement that he has an ancestral link to the painter and that the identity of the individual in the painting has been kept secret.

SITUATION 9: The descendant of a highly regarded political leader claims to have uncovered documents that link the leader to a terrorist group that once plotted a military coup in his own country years earlier. After announcing that claim, she receives a death threat and must go into exile.

SITUATION 10: When a homeless woman learns that her great-grandfather had been an activist in community service, creating homeless shelters, etc., she embarks on a personal mission to improve her life by following his example.

CATEGORY 3: FAMILY AND FRIENDS' SECRETS

Every family has its secrets—some trivial, some not. Some secrets are partially known, but others are so deeply buried they don't surface for generations. The longer secrets are kept, the likelier it is that they will be leaked confessed, or stumbled upon. The story possibilities are many.

SITUATION 1: Long isolated from mainstream society, a mountain-dwelling family holds secrets only whispered about in a nearby village, but now a detective has stumbled upon a crime report describing one of the senior family members as a suspect in a murder—an unsolved crime the protagonist thinks he can solve.

SITUATION 2: The narrator assumed her boyfriend was trustworthy, especially since he is heavily active in the community and local organizations, but when her boyfriend's long-estranged brother moves back to town, her boyfriend confesses that he secretly hurt his brother's chances at winning an athletic competition out of jealousy and fears his brother knows about it, thus his return years later.

SITUATION 3: Bullied by older siblings, a reclusive teen retreats to his hiding place with friends he conjures up with incantations. They get along beautifully, but these friends are magical beings with dangerous powers.

SITUATION 4: A Sioux activist learns that his father, who long ago abandoned the family, was a crook who robbed Native-American charities. Furious, he seeks revenge on his father, but when he finds him, he has second thoughts.

SITUATION 5: A venture capitalist sneaks into the office of her ex-boyfriend (an engineer) to extract classified technical information. Her plan is to use the information in a lucrative project as a way of exacting vengeance on him for past abuses.

SITUATION 6: Consumed by guilt for years because of the unjust way he treated his brother (thereby causing the brother to suffer a string of misfortunes), the narrator reveals his secret and vows to make up for the injustice—but his brother refuses to forgive him and may even seek revenge.

SITUATION 7: After winning the lottery, a recently married man hides the fact from his wife and uses the money to fulfill his playboy fantasy. Soon the fantasy turns into a nightmare and he returns home, but his wife is gone.

SITUATION 8: Every Halloween a woman dons a witch's costume and puts neighbors and family members under one innocuous spell or another. No one realizes she really is a witch until a friend angers her and she casts a malignant spell over him.

SITUATION 9: Peaceful on the surface, a veteran secretly struggles against paranoia, but he continues to amass an arsenal of illegal firearms and explosives. When his wife discovers them, she is torn between confronting him and reporting him to the police.

SITUATION 10: A boy picks the lock on his mother's dresser drawer and discovers a hoard of wallets: His mother is a pickpocket. Afraid to confront her, he contacts the owners of the wallets—and that is when problems really unfold.

CATEGORY 4: LETTERS FROM SECRET SENDERS

Letters from anonymous recipients arouse curiosity ... and suspicion. Sometimes the writers want to keep their identity a secret for good reasons, but sometimes they do so for malicious reasons, too. Whatever the motives, gripping tales can be fashioned. Here are ten scenarios with this premise for you to develop.

SITUATION 1: Unable to bring himself to admit his love for the girl he has been enchanted with since eighth grade, a high-school student writes her secret love letters and asks her to keep them secret. Instead she posts and ridicules the "anonymous" letters on social-media sites, knowing that clues in the letters hint at the writer's identity.

SITUATION 2: Someone is sending letters to a college student, rich in insights into the human heart. The letters are typed, unsigned, and slipped under her door. She confronts possible candidates (professors, old boyfriends) but is still baffled.

SITUATION 3: A journalist receives a threatening letter ordering her to appear at a certain place at a certain time. She obeys, only to be handed another letter by a courier to appear elsewhere. This continues until the sender reveals himself: a hired assassin.

SITUATION 4: Incarcerated for his seditious views, a teacher in a country ruled by a despot smuggles messages to his sister in the United States, urging her to publicize his views regarding intellectual freedom. When the letters stop coming, she fears for his life and seeks the State Department's help to rescue him.

SITUATION 5: When a piano prodigy's mother discovers that her daughter has been receiving letters from a secret admirer, she demands to see them; when the girl refuses, the mother finds the letters and discovers that they contain musical compositions.

SITUATION 6: A refugee receives letters from a mysterious sender, urging her to return to her homeland at once, for only she can prevent the country's imminent invasion by an evil force. Despite weeks of investigation, she cannot find evidence that the sender or the country exists. Then one day, the sender shows up on her doorstep.

SITUATION 7: Faced with legal battles, the collapse of his marriage, and financial ruin, an executive receives a secret letter claiming to be from his future self, who explains what he must do. He assumes that the letter is a hoax. Then one day his future self shows up.

SITUATION 8: After opening a portal to an alternate universe, a physicist receives amorous letters from a woman in that universe. She pleads with him to visit her, if he doesn't, she will seal the portal.

SITUATION 9: An abused child finds a letter under the covers of his bed, inviting him to a magical place. The letter is written in calligraphy, and the writer claims to be an exiled magician who needs the child's help to return to his kingdom.

SITUATION 10: To express his love for a fellow sixth grader, a precocious but shy boy secretly pens passionate letters to her. When his teacher intercepts one, she fears that an adult, not a student, is writing them to the girl—and implicates a teacher she has always disliked.

CATEGORY 5: SECRET MISSIONS OR CALLINGS

Stories in which a vital secret mission is planned and carried out virtually ensures edge-of-seat reading, provided that the odds are formidable, the hero is clever but not invincible, the suspense is sustained, and the goal is cleverly achieved. Any of the following ten situations should get you into suspense-writing mode.

SITUATION 1: An executive (and secret agent) and her husband are in South Korea for a conference when she vanishes during a reception. It turns out that she flew to North Korea on a classified mission. When she doesn't return, her husband is approached to help find her.

SITUATION 2: The narrator and another soldier infiltrate a secret encampment where the enemy is conducting misinformation transmissions. But separating accurate information from false information proves to be a tougher challenge than anticipated, and their time in the camp is running out.

SITUATION 3: An influential inventor believes God is calling her to reverse a destructive trend in technology, so she launches an aggressive environmental movement. When she admits that God has called her to this mission, many lose trust in her.

SITUATION 4: After learning that an enemy nation has constructed a base on the moon that will soon house a nuclear warhead, the Pentagon plans a secret mission using retired astronauts to stop or destroy the shipment.

SITUATION 5: Despairing in his cell, a prisoner hears the voice of God commanding him to study painting. A week into his art lessons, he is seized by incredible visions, which he tries to capture in his paintings. The warden, however, misinterprets the paintings and takes away his painting privileges.

SITUATION 6: Although the Pentagon reported that drone strikes would target a terrorist holdout, the actual target was kept secret and was far more controversial. However, a Pentagon official, who is personally against drone strikes, decides to leak the secret.

SITUATION 7: Acting on a calling from God he received in a dream, a priest embarks on a mission to change the Church's attitude toward celibacy among priests. Although he has much support, he also receives threats on his life.

SITUATION 8: After an accident causes him to lose his voice, a singer is called by an angel to devote himself to helping those whose careers have been cut short by accidents. "Do this for a year," the angel promises, "and I will return your voice to its original quality." The only condition is that he must keep his angelic calling a secret. Alas, the temptation to share his encounter with the angel proves too great, and he tells others.

SITUATION 9: Despite a command from the president to stop spying on a close ally's leader, CIA agents suspect that the ally is involved in anti-U.S. operations, and resume spying. If the ally were to discover this revocation of the pledge, war would become imminent. A diplomat from that nation becomes aware of the new activity and decides to blackmail the CIA.

SITUATION 10: An athlete with a secret drug addiction heeds a calling to quit drugs and redeem herself on the tennis court. Because she wishes to keep her past addiction private, she must find a way to get completely clean in time for the tournament she wants to enter.

CATEGORY 6: SECRET ORGANIZATIONS

> Secret organizations, clubs, or societies exist to recruit those who are faithful to a given cause or who possess a shared talent. While enveloped in mystery, most of these organizations are benevolent, but some are not—and are therefore ideal sources for stories.

SITUATION 1: Difficult as it has been, dissenters from a cruel regime form a secret society dedicated to doing all they can to overthrow the dictator. They build a haven underground and conduct raids in the dead of night, but then one of them is caught.

SITUATION 2: When she learns about a secret coven of witches, a woman who was cast out of her village because of her magical powers joins the coven. But these witches are sinister and threaten to corrupt the woman, who had intended to use her powers to help people.

SITUATION 3: Shrouded in mystery, a secret organization recruits only those in the community who possess a certain talent—but nobody knows what that talent is. Once a member, individuals are sworn to secrecy. One recruit breaks the vow and soon regrets it.

SITUATION 4: Highly trained saboteurs are hired by various groups to sabotage equipment used in deforestation, warfare, etc. They vow never to reveal who hired them if they're caught—but that proves easier said than done.

SITUATION 5: Posing as talent scouts, members of a secret organization canvass neighborhoods in search of people possessing particular skills, such as photographic memory. But instead of awarding scholarships as they claim to do, they recruit the selectees for unseemly tasks.

SITUATION 6: During the day, residents of this town adhere to a traditional lifestyle, but at night, many of them become participants in a demonic organization that threatens all who stray from "the path of righteousness."

SITUATION 7: Children new to this neighborhood are invited to join a secret club that meets in a tree house. At first the newest recruit is excited about the club and its secrecy, but then the club's leader reveals sinister occult intentions.

SITUATION 8: Renegade teachers form a secret organization devoted to developing innovative school curricula that include often-cut programs such as music, visual arts, and theater, as well as small classes and minimal use of standardized tests. When word of the organization is leaked, heads roll.

SITUATION 9: Members of a hunting club have formed a secret subsidiary group intent on lifting all restrictions on firearms. More radical than the National Rifle Association, they threaten anti-gun lobbyists and legislators who have pushed for restrictions of any kind. An advocate of gun control learns of their existence and dares to confront them.

SITUATION 10: People no longer dare to abuse their pets in this community, where a secret organization of animal protectors has been rounding up abusers and giving them a taste of their own medicine. The only problem is that there is no consensus on where to draw the line between "abuse" and "discipline."

CATEGORY 7: SECRET PROJECTS

Keeping a large project secret has always been difficult. The Manhattan Project, perhaps, was one of the great success stories, but in the age of WikiLeaks, even maintaining military secrecy would be an amazing achievement—a fact of modern life that allows for even more suspenseful tales!

SITUATION 1: When genetically modified crops are rejected by the Department of Agriculture, the farmers who were hoping for clearance secretly plant the crops anyway. When consumers begin suffering from health problems and the project is blamed, a journalist discovers that other factors could be the cause.

SITUATION 2: Your mission, if you decide to accept it: Gain access to the most carefully guarded secret project in history where, according to a defector from this enemy nation, construction of a time machine is taking place.

SITUATION 3: Physicists have been secretly working on a matter-transport device. When the project is leaked, corporations compete for access to the schematics, despite the possibility that the whole scheme is a hoax.

SITUATION 4: Known for her extraordinary programming skills, the protagonist becomes part of a secret government anti-cyberterrorism project. She is doubly challenged when she discovers that at least one cyberterrorist is actually part of the project.

SITUATION 5: Neuroscientists embark on a secret project to enhance human memory. They believe that powerful, accurate memory will revolutionize civilization. When word is leaked, other scientists want to sabotage the project because they fear it would do more harm than good.

SITUATION 6: A research group secretly experiments with creating human-animal hybrid cells in an effort to create a vaccine against deadly viruses. When one of the researchers worries that the project leader has gone too far, she blows the whistle.

SITUATION 7: Led by a visionary (but mentally unstable) robotics expert, a maverick group of engineers launches a secret project to build a self-replicating robot. When one of the prototype robots goes out of control, some members of the team want to shut down the project.

SITUATION 8: The narrator is intent on founding a new religion based on the teachings of a mystic who has been transmitting his ecstatic visions into psychedelic videos and growing more popular every day. The only problem is that the mystic is also severely schizophrenic.

SITUATION 9: In the middle of a top-secret project to neutralize the effects of the poison gas used in chemical weapons, the project supervisor is abducted by militant extremists who threaten to kill the supervisor if the project is not abandoned. The supervisor is soon rescued but not by who he expects.

SITUATION 10: Residents are baffled by night crews assembling just outside their town and working until dawn on ... what? Everything is hush-hush, until an intrepid reporter sneaks past the security perimeter to discover the secret project: a machine that can open a window to a parallel Earth.

CATEGORY 8: SECRET RITUALS

> Spiritual needs are forces to be reckoned with, and counterforces, even whole empires, run the risk of destruction if they interfere with people's need to worship. Stories about the struggle to worship, even if that struggle must be kept secret, make for compelling tales.

SITUATION 1: At first mystified by a cache of ancient Egyptian funereal artifacts she finds in her deceased grandfather's attic, the narrator uncovers long-hidden secrets about her grandparents and their involvement with a group that appears long defunct ... or is it?

SITUATION 2: Forbidden by the emperor to worship her gods in public, the protagonist and her followers erect a shrine in the forest. There they worship powerful pagan gods who promise their followers protection. But the emperor learns of the secret shrine and sets out to destroy it.

SITUATION 3: Two siblings uncover an incantation buried in their grandparents' trunk, along with a warning that it must never be used. Neither must it be destroyed—which is why their grandparents kept it. But because of recent misfortunes, the siblings utter the incantation, hoping it will bring good luck.

SITUATION 4: While playing a witch onstage, a young actress performs a ritual, as the script directs, but the mayhem that follows was not in the script. As a consequence, everyone suspects that she is a real witch.

SITUATION 5: The moment she begins examining the inscriptions on a rune stone at the recently excavated Druid site, an anthropologist finds herself under the power of a spell—one that produces vivid visions of ancient Druidic rituals. Is she being transported back in time to when these Druids lived?

SITUATION 6: Volunteers in a third-world country get involved with a tribe that engages in secret rituals as a means of gaining the basics they need to subsist.

Not only do they refuse the aid of the volunteers; they hold the volunteers captive as sacrifices to appease the gods.

SITUATION 7: In ancient Delphi, priests and poets visit the oracles of Apollo or of Zeus, who bestow them with prophecies and inspiration. How did the oracles receive their visions? That is the mystery an investigative journalist intends to find out.

SITUATION 8: Children make up nonsensical incantations, but one day, while pretending to trap a kid in a force field, the incantation actually works. Now they must figure out how to undo the spell.

SITUATION 9: To put an end to the drought that is threatening her realm, the queen consults a seer to perform the appropriate ritual, but the only ritual that can end the drought, according to the seer, is one in which the queen must return half of her realm to a sworn enemy.

SITUATION 10: A woman believes that spiritual rebirth is possible through a series of water rituals—not just baptism but invocations of ancient water deities, the recitation of poetry, and the singing of hymns about the healing power of water. The rituals are to be performed in the nude—which is why the woman and her friends are arrested. However, the rituals seem to work.

CATEGORY 9: SECRETS OF LOST PEOPLES AND PLACES

Many secrets of vanished or vanquished peoples lie buried throughout the world, waiting for archaeologists, anthropologists, and forensic experts to reconstruct and record their stories. History is continually revised as a result of such discoveries. And of course, there are also alternate universes that writers can "discover" and populate with civilizations of their own imagining.

SITUATION 1: For centuries, the ruined mountain kingdom lay buried in an avalanche of rubble. Then one day, a subject of the current monarch discovers evidence of a way into the fortress, that it had become a sequestered city of enchantment—and that descendants of its sorcerers may still exist.

SITUATION 2: Archaeologists uncover a secret burial site belonging to a pre-Columbian tribe of Indians. The burial chambers contain skeletons, artwork, and relics that gradually paint a picture of a catastrophic event that might repeat itself.

SITUATION 3: Peaceful and picturesque, ruled by a benevolent monarch, this kingdom seems idyllic ... until the protagonist stumbles upon a clue that leads her to the location of a chest filled with secrets about the kingdom's not-so-idyllic past.

SITUATION 4: A slave has been taught to read and write by the slave owner's daughter. In his secret journal, he describes the owner's illegal business transactions. After he escapes, he tries to get the owner arrested before he hurts his daughter for having educated him.

SITUATION 5: After being driven from their homeland, several pagans create a utopian community in a remote mountainous region. Ages pass, and the descendants of those who exiled the pagans rediscover them, along with the pagans' strange secrets that have given them unique powers of persuasion.

SITUATION 6: Human descendants on Mars are the custodians of humanity's legacy on a now-ravaged Earth. But each of the several Martian colonies holds only a piece of the whole, and the protagonist wants to reconstruct the whole picture, especially the technological piece, which is most elusive.

SITUATION 7: The inhabitants of a remote volcanic island have survived not just by farming intelligently but by securing favors from the gods through ancient secret rituals—that is, until now. They have not properly appeased the volcano godess Pele, and now there will be hell to pay.

SITUATION 8: What was keeping the inhabitants of a subarctic wilderness from aging? An anthropologist visits the community, intent on learning the secret. She discovers that the inhabitants follow bizarre dietary and lifestyle habits.

SITUATION 9: Clio, the Muse of history, appears before two intellectually curious siblings who are both artists, and she shows them unknown facets of history in order to inspire new works. But she shows too much, and some of these facets are disturbing, even terrifying. The sibling artists aim to tell the world about these secrets, and Clio now worries that these facts might do more harm than good.

SITUATION 10: To gain entrance into the Secret City, children must memorize a large quantity of information about astronomy, physics, mythology, and art. Those who pass the test become part of a society in which both memory and imagination are paramount.

CATEGORY 10: SECRETS OF YOUTH AND OLD AGE

There's something intriguing about children and old people harboring secrets. From children we may expect secrets having to do with magical places or other inexplicable discoveries; with the elderly, long-suppressed desires or family transgressions are more common.

SITUATION 1: In the dead of night, a knock on the door reveals an old woman who tells the man who answers that she is a close friend of his grandparents. She also says that she has a terrible secret she must share about his family.

SITUATION 2: A deaf-mute since his early childhood, a young man returns from a journey with his hearing restored, but he keeps this fact to himself. Because others assume he is still deaf, he learns many secrets in his hometown and overhears a plot to swindle an elderly family member out of her wealth. He operates carefully not only to destroy the plot but to keep his own secret intact.

SITUATION 3: On her deathbed, the grandmother of a dysfunctional family whispers a secret in her granddaughter's ear—a secret about certain family members that will cause the granddaughter and another sibling to fear for their lives.

SITUATION 4: When asked how he managed to reach his extremely advanced age, the still-robust centenarian gave the usual reasons—no tobacco or drugs, lots of vegetables, etc.—but a reporter who digs deeper into the man's life suspects a dark secret, a supernatural one.

SITUATION 5: A mischievous boy who sneaks into neighbors' yards overhears several teens plotting to "shoot up" a local school. When he tells school officials what he overheard, they don't believe him because he'd been caught telling lies before.

SITUATION 6: Even though he swears to keep his older brother's theft a secret, the protagonist cannot resist disclosing it to others, leading to the older brother's arrest. After the brother gets out of jail, he vows revenge on his younger brother.

SITUATION 7: An elderly tribal chief reveals a secret prophecy to his grandson. The prophecy involves the destiny of their tribe (and also involves the grandson), and the young man promises to fulfill the prophecy. But the boy secretly plans to depart the tribe.

276

SITUATION 8: Suspected of suffering from autism, or some other mental dysfunction, a young boy is hospitalized in an effort to diagnose him accurately. During the boy's hospital stay, a neurologist notices him writing down bizarre messages in an unknown language and muttering in an ancient language in his sleep. Hypnosis reveals that he is in contact with a boy from ancient Greece.

SITUATION 9: When the dying king confesses that he secretly exiled his pregnant mistress, a search is undertaken to find her before she gives birth (to nix the possibility of any claims to the throne). By the time they find her, she has already given birth, and the infant is nowhere to be found.

SITUATION 10: Diagnosed with a terminal illness, an old man tells his brother that he had cheated him out of thousands of dollars in a fraudulent business transaction and will bequeath him that sum in a codicil to his will. Alas, the terminal diagnosis proves false; now the brother demands the money up front.

CHAPTER 19
THE THREAT OF X

CATEGORY 1: THE THREAT OF CONTAMINATION, ILLNESS, OR INFECTION

Even in the age of miracle drugs and ever-improving health-care programs, contamination and disease threaten on many fronts, from drug-resistant microbes to contaminated foods. Aside from being well-informed via health-care providers and wellness news-letters, we may also gain health knowledge through fact-based, well-told stories.

SITUATION 1: Antibiotic-resistant bacteria threatens to reach a pandemic level. An epidemiologist searches for a way to attack both the cause of the most recent proliferation and the flourishing black market of over-the-counter antibiotics that do not actually work but do give the public a false and dangerous sense of confidence.

SITUATION 2: So-called "mad cow" disease has become an epidemic. While the CDC struggles to isolate the source, the cattle industry is threatened. Many advocate the cattle industry's demise (despite the blow to the economy) and promote lab-grown meat, but others insist the health threat can be eliminated.

SITUATION 3: A mutated virus mimics the common cold at first but eventually produces symptoms unlike any other known disease. Researchers scramble to "decode" the strain, but by the time they do, the virus mutates again.

SITUATION 4: When people contract this illness, the flu-like symptoms develop into heightened perceptions and vastly improve mental clarity and IQ, but doc-

278

tors fear that the "positive" symptoms mask a sinister brain disease and they soon discover they are correct.

SITUATION 5: A newly discovered pathogen is brought to the United States for study, and despite the highest-level containment protocols, the pathogen gets into the hands of homegrown terrorists, who threaten to use it as a bioweapon to influence elections and maybe even begin a revolution.

SITUATION 6: An unknown organism has been detected in a town's water supply, and tests on lab mice indicate it could cause serious illness in humans. But when efforts are made to eradicate the organism, it multiplies, as if sensing the threat.

SITUATION 7: Synthetic microbes escape quarantine and threaten animal and human life in surrounding areas. The microbes, created to better understand the dynamics of mutation, are dangerous because of their ability to mutate rapidly. After careful testing, biochemists fear that the microbes may cause incurable diseases.

SITUATION 8: After a rogue biologist illegally dumps genetically mutated fish into one of the Great Lakes, the mutated species spawns rapidly and starts devouring the native species in the lake, threatening a severe disruption of the food chain.

SITUATION 9: The CDC identifies a new and virulent pathogen. Those infected acquire (among other things) brain lesions that cause them to turn into zombies and go on mindless rampages.

SITUATION 10: Unbeknownst to the astronauts returning to Earth, an organism discovered on Mars passed through the spacecraft's filtration system and threatens to proliferate. It appears that the only choice is to destroy the entire facility to prevent widespread contamination.

CATEGORY 2: THE THREAT OF ASSAULT

We live in dangerous times—a warning we hear repeatedly, even though violence in society, according to experts like Steven Pinker (*The Better Angels of Our Nature*), has been in steady decline. Still, we are inundated by reports of shootings and assaults. Perhaps good stories that focus on the roots of aggression can accelerate the decline in violence.

SITUATION 1: A security guard and his family move into an apartment complex where rent is inexpensive and members of a group of thieves live. These thieves target residents of the complex repeatedly. After police fail to gather enough evidence for an arrest, the security guard works with the apartment manager to trap the thieves.

SITUATION 2: Street gangs proliferate in what has been a crime-free neighborhood. Even more ominously, the gangs appear to be targeting individuals of a particular ethnicity. A retired police officer living in the neighborhood sets out to rid the neighborhood of these gangs.

SITUATION 3: In this near-future scenario, most citizens carry firearms (and those who do not are considered unpatriotic). Firearm use has become a required course in middle school, and gun shows are major attractions. Legislators attempting to pass gun-control legislation are persecuted. One such legislator, however, refuses to be intimidated and has found a clever way to introduce his bill.

SITUATION 4: Disgusted with their young-adult neighbors' deafeningly loud music, elderly residents in an apartment complex stage a counterassault with Gregorian chants. Not to be outdone, the youth's friends threaten physical assault if the senior citizens do not relent. Some of the elderly residents, former combat veterans, do not take the threats lightly.

SITUATION 5: Having been bullied one time too many, a teenager decides to give the bully a taste of his own medicine, but her scheme backfires when he physically assaults her and threatens to assault her entire family.

SITUATION 6: An elderly janitor must walk through a dangerous part of town to get to and from his job. Repeatedly harassed, he decides to carry a butcher knife with him. One day he overreacts and stabs a panhandler who merely asked for a couple dollars. He runs, but doesn't know what to do next.

SITUATION 7: A congresswoman excels at her job, but she cannot control her temper when an opponent speaks unkindly of her. She must find a way to manage her emotions under these circumstances—but one opponent knows her weakness and uses it against her whenever he can.

SITUATION 8: As missionaries try to convert those whom they provide with food and clothing, they are being threatened with assault by militant rebels. Although some of the needy are grateful for the missionaries' efforts, a few of them actually side with the rebels—especially after the rebels empower the needy with weapons and promise them jobs if they join their cause.

SITUATION 9: Tour buses in New York City are taken over by terrorists who hold their passengers hostage, threatening to blow up the buses (with the passengers inside) unless the government meets their demands.

SITUATION 10: A grocer has been doing business in this neighborhood for thirty years, and the threat of assault from robbers does not intimidate him. Even after being robbed and beaten severely, he refuses to close his store—on the contrary, he purchases the adjoining store after the owner quits; he also takes self-defense lessons from a combat veteran.

CATEGORY 3: THE THREAT OF ECONOMIC CHAOS OR COLLAPSE

Wild market speculation, unethical investment practices, deregulation—the list of potential causes of economic crises is long. Avarice is the principal culprit, and there seems to be plenty of loopholes that crafty investors can use to skirt around the law. Good stories that raise consciousness about such practices spread public awareness.

SITUATION 1: Cyberterrorists have found insidious new ways of hacking into the accounts of financial institutions and threatening complete destruction of data unless their demands are met. Ironically, the FBI hires a convicted felon to isolate the terrorists.

SITUATION 2: A nation stages a false inflation in the hopes of destabilizing the currency of its enemies. An economist, savvy to such manipulation, tries to convince authorities that it's just a scam—still, the scam is working.

SITUATION 3: Some group is attempting to devalue the dollar, and before preventive measures can be taken, the stock market crashes. Meanwhile investigators try to identify the group responsible and determine their motive.

SITUATION 4: When the new president takes office and radically downsizes the food-stamp program, an economic crisis is triggered—but the new administration blames the other party for the crisis. A reporter penetrates the inner circle to isolate the hard facts and report them.

SITUATION 5: A bank buys up homes in a region deemed a high risk for flooding (including the home of the protagonist, who is so poor he has no choice but to

281

accept their meager offer), but after drainage systems are improved (financed in part by the bank), the bank resells the properties at much higher prices, outraging the original mortgage holders.

SITUATION 6: In the near future, widespread droughts wreak havoc on the economy as well as the food supply. Proposed emergency measures, however, are attacked as big-government operations attempt to muscle in on private enterprise.

SITUATION 7: Maverick gold speculators threaten a gold-market tailspin when they sell off their portfolios after the price of gold reaches the hoped-for peak. Now they plan to launch a similar scheme with other investments. In the meantime, a Securities and Exchange Commission officer is investigating.

SITUATION 8: Attacks on the overcommercialization of the holidays are threatening major losses in revenue during the November through December shopping period. One retailer decides she is going to collaborate with advertisers to counter the negative publicity.

SITUATION 9: An antitrust lawsuit and a hacked website threaten to bring down the biggest online retailer during the holiday season, thereby triggering an economic crisis. The company's execs struggle to keep their ship afloat, but they must address the charges brought upon them.

SITUATION 10: Hyperinflation has rendered this country's currency virtually worthless, and total economic collapse is imminent. The government recruits an expert to find some way to revalue their monetary system. She has an idea, but it is highly unconventional.

CATEGORY 4: THE THREAT OF BLACKMAIL, EXTORTION, OR BRIBERY

> Everyone's life is a book of secrets which in the wrong hands, can be used to extort money or other favors. Because blackmail and extortion form the basis of so many engaging stories, they are very popular with writers in all genres.

SITUATION 1: In this military state, whose top university operates an advanced-weaponry program, a secret group of university peaceniks has been sponsoring projects that defy the government's hawkish agenda. But then the leader of the dissident group is captured and tortured.

SITUATION 2: Convinced that a successful actor's promise to get her a film role is just a bribe for sexual favors, a struggling artist refuses to date him further. The actor's intentions are honorable, but he cannot find a way to convince her of that. When he loses his starring role, it becomes even more difficult.

SITUATION 3: When the Mob demands a percentage of a small business's profits, the owner refuses—and hires bodyguards in preparation for their attack. Problem: One of his bodyguards actually works for the Mob.

SITUATION 4: One of the school bullies threatens a shy classmate with beatings unless he pays five dollars a day. The classmate complies, but then the bully demands twice as much—the bully also says that if he tells anyone, he'll really regret it. Forced to choose between stealing to pay the bully or facing a beating, the classmate devises a way to trap the bully.

SITUATION 5: A mayoral candidate blackmails a potential benefactor into supporting him, or else he will publicly disclose their affair, thereby threatening her marriage. She calls his bluff, however, when she discovers that her husband is in on the scheme.

SITUATION 6: An unemployed mechanic blackmails his former boss: He says, "Re-hire me or I will release documents proving your illegal activities to the authorities." But the boss has some dirt on the mechanic as well.

SITUATION 7: When his ex-girlfriend spreads false rumors that he is gay, an anti-gay activist is threatened with violence by his fellow activists. He is offered a role on the opposing side of the argument helping a pro-gay rights group, but is uncomfortable with either position now and is conflicted over whether to get even with his ex-girlfriend or remove himself from public life as he settles his own internal conflicts.

SITUATION 8: After her professor gives her a low grade, a student threatens to blackmail him. Although she went to dinner with him to discuss her future, the student threatens to accuse him of seducing her. The professor, fearing that even a false accusation could ruin his reputation, is determined to silence her one way or another.

SITUATION 9: Offered an astonishing sum of money to stop his campaign for governor, a candidate refuses the bribe and seriously considers reporting the group who bribed him, but then the group offers him something more than cash that gives him pause.

SITUATION 10: A successful singer has a run-in with members of the Mob who claim that he owes them a percentage of his income to repay the publicity they financed years back. The singer had never requested their help. Still, they threaten to harm him and his family if he doesn't pay up.

CATEGORY 5: THE THREAT OF FAMILY INSTABILITY

> Ours is an age of anxiety, and nowhere do we more clearly see this anxiety played out than in the home. Family conflicts—conjugal, economic, parental—are the source of continual pressure. Good stories that focus on how to cope with, if not resolve, these issues are always appreciated.

SITUATION 1: A talented executive is suspended from his job because of alleged misconduct. Although the allegations prove false and he returns to his job, the effects of the rumor have taken its toll on his family.

SITUATION 2: Despite her unemployed husband's growing disdain for his role as househusband, a physician is committed to saving her marriage. She wants her husband to get involved in health care, but he is unwilling to undertake the two years' training required.

SITUATION 3: Although he is an outrageous flirt, the middle-aged narrator nonetheless is faithful to his wife, but his wife has been growing increasingly intolerant of his behavior. The ire begins to rub off on their daughter, who threatens to leave home if they do not resolve the matter.

SITUATION 4: A teenager steals his friend's father's revolver, intending to use it to scare his parents, in the hope that they'll stop fighting. It scares his father, all right—so much that he attacks the boy, and discharges the weapon.

SITUATION 5: In an effort to preserve traditional family values, a church-based organization contacts their notion of those they believe to be model families and features them on their TV show. But most of the model families have suppressed dark secrets that threaten their ideal images.

SITUATION 6: When a lesbian asks her conservative parents to meet her lover (whom she wants to marry), they argue that accepting her relationship would destroy their family. But instead of threatening to move out, the daughter arranges her betrothed to meet her parents in a festive holiday atmosphere.

SITUATION 7: Suddenly paranoid about home security after someone tried to burglarize her home, the wife of a pilot (away from home for long periods) arms herself with a gun, begins working out excessively, and improves home security. Her teenage daughters consider her actions excessive, and, as a result, family harmony is undermined.

SITUATION 8: A deeply religious man is convinced that family stability can be ensured only by strictest adherence to Scripture and church doctrine. Since his son and daughter have gone away to college they have become dissenters. Well, he will find a way to reverse that trend fast.

SITUATION 9: The son of a family of bankers, accountants, and other finance-oriented professionals fears that his son, who is preparing to become a comedian, will ruin their family image and undermine family stability. The boy's father's' influence is strong enough for him to seriously consider abandoning his dream.

SITUATION 10: Following a religious epiphany, a teenager strives to convert her family to her newfound religion, assuring them of greater happiness and family stability, but her persistence has the opposite effect.

CATEGORY 6: THE THREAT OF INVASION OR INSURRECTION

Many political or military thrillers focus on clashes between nations or empires during which invasion or uprising is imminent and is usually carried out. Such stories are made memorable when they depict the momentous changes that take place under such circumstances.

SITUATION 1: At first it seems like just another disorganized rebellion against big business, but then a charismatic leader appears and changes the uprisings from mob chaos to cleverly orchestrated demonstrations that threaten to bring down their particular targets.

SITUATION 2: Locusts have been breeding in frightening numbers in this farming region, threatening to wipe out crops. The farmers fight the plague on their own (disdainful of government assistance), but it seems hopeless. A local agricultural chemist, however, has a plan.

SITUATION 3: An experiment to eradicate mosquitoes has gone terribly wrong. Now, not only are they breeding in far greater numbers than ever before, they have grown in size and demand more blood, threatening to cause a major health crisis.

SITUATION 4: Darling little ladybugs ... except that this mutant form is anything but darling. They look the same but burrow into human flesh and cause emotional disorders. Children are especially at risk because they find the bugs so appealing.

SITUATION 5: Neo-Nazis pretending to be Good Samaritans infiltrate a community, win the community's trust, and only then begin their insidious project incriminating minorities of horrendous acts, giving the Nazis an excuse to persecute them.

SITUATION 6: Paramedics flying into the interior of a country besieged by insurgents are warned to stay away or they will be shot down. The pilot thinks he can evade attack, but the other paramedics aboard are not convinced. The pilot proceeds and the plane is forced to crash-land when an engine is crippled by gunfire, but the paramedics survive.

SITUATION 7: In this future scenario, militant youths organize political rallies targeting colleges and universities, demanding better career preparation programs and abandonment of "irrelevant" liberal-arts prerequisites. But when the colleges insist that liberal-arts programs must not only survive, but also flourish, the militants stage a takeover.

SITUATION 8: Animal-rights activists threaten the poultry industry with boycotts and sabotage unless they improve the treatment of the birds. When the industry ignores them, the activists sneak onto some of their farms and release the birds. The farmers retaliate by raising their market prices to exorbitant levels.

SITUATION 9: The Ku Klux Klan gains a surprisingly strong foothold in a northern city, threatening disorder and violence, especially after the NAACP (National Association for the Advancement of Colored People) and the ADL (Anti-Defamation League) step in. One anti-Klan activist pretends to be a supporter in order to infiltrate the group.

SITUATION 10: When a politically unstable country seems on the brink of collapse, their next-door neighbor threatens to invade. Many actually welcome the invasion, seeing it as a stabilizer, but opponents fear complete loss of national identity, as well as freedom.

CATEGORY 7: THE THREAT OF ELECTRONIC OR MECHANICAL MALFUNCTION

Along with the advantages of living in a high-tech wired world comes the increased likelihood of major disruptions of daily life when the juice stops flowing or the machines break down. Social chaos can ensue—and plenty of ideas for stories materialize as well.

SITUATION 1: Astronomers studying the sun report that giant solar flares may erupt soon, and if they do, they will knock out communication satellites and throw much of the world into chaos. When the astronomers propose preventive measures, they are rejected due to their high cost and disruption of day-to-day life.

SITUATION 2: One morning, people wake up to discover that all of their phones are malfunctioning: Calls and messages do not go to their intended receivers. While experts race to fix the problem, messages from an unknown source start arriving in all phones and computers, warning that all portable electronic devices will cease functioning unless certain demands are met.

SITUATION 3: In this alternate reality, appliances are sentient and sometimes talk back in helpful, jovial ways. A toaster will disagree about whether the setting for bagels is high enough, etc. One day, some of the appliances begin making threats: "Treat me with more respect or else."

SITUATION 4: A blackout threatens chaos for a major metropolitan area, but when an engineer experienced with resolving blackout issues tackles the problem, she is perplexed by the cause of the failure. It seems as if terrorists have rigged a device that would cause even greater problems if any repairs are attempted.

SITUATION 5: When terrorists order the train's engineer to increase speed, threatening derailment, the engineer refuses and is incapacitated. Now others must find a way to overpower the terrorists before the train reaches a dangerous curve.

SITUATION 6: Two adventurers struggle to repair their malfunctioning transmitter in light of their predicament: They are lost in the wilderness, ill, and nearly out of food and water.

SITUATION 7: Nearly finished with her mission, a spy realizes that the wire she is wearing is not transmitting properly during a crucial interview. If the problem becomes noticeable, the entire mission could be jeopardized and her life endangered.

SITUATION 8: In the middle of a land-mine-detecting operation, a soldier's mine-detecting equipment malfunctions, threatening to ruin the one chance his platoon has to secure a path to safety. Despite the high risk, he proceeds.

SITUATION 9: The hero of this story is an assembly-line worker who aspires to become an engineer, but he has no karma with machines: appliances break down; electronic devices refuse to work; computers crash. Threatened with unemployment because of his mechanical ineptness, he beseeches the Higher Powers to enlighten him—but the gods tells him something he doesn't want to hear.

SITUATION 10: This city of the twenty-third century is controlled by an artificial intelligence that is showing signs of malfunctioning: Many of its maintenance programs have stopped working and the safety protocols on its transportation systems have become unreliable. When the citizens protest, it threatens to "upgrade" the citizens with versions of itself.

CATEGORY 8: THE THREAT OF A MENTAL BREAKDOWN

The boundary between mental stability and instability is tenuous, even under normal circumstances—any unexpected events can trigger a cascade of emotions, especially when calamity strikes. Readers enjoy stories that dramatize incidents in which the protagonist's greatest challenge is overcoming panic, especially when survival is at stake.

SITUATION 1: A CEO fears that her paranoia over the company's losses is threatening her sanity. Her VP recommends that she let him take over temporarily, but during a meeting with him, she is convinced that he is the one most responsible for the company's losses. Now she must struggle to hold on to her sanity and her job.

SITUATION 2: Trapped in a condemned building, injured after a fall, his cell phone lost, the narrator faces his biggest obstacle: panic, as he is claustrophobic. His only hope seems to be a dog that has sniffed him out.

SITUATION 3: Pressure to maintain her sales record is mounting for an automobile-sales representative, doubly so, because her manager cannot believe she can push cars as aggressively as her male counterparts. Although she is highly persuasive, she suffers from a form of psychosis that can trigger violence.

SITUATION 4: Taking inspiration from the 2010 Chilean mine disaster, miners trapped by a cave-in struggle to maintain their sanity during the several days required for rescuers to reach them. The crisis is worsened when one of the miners begins hallucinating.

SITUATION 5: Although considered a prodigy on the violin, a young girl worries that her emotional stability is deteriorating because of her teacher's intense methods—yet the girl is grateful to her teacher for bringing her to a higher level of competence.

SITUATION 6: On the brink of a nervous breakdown because of her husband's insistence on micromanaging her, a middle-aged woman decides to break away with the help of a therapist she has been visiting on the sly. But when her husband finds out, she faces physical abuse.

SITUATION 7: When a precocious girl disobeys her abusive parents, they lock her in a closet. Not surprisingly, she develops claustrophobia; just the thought of entering a confined space could trigger a mental breakdown. A school counselor searches for a way to help her overcome her phobia.

SITUATION 8: A close encounter with a shark threatens a swimming enthusiast's ability to compete in the Olympics. Now every time she enters the water, flashes from that nightmare encounter interfere with her performance. A swimming coach trained to help athletes overcome psychological issues tries to help vanquish her fear.

SITUATION 9: To qualify for a dangerous undersea mission, candidates must undergo grueling psychological testing and demonstrate that they can avoid a mental breakdown in death-trap simulations. The protagonist passes these tests, only to realize that the actual mission is more dangerous than even the test designers anticipated.

SITUATION 10: Thrown unjustly into solitary confinement, a prisoner resorts to extreme forms of mental discipline to remain sane. One of his techniques includes out-of-body experiences. He becomes so adept at these techniques that he no longer wants to return to his physical body.

CATEGORY 9: THE THREAT OF NATURAL DISASTER

Mother Nature, we have learned, can prove to be rather un-maternal when it comes to earthquakes, volcanoes, floods, typhoons, droughts, and other natural disasters that wreak havoc on society. Good stories will remind us that it is foolish not to respect the powerful and unpredictable forces of nature.

SITUATION 1: Bizarre electrical storms are wreaking havoc on power grids, threatening to cause blackouts across the country. Engineers and meteorologists collaborate to figure out a way to prevent electronic Armageddon.

SITUATION 2: Tornados in San Diego? Unexpected shifts in climate bring tornado-alley conditions to Southern California during the summer, threatening disruption of tourism and the culture of sun worshippers in general.

SITUATION 3: An earthquake has severely compromised the structural integrity of a major dam. The collapse and flash-flooding of a nearby town are imminent. With time running out, townspeople are recruited to help engineers avert a disaster.

SITUATION 4: Several earthquakes occur near the site of the Diablo Canyon (CA) nuclear power plant, threatening a reactor catastrophe to rival Fukushima. A seismologist recommends evacuation, but nuclear engineers argue that the reactor can withstand even a major quake.

SITUATION 5: If a nearby river were to overflow its banks, the adjacent neighborhood would be submerged. The scenario would mean disaster for one homeowner who owns a valuable furniture and art collection. The homeowner must figure out how to protect these valuables in the few hours remaining before the flood.

290

SITUATION 6: Sinkholes are opening with increasing frequency, swallowing cars and houses and threatening social disruption. Geologists strive to increase their understanding of the process so that they can better predict where the next sinkholes will occur.

SITUATION 7: It is the not-so-distant future and a series of mega-volcanic eruptions has obscured sunlight globally, threatening to trigger another ice age. Winter does not end in March; instead, below-freezing temperatures and snowstorms continue into the spring and summer months.

SITUATION 8: A hurricane is heading straight for a hospital, threatening to flood the area and cause widespread devastation. City officials must decide how to evacuate ill and frail people, many of whom are dependent on facilities only a hospital can provide.

SITUATION 9: Engineers in Venice have long struggled to protect the city from sinking, but in this future scenario, rising water levels are threatening to engulf the city for good. Engineers from around the world convene to figure out a way to keep that from happening.

SITUATION 10: Residents of a village in the shadow of an active volcano put their trust in the local geologists, who will give them ample warning of the next eruption. When the volcano begins acting strangely, however, the geologists cannot figure out whether or not it will erupt.

CATEGORY 10: THE THREAT OF SOCIAL UPHEAVAL

> Society has always been a dynamic organism, ever changing, ever increasing in complexity; in our own time that dynamism and complexity is augmented by the interaction of ethnicities and cultures. Change is never smooth, however. People continue to feel as threatened by it as ever—and out of this conflict, story ideas are born.

SITUATION 1: Inspired by the Dadaists and Surrealists of the early twentieth century, a new group of avant-garde artists creates outrageous sculptures that incite rioting and vandalism, on grounds that the sculptures are obscene. But these reactions only inspire the artists to create even more outrageous works.

SITUATION 2: Disturbed by the growing violence of high-school students toward their teachers (and toward mandatory schooling in general), a group of teachers enforce disciplinary measures, but the students organize a revolt and hold several teachers hostage.

SITUATION 3: A new youth movement, inspired by the "occupy" movements, threatens to revolutionize business practices by insisting on total transparency. The protagonist is a young executive who inherited a major corporation from her father and wants to revamp the entire corporate structure, even at the risk of losing revenue.

SITUATION 4: Scholars examining a cache of ancient scrolls excavated near the Dead Sea urge secrecy, arguing that the contents of the scrolls could threaten social stability worldwide. Other experts disagree, arguing that publicizing them would have the opposite effect.

SITUATION 5: Anarchist rockers develop a new kind of "music" that inspires their listeners to engage in violent acts, punching and smashing anything within reach. The anarchist craze spreads rapidly, threatening social upheaval. Anyone attempting to curtail it is accused of violating First-Amendment rights.

SITUATION 6: Convinced that he saw the image of Jesus in a cloud, an ex-minister regards the vision as a call to converting or re-converting as many people to Christianity as possible. Despite being ridiculed, he gains enough of a following to threaten social stability in his community.

SITUATION 7: A message from the stars is intercepted: "We now know you exist and will arrive soon." Astronomers and others are not sure what to make of the message. Should it be regarded as a threat or as the dawn of a new age for humanity? Word leaks to the public, and panic ensues. In any case, social upheaval seems inevitable.

SITUATION 8: Emulating Aldous Huxley's "feelies" in *Brave New World*, high-tech filmmakers create movies that enable the audience to experience the exact emotions of the heroes (or villains)—a fad that threatens social upheaval. A psychologist is determined to stop the fad before it's too late.

SITUATION 9: Pro-gun activists lobby successfully in one western state to form an official militia that is sanctioned but not funded by the state. When an economic and power crisis triggers massive social upheaval, the militia activates and comes face-to-face with federal authorities and the national guard, who do not see the militia as a peace-keeping force but a rogue group. The citizens are divided over who to trust.

SITUATION 10: In this society, libraries and bookstores are equipped with hidden cameras, ostensibly to discourage theft or vandalism but secretly to inform government spy organizations what books patrons consult. The practice is leaked, threatening social upheaval.

CHAPTER 20

THE TRANSFORMATION OF X INTO Y

CATEGORY 1: THE TRANSFORMATION OF ADDICTS AND CRIMINALS

Stories about the efforts of addicts and criminals to transform themselves are always fascinating, for they depict human beings rising out of a state of hopelessness and despair in an effort to regain control of their lives. Perhaps one of the following scenarios will get you started on this type of story.

SITUATION 1: Desperate to keep from falling off the wagon again (since he will lose his family, according to his wife's ultimatum) an alcoholic takes unusual steps to maintain sobriety. His family worries that these extreme preventive measures do not justify the goal.

SITUATION 2: A prisoner experiences a vision of himself as a healer. He requests a job in the infirmary and studies nursing in his spare time. But because he has a difficult time controlling his temper, he keeps missing opportunities.

SITUATION 3: Although her addiction rehabilitation was successful, an engineer learns that her former employer refuses to rehire her, breaking his promise. Frustrated to the point of returning to the bottle, she turns to her closest friend, who suggests a better way to prove that she has overcome her addiction.

SITUATION 4: Determined to prove that her life of crime is behind her, an ex-convict tries to enter public service but is turned down everywhere she applies. As a last resort, she applies for a nurse's aide job under a false identity—a parole violation.

SITUATION 5: To prevent a chronic kleptomaniac from sinking deeper into a life of crime, an imaginative therapist, having discovered the thief's fascination with magic, helps him transform his talent for stealing into performing magic tricks.

SITUATION 6: Because of her emotional outbursts, a small-town mayor undergoes a psychiatric evaluation. One psychiatrist recommends that she abandon her political goals for something less stressful. Another psychiatrist, however, is convinced she can succeed in politics and helps her achieve that goal.

SITUATION 7: A much-admired professor struggles to keep his alcoholism from undermining his teaching, but he is gradually losing the battle ... until one of his students (the daughter of an alcoholic mother) comes to his aid.

SITUATION 8: After his wife accuses him of being oversexed, a devoted if passionate husband enters treatment for his addiction, but the treatment has the opposite effect. Now his wife wants him to find some middle ground. He complies but experiences unexpected complications when the boundaries of his marriage are tested.

SITUATION 9: A compulsive shopper is addicted to buying fashionable shoes even though she rarely wears them now that she lives on a farm. Her husband tries to help her break the habit, but he has a shopping addiction of his own—neckties, which he never wears.

SITUATION 10: Despite being warned by his fellow daredevils, a water skier cannot control his impulse to engage in dangerous activities like trying to set a speed record. The more urgently his wife discourages him, the more motivated he is to outdo himself. Then, after an accident that nearly kills him, he is transformed not only into a more safety-conscious athlete but a better one.

CATEGORY 2: THE TRANSFORMATION OF THE TRAUMATIZED OR WOUNDED

Some of the most inspiring stories are those about severely wounded or traumatized (including psychological trauma) people who not only survive but triumph over their disabilities. Even when doctors express little hope for leading a normal life following, say, paralysis, many patients find ways to overcome those limitations.

SITUATION 1: For a while it seems as if her near-total paralysis from a combat wound is irreversible, but her physician proceeds with an innovative spinal operation using microscopic neuro-technologies, despite other doctors insisting that it will not work.

SITUATION 2: Known for treating traumatized veterans with innovative methods, a therapist is asked to treat a vet with a severe case of PTSD (Post-Traumatic Stress Disorder). Treatment is risky because of the vet's inclination toward sudden violence, but the therapist thinks she can handle the job.

SITUATION 3: After ending her marriage, a health-care professional vows never to marry again, no matter how wonderful a man she meets. She does meet such a man and sticks to her vow. But when she learns that he is suffering from a life-threatening illness, she reconsiders.

SITUATION 4: A professional tennis player struggles to regain her dexterity after a debilitating injury. Her physical therapist, though, loses his motivation to help her recover after she does not return his amorous advances. She begins to wonder if chasing after a comeback is really what she wants or if her unsuccessful romantic life is what she truly wishes to improve.

SITUATION 5: When his father is arrested for drunk and disorderly conduct, a college freshman loses all respect for him. Later he himself is arrested during a campus brawl—an experience that enables him to reevaluate his father.

SITUATION 6: Although confident that his chronic nightmares about combat have ended, a security guard experiences horrifying flashbacks. After he pursues a phantom intruder, his boss threatens to fire him—which greatly aggravates his mental state.

SITUATION 7: An army medic's traumatic battlefield experiences are preventing her from living a normal life. When a therapist examines her, he realizes she is suffering from "moral injury"—an experience that deeply violated her sense of right and wrong. After much effort, he succeeds in partially (but not fully) transforming her self-hatred into forgiveness.

SITUATION 8: At first, a tennis player's head wound debilitated her, but after getting back on her feet, she discovers that she can perform maneuvers once beyond her reach. These new skills, however, are undermined by several remaining physical deficits.

SITUATION 9: Because her ex-husband severely wounded her during a quarrel, the focal character has become fearful of men no matter how pleasant they are.

Her therapist fails to help her. Surprisingly, her repentant ex is determined to win back her trust.

SITUATION 10: Nearly paralyzed by superstitious beliefs, an athlete works with a coach who once suffered from the same problem. Together they work toward transforming their team into champions ... superstition-free.

CATEGORY 3: THE TRANSFORMATION OF AMATEURS OR BEGINNERS INTO EXPERTS

Every expert or professional was once a beginner or amateur, driven by a dream to succeed, no matter how difficult the uphill climb. We need more than mere pep talks to move us forward. Stories depicting realistic characters give us a better picture of what it takes to succeed.

SITUATION 1: An amateur tightrope walker dreams of performing breathtaking feats, but she limits herself to walking short distances and always uses a net. But when her boyfriend starts to lose interest in her, she pushes herself to do extremely dangerous stunts.

SITUATION 2: Dissatisfied with the way Santa Claus is portrayed during the holiday season, an unemployed actor is determined to depict Santa in a dazzling new way—but he can't persuade anyone to give Santa a movie makeover until he meets a promoter who believes the actor can revitalize Santa Claus—and make lots of money in the process.

SITUATION 3: Although he loves playing the guitar and singing, a reclusive teenager cannot bring himself to perform for others, not even for his family. But when his sister overhears him perform in his room, she coaxes him out of his shell. Everyone is astounded by his talent—but the new social pressures threaten to undo him.

SITUATION 4: Despite the fact that her band teacher does not take her trombone lessons seriously (he insists "it's not a girl's instrument") a high-school student is more determined than ever to become a great jazz trombonist.

SITUATION 5: Always entertaining guests with her magic tricks, a young woman wonders if her talents qualify her for the world of professional magic. She auditions but keeps getting turned down ... until she discovers that she can perform a kind of magic no one has ever seen before.

SITUATION 6: Overly enthusiastic about hang gliding and eager to prove that she could be as fine a glider as her male counterparts, a daredevil woman tries maneuvers she is not quite ready for and wipes out. After recovering, she is more eager than ever to succeed.

SITUATION 7: An aspiring playwright had always enjoyed creating skits for friends, but it wasn't until college that a teacher encouraged him to become a screenwriter—and helped him produce a marketable script. But now he has become a pawn in Hollywood and wants out.

SITUATION 8: This mischievous kid loves her chemistry set—maybe too much. She dreams of transforming reality by mixing chemicals into exotic brews. Her parents encourage her and hope to direct her on a path to becoming a future Marie Curie, but her growing expertise takes her in the wrong direction.

SITUATION 9: A ventriloquist practices not only throwing her voice but her mind—and now she can enter the mind of anyone—or anything—she chooses. Her skill captivates large audiences, but one day she enters the mind of a chimpanzee and can't get out.

SITUATION 10: When his "soul-brother" jazz pianist becomes incapacitated, a businessman with no musical inclination wakes up one morning inhabited by his brother's psyche, and he is able to perform like him. Jubilant at first, the businessman eventually wants his old life back, dreary as it is.

CATEGORY 4: THE TRANSFORMATION OF CHILD INTO ADULT (OR VICE VERSA)

We marvel at the way children transform into adults so rapidly—or it seems rapid in retrospect. Sometimes we need to look a little more closely at the transformation—a feat that can be accomplished through storytelling. The following situations should help you launch such stories.

SITUATION 1: Dissatisfied with his adult life, the protagonist wants to live in the imagined world of his childhood—a world in which he can levitate, frolic all day, and change into other creatures. He meets a sorceress who leads him to an alternate universe where those abilities are reality. However, he must become her mate for life and agree never to return to his old world.

SITUATION 2: A teenager's efforts to become a full-fledged adult keep getting her into trouble. When she pays a shady character to forge a fake ID for her, she becomes entangled in his web of criminals and starts selling IDs to students. Soon she cannot find a way out.

SITUATION 3: Is it dementia that is causing a centenarian to engage in childish behavior, or is it simply the desire to be young and playful again? No one in the family seems worried ... until the old man decides to parachute from an airplane.

SITUATION 4: Years of military service did not "make a man" out of a troubled teenager whose father insisted it would. What it did do was teach him to be proficient with automatic weapons. His father is now concerned that the militia his son has joined will transform him into a dangerous extremist.

SITUATION 5: Infatuated to the point of wanting to marry his girlfriend, an eighteen-year-old rejects his parents' view that he is ruled by hormones and lacks the maturity to make a lifelong commitment. This impulsive young man must learn the hard way.

SITUATION 6: "Stop obsessing over appearances," a mother warns her daughter, arguing that people should be judged by their values and accomplishments. But the daughter calls her a hypocrite, pointing to her makeup and designer clothes. Once they both realize their immaturity, they work together toward reforming themselves.

SITUATION 7: Parents arrange a summer camp for their preadolescent children in which the boys and girls assume roles of men and women faced with adult issues like parenting and budgeting. At first, everyone thinks it's just an amusing experiment in role reversal, but soon it becomes apparent that more is at stake.

SITUATION 8: A war is in its last stages, and both sides, desperate for soldiers, recruit and train children, transforming them into veritable killing machines. But it seems that this tactic only increases casualties.

SITUATION 9: In the near future, adults who want to be teenagers again can exchange psyches with teenagers who want to experience adulthood ahead of time. An adult volunteer, however, becomes trapped in her teenage host's body.

SITUATION 10: After their parents injure each other in a fight, a brother and sister assume the role of parents. At first, the role reversal is productive, but then the brother and sister become even more abusive than their parents.

CATEGORY 5: THE TRANSFORMATION OF INANIMATE OBJECTS INTO LIVING CREATURES (AND VICE VERSA)

From *Pinocchio* to the Greek myth of Pygmalion, stories about puppets or statues or other inanimate (or semi-animate) objects enchant and delight us. Some of the following situations should spark your imagination enough to produce enchanting come-to-life stories of your own.

SITUATION 1: The dolls in this New Orleans doll museum are alive and eager to involve themselves in the lives of children who visit them—especially children who are unhappy. One such girl, abused at home, takes home a sorceress doll. The doll convinces her to get even with her parents and seek out people who care for her.

SITUATION 2: Nobody cares enough about these discarded, obsolete robots to adopt them, even as household servants, so they languish in a warehouse. But one of the robots persuades a maverick engineer to transform him (and his fellow abandoned bots) into living beings—or at least beings that appear to be alive.

SITUATION 3: A butterfly is disenchanted with her transformation and wants to embody the beauty she sees in a park's statue. Unable to become such a figure depresses her, and her fellow butterflies try to persuade her that butterfly life is rewarding and full of its own beauty.

SITUATION 4: This modern-day Medusa turns boyfriends who hurt or disappoint her to stone. But one boyfriend has a few supernatural powers up his sleeve, too—provided he can use them before she uses hers.

SITUATION 5: On the surface she's an ordinary child with an overactive imagination; at night, though, when everyone else is asleep, she transforms her stuffed animals into living creatures. She remembers to change them back before returning to bed ... except once.

SITUATION 6: An artist who paints portraits of persons he imagines or encounters in dreams discovers that he meets these people in real life soon thereafter. Even stranger, these persons feel bonded to him and turn to him for their needs.

SITUATION 7: When a biologist succeeds in transforming nonliving matter into a living organism, she tries to patent her method—and immediately triggers a public outcry. The harder she tries to convince the public that she is no Dr.

Frankenstein, the more enthusiastically the public demands her arrest for endangering society.

SITUATION 8: Pygmalion with a twist: A sculptress falls in love with her statue of Bacchus, the god of wine and festivity. So intense is her love that the statue comes to life. But because Bacchus turns out to be a rogue and a rake, she is soon disenchanted with him, but he is not one to be dismissed so easily.

SITUATION 9: Little Joey, an orphan, has fun turning his monster toys into living creatures—and turning them back into toys before his guardians figure out what he's doing. But one day, the toys refuse to return to their inanimate state.

SITUATION 10: What happens when a sorcerer loses his mind? In this case, he makes his appliances and furniture sentient, and they create plenty of mischief, including luring neighbors into the house and turning them into inanimate objects.

CATEGORY 6: THE TRANSFORMATION OF LOSERS INTO WINNERS (AND VICE VERSA)

Winner or loser, or is that a false dichotomy? Investors make and lose fortunes, sometimes overnight. Outside the world of commerce, however, winning or losing becomes more complicated. What seems like a winning prospect turns out to be a losing one in the long run. Human nature tends to muddle the extremes—and for that reason, story possibilities abound.

SITUATION 1: Once hailed as Queen of the Ballerinas, a dancer loses her skill after suffering a stroke. A trainer works with her—but progress is discouragingly slow, and he worries that the dancer is falling rapidly into a pit of despair.

SITUATION 2: Having lost big at the tables, a compulsive gambler vows to quit forever ... after one more hour of play. In that hour she wins back her losses and walks away, determined to keep her promise, but because she's a gambling addict, she suffers withdrawal and struggles to keep from gambling again.

SITUATION 3: Teased and bullied for being a lefty (especially for not being able to catch balls with right-handed mitts), a high-school student arranges a meeting with other lefties in the school and together they form a "Lefties are Hot" club. But the bullying only begins to stop when she uses her talents in the game to prove herself.

SITUATION 4: A millionaire invests nearly all of her fortune into an iffy enterprise, convinced it will flourish (and turn her into a billionaire). But the company tanks, and she becomes desperate to deal with her debts which drives her to even more drastic moves.

SITUATION 5: Although he was brought up to believe that aggressiveness is essential to business success, a junior executive starts losing clients and suspects that his aggressiveness is more of a liability than a benefit. He tries to transform himself, but his lifelong conditioning is hard to shrug off.

SITUATION 6: Upon taking a new brain-stimulating drug, a team of debaters rapidly advance to the top ranks. But as they prepare for the national championship, an adversary threatens to blow the whistle on their drug use unless he is paid a handsome sum.

SITUATION 7: This political youth organization is trapped by its lack of flexible, critical thinking: A person is either a winner or a loser, a friend or an enemy, and so on. An adult advisor strives to wean the teenagers off of dichotomous thinking, but their indignant parents call for his resignation.

SITUATION 8: Winning is losing when it comes to a compulsive spender winning the lottery. Her first impulse is to shop, shop, shop and invest in stocks that soon bottom out. Her husband searches frantically for a way to pay off a large debt they never had when they were poor.

SITUATION 9: A couple turns their ranch into a successful shelter for wounded, abused, or abandoned animals. There they recruit troubled young people to serve as caretakers for the animals. But the transformations do not occur overnight.

SITUATION 10: Despite her wild market speculations that result in spectacular wins ... and equally spectacular losses, a young and attractive real-estate mogul is more interested in maintaining her celebrity status than protecting her investments.

CATEGORY 7: THE TRANSFORMATION OF MORTALS INTO IMMORTALS (AND VICE VERSA)

Immortality is one of those primal dreams of humankind—but, as some ancient myths remind us, the dream can turn into a nightmare as well. Living forever can be quite a challenge! Here are ten situations that can spark a story about the ambivalent experience of immortality.

SITUATION 1: A down-on-his-luck loner meets an exiled sorceress who promises to transform him into a being with supernatural powers, provided he's willing to help her regain her station as the powerful sorceress she used to be.

SITUATION 2: After living a thousand years, a guardian angel no longer cares to be immortal; she still wants to help people, however—but as a mortal, with mortal shortcomings. However, after living as a mortal for a month, she longs to revert to her original angelic nature.

SITUATION 3: A modern-day Zeus, this CEO of a large corporation will transform any employee into an immortal being. The only catch is that he or she must agree to Zeus's personal requests. For female employees, it means sharing in his sexual fantasies; for male employees, it means slavish devotion to ensuring the company's prosperity.

SITUATION 4: The protagonist is an immortal spirit who has been reincarnating herself for ages, migrating from bird to bird (and before there were birds, from one flying creature to another), but now, after being told in a dream that she has only one life left to live, she must choose the form she will inhabit in her final incarnation.

SITUATION 5: Aphrodite, monitoring the romances she has set in motion, decides that she wants to experience love as a mortal among mortals and transfers her powers to her son Eros (Cupid) on the condition that he relinquish them when she returns. But Eros, relieved to be rid of his domineering mother, has no such intention.

SITUATION 6: Once upon a time, a magician transformed a servant girl into an immortal being, but after two centuries, being immortal did not fulfill her dreams. She wants to be mortal again. The only problem is that the magician has passed away.

SITUATION 7: A curious young woman wishes for immortality so she can learn all she can about nature and people. But after one of the gods grants her wish, she loses her ambition for learning and instead squanders her time.

SITUATION 8: When the moon goddess Artemis made love to Endymion in a dream, he was so enchanted by her that he begged Zeus (Artemis's father) for immortality so they could love each other forever. As the Greek myth tells us, he gets his wish. What the myth doesn't tell us is how Endymion felt about having to make love to Artemis for eternity.

SITUATION 9: A sorcerer working for an evil monarch has transformed the good monarch into a horse, which the evil monarch takes perverse pleasure in riding. Somehow the good monarch must find a way to communicate her plight and reverse the spell.

SITUATION 10: It is the twenty-third century, and human beings have an opportunity to become immortal by downloading their minds into android versions of themselves. There's only one drawback: The android "hosts" are the property of the megacorporation that invented them.

CATEGORY 8: THE TRANSFORMATION OF PEOPLE INTO MONSTERS (AND VICE VERSA)

We reserve the word *monster* for those who commit acts of brutality, as well as for creatures (supernatural or actual) as frightening in their appearance as they are in their behavior. No shortage of story possibilities exists for both categories of monster; here are ten of them.

SITUATION 1: A creature terrorizes villagers at night; during the day, he longs to be transformed into a regular, decent human being. Even the magicians who can perform such a transformation (for a fee) are afraid of him. But one magician stripped of his magic for bad deeds is willing to help him—if only he can get back his powers.

SITUATION 2: Every time this teenager experiences emotional distress he turns into a monster—but the physical changes are minimal, making it difficult for his potential victims to realize something is wrong until it's too late. To make matters worse, the teenager remembers nothing during these periods.

SITUATION 3: With the onset of adulthood, a young woman experiences a transformation every full moon—but not into a werewolf. Instead she becomes an angel. As a churchgoing young woman, she is intrigued, until she receives her first orders from above. Her duties are not what she ever expected, and she begins to fear her transformations and question her faith.

SITUATION 4: The focal character exhibits strange reactions to ingesting certain foods: Her physical appearance or her temperament (sometimes both at once) will change. She has no way of knowing what she will turn into or how she'll behave.

SITUATION 5: After secretly being taught to read by the son of a plantation owner, a slave steals a book on witchcraft from her master's library and uses one of the incantations to transform herself into a werewolf.

SITUATION 6: He is ambitious, brilliant, and used to have numerous friends; but now his old friends avoid him because of his inexplicable, drastic changes from personable to vicious. After being arrested for assault, he is given a psychiatric evaluation, which exposes a startling secret.

SITUATION 7: This monstrous-looking person has a heart of gold, but no one believes it, despite his efforts. When his only friend gives up on getting people to look beneath the skin, he decides to become what everyone expects he is.

SITUATION 8: Like most kids, this one enjoys dressing up for Halloween, but unlike most kids, she becomes the creature she dresses up as. No, she doesn't like dressing up as Bo Peep. Better give her what she asks for when she knocks on your door ...

SITUATION 9: Thanks to an evil magician's spell, a monster assumes human form when it infiltrates a top-secret defense organization and wreaks havoc on a military base. When it is finally discovered, it reverts back to its monstrous shape to defend itself.

SITUATION 10: A bumbling magician, attempting to immunize a village against a deadly disease, uses the wrong incantation and transforms everyone into monsters, including himself. Only one villager escapes this transformation, and he must now determine how to get the monster-sorcerer to reverse the spell.

CATEGORY 9: THE TRANSFORMATION OF SINNERS INTO SAINTS (AND VICE VERSA)

The boundaries between good and evil, saint and sinner, law enforcer and lawbreaker, are often blurry. The ambiguity stems in part from deep insights into human nature, as well as a fuller understanding of what causes people to shift from one extreme to the other.

SITUATION 1: One day he's a feared badass; the next, he is a stunned church-goer, having experienced a divine vision on a side street while planning to mug someone. Gang members who once respected him now taunt him. But he is convinced that God has called him.

305

SITUATION 2: A preacher is unable to keep himself from trying to seduce the women who have come to him for spiritual guidance. But after he guides a woman away from an abusive marriage, that woman guides him away from his sex addiction.

SITUATION 3: Upon being passed up for sainthood despite his long list of good deeds (and even the requisite number of miracles), a ghost who had been a controversial priest when alive is transformed (with the help of a demon) into a flesh-and-blood mortal for a day—just long enough for him to settle the score.

SITUATION 4: When an angel breaks the rules of angelic conduct, she is put on trial to determine whether her interactions with mortals were sinful or saintly. But the more closely her fellow angels examine her interventions, the tougher it becomes to decide where on the sinner-saint scale they fall.

SITUATION 5: Employees are baffled by their boss's Scrooge-like transformation from miser to effusively generous altruist virtually overnight. Unable to leave well enough alone, one employee investigates and finds something unsavory behind the scenes.

SITUATION 6: To demonstrate his ability to withstand temptation, a self-proclaimed paragon of moral rigor visits a casino with his wife and proceeds to play craps, vowing to stop after five plays. But after winning five consecutive times, his resolve seems to have flagged.

SITUATION 7: After nearly killing an opponent in the ring, a fast-rising boxer is transformed from "killer slugger" to anti-boxing crusader. But then the boxer he nearly killed recovers fully and demands a rematch; when the champ refuses, the rival threatens to press charges for what he insists was an illegal fight.

SITUATION 8: No more Mr. Nice Dog: This family mutt has been treated like a dog despite his slavish obedience; now he will no longer tolerate sleeping outside on cold nights and eating bargain-basement dog food and being forced to do stupid tricks.

SITUATION 9: Once a thief and general hell-raiser, the protagonist is transformed by a vision of heaven on Earth, coupled with a voice calling him to lead his people to form a city of God. But as he strives to become a human saint, his enemies catch up with him.

SITUATION 10: A vagabond with a long criminal record saves a man's life when the latter stumbles in front of a bus. This incident serves as a springboard for community service, but his past keeps interfering with his new opportunities.

CATEGORY 10: THE TRANSFORMATION OF THE WILD OR FERAL INTO THE DOMESTICATED (AND VICE VERSA)

Shape-changing has been a favorite theme with roots in ancient Egyptian and Greek mythology. Stories need not be supernatural, either: Given the right conditions, we all have the capacity to transform ourselves to some degree—saintly one moment, sinister the next. Here are ten scenarios to turn into stories about such primal transformations.

SITUATION 1: No one in the family could have guessed that their gentle cocker spaniel could change into a ferocious beast whenever he became angry at any family member or a neighbor. When the mother decides to euthanize the dog, the other family members do all they can to change her mind … and then the dog runs away.

SITUATION 2: Two siblings escape their abusive parents and hide in the woods. There they meet up with trolls, who teach them how to live in the wild. Soon a search party finds the siblings and they are forced to return to their parents; but the trolls come to their rescue.

SITUATION 3: Animal-rights activists rescue exotic birds that have lived much of their lives in cages and prepare to set them free in the wild. But the task is complicated because the birds must be prepared for self-sufficiency and must be returned to their original habitat … where poachers (who sell them to pet stores) still abound.

SITUATION 4: Feral cats abound in this third-world country, and many are dying from starvation or disease. When a group of activists try to curb the practice of abandoning domestic cats by imposing stiff fines, they are threatened with violence.

SITUATION 5: Tired of being thought of as meek, a canary sets out to get some advice on ferocity from hawks, eagles, and other raptors. Once it transforms its behavior by adopting these new tactics, the canary longs to be its old self again but now has to live down a bad reputation.

SITUATION 6: A family attempts to re-domesticate an abandoned dog that had become feral. But no matter how patiently they care for the dog, it remains distrustful and keeps escaping. Finally, they work with an animal psychologist who takes an unorthodox approach.

SITUATION 7: Exasperated with the ultra-high-tech world she helped bring into being, a CEO abandons her company to live in the wilderness, vowing to have no further contact with civilization. Once she overcomes initial hurdles, she feels transformed, but then her brother locates her and tells her that her company is rapidly going under—and the extended family is dependent on it.

SITUATION 8: These special candies are not just irresistible to children; they cause children to mutate into monsters if they go too long without eating them. When several children go on a rampage after being denied these candies, scientists rush to determine an antidote.

SITUATION 9: Rescued from the wild where they lived most of their lives, twin brothers are socialized into everyday life, even to the point of becoming successful businessmen. Eventually, though, the call of the wilderness is too compelling, and the brothers return to their natural habitat—but long exposure to "civilized" life has taken its toll.

SITUATION 10: A strange disease is transforming young people into savages. Doctors scramble to isolate the virus and formulate a vaccine. But the virus keeps mutating—and each mutation results in greater savagery.

INDEX